RETHINKING

MEDIA

THEORY

Media & Society

Richard Bolton, series editor

Armand Mattelart

$\oplus$

Michèle Mattelart

SIGNPOSTS AND NEW

DIRECTIONS

RETHINKING

MEDIA

THEORY

Translation by James A. Cohen and Marina Urquidi

MEDIA & SOCIETY 5

University of Minnesota Press

Minneapolis

Originally published as *Penser les médias*, Copyright 1986 by Editions La Découverte, Paris.

Library of Congress Cataloging-in-Publication Data

Mattelart, Armand.
  [Penser les médias. English]
  Rethinking media theory : signposts and new directions / Armand Mattelart and Michèle Mattelart ; translated by James A. Cohen and Marina Urquidi.
    p. cm. — (Media & society ; 5)
  Translation of: Penser les médias.
  Includes bibliographical references and index.
  ISBN 0-8166-1908-5 (hc). — ISBN 0-8166-1910-7 (pb)
  1. Communication. 2. Mass media. I. Mattelart, Michèle.
  II. Title. III. Series.
  P90.M34413 1992
  302.2—dc20   91-35874
                                                           CIP

Published by the University of Minnesota Press
2037 University Avenue Southeast, Minneapolis, MN 55414
Printed in the United States of America on acid-free paper

The University of Minnesota is an
equal-opportunity educator and employer.

CONTENTS

Preface to the English Edition

In the course of the past decade, new modes of seeing and thinking critically about information, communication, and culture have appeared. These radical changes are at once the culmination of a process and the beginning of another. The main goal of this book is to locate points of reference that will make it possible to understand the breaks and the continuities of this period, during which the major paradigms have entered into crisis.

The realities of "communication" have evolved considerably, as witnessed by the processes of privatization and deregulation of audiovisual institutions and telecommunications networks, the construction of a system of "world-communication" in the context of a "world-economy" (in Braudel's sense of the term), and the mercantilization of sectors such as culture, education, religion, and health care, which had up to now remained on the margin of commodity circuits and had hardly been affected by the law of value. The new technologies of communication have not only assumed a central place in the industrial network—they are at the very heart of the strategies of reorganization of the relations between the state and citizens, local and central powers, producers and consumers, workers and managers, teachers and students, experts and those who execute their plans. In this context of scientific and technological change, new historical actors have emerged in industry and trade, of course, but also in strategies of social resistance; and in the Third World as well as in the "First."

The point of departure of this book is therefore the analysis of the evolution of thought and research on information, communication, and culture in France. But reference to the case of France does not by any means indicate a confinement to it. Indeed, this work raises questions that transcend the limits of any geographical perimeter. There is no denying that French philosophers and sociologists have elaborated theories of communication and culture that have exercised, and still exercise, a profound influence on contemporary critical thought in their domain. However, there has hardly been any analysis of the concrete conditions under which these concepts and theories, abundantly exported by the French schools, have been produced. Concepts and theories have been disseminated outside France stripped of their original frameworks and contexts.

In the face of rising neopositivist currents of thought and the fascination for technological tools that accompanies them, this book seeks to emphasize the importance of epistemological reflection. It postulates the necessity of establishing theoretical distance in order to understand to what degree the refashioning of communications systems affects our societies and our ways of conceiving or reflecting upon them.

These analyses have led us to question, successively, the linear mode of thought and its consequences not only in theory but in models of growth and development; and the construction of new perspectives and conceptual matrixes (e.g., the return to the subject, the return to "ordinary culture" and the procedures of consumption, the relation between meaning and pleasure, the revision of monolithic theories of power). While emphasizing the limits of old ways of perceiving communication processes, this book further points out the ambiguities and ambivalences of the breaks within critical theory in the past several years. Thus, it shows how neofunctionalist perspectives and their attendant cybernetic conception of social organization have gained renewed strength.

With the advent of new forms of seeing and thinking about communication and the world, we detect profound changes in the relations between the class of intellectuals and mass cultural production as well as the groups that consume it.

Finally, we wish to make it clear that as we rethink the history of research about communication, we are also retracing our own personal itinerary.

Armand and Michèle Mattelart

Preface to the Original French Edition

In barely five years, France has reconciled itself with the media. Who would recognize in today's France the country that had so much trouble making its entry into technological modernity? By doubling its number of television channels, it made the definitive move from a scarcity of images to an abundance of them. The France of the seventies, which criminalized freedom of choice on the airwaves by confiscating the equipment of "free radio stations" (*radios libres*), the France that shut down the studios of its first experiments in cable TV in the new urban residential developments— this is nothing but a distant memory. It is a memory that does not so much evoke the traditional France of yesterday as the obscurantist regimes throughout the world that persist in refusing to tolerate a plurality of discourses and in rejecting innovation.

The left succeeded where it was least expected to do so. What the right, with its doctrine of liberal capitalism, had prohibited, the left actually liberalized.

The paradox is that this same government of the left was not able to communicate with its citizens. It has singularly lacked effectiveness in rallying a consensus around those of its realizations that have deeply marked the evolution of institutions, from the abolition of the death penalty to penal reform, or, in the area of culture, the rights of authors and creators. The left government has not succeeded in "selling" its policies. On the other hand, it can boast of having inspired the unanimity of consumers regarding its generosity in the legalization of new television channels.

And yet in its communication with the public, the left in power has not been skimpy in the use of modern sales and demand-stimulation techniques. It has sharply increased its public relations budget in comparison to that of its predecessors. Certain television appearances by the president or the prime minister have shown that the governmental left, having been seduced by the media, sought in turn to seduce the public. Although during election periods it behaved in a different way, returning to its old policy of meeting citizens on the concrete terrain of their daily concerns, its ordinary mode of governing, meeting the people and managing its relation with the country, has tried to adopt the logic of the media—with no success, however. Nonetheless, in its years of government, the left has done what capital and market forces had not been able to do: helped confer full legitimacy on this logic. The idea that the public sphere, the space for democratic debate, is the same as the space occupied by the media has lodged itself in collective references. The media are no longer that "fifth power" (*cinquième pouvoir*) that the left had demonized; they have become the sphere of "transparency." The reaction of the media has thus become the key criterion for judging political effectiveness or the validity of an idea or argument.

One does not theorize transparency, one lives it—for the logic of the media is first of all a technique of action. To subscribe to it means adopting empiricism and pragmatism as methods. (Pragmatism: the unmentionable word has been spoken.) Just as the left in power has refused to reflect on the media apparatus, it has also minimized reflection on its technological project for overcoming the economic crisis. One logic hides another; pragmatism regarding the media masks another, much more fundamental sort: the pragmatism of a project for overcoming the economic crisis whose only perspective is, indeed, overcoming the crisis. This is a project imprisoned in a sophism according to which more technology implies more modernity, and vice versa . . .

Pragmatism, the things people do in thy name! The left government, invoking the constraints—and they were real ones—of the economic crisis, narrowed its range of options by being pragmatic. The claim "we have no alternative" justifies having only one discourse. And yet, in civil society, seamless, single-vision discourse has never been so much in crisis as it is now.

No one asked the left to resolve problems that were impossible to resolve. People only asked it to demonstrate why all courses of action were in fact not possible.

No one asked the left to eliminate all inequalities. People did, however, ask it not to develop a discourse that seemed to claim that inequalities had ceased to exist, and that submitting to constraints would result in liberation.

No one asked the left to escape, as if by miracle, from the deep trends of the internationalization of cultures and economies. People did ask it, however, not to present the ambition of a certain Italian entrepreneur to launch the first private TV channel in France as an inevitable choice by invoking professionalism and technology above all considerations of a cultural nature.

No one asked the left to tell Disneyland: "Go home!"; people did ask it, however, not to present the building of a Euro-Disneyland in the Paris area as an inevitable solution, in the name of the struggle against unemployment.

No one asked the left to ban the Smurfs entertainment park at Longwy (a city hard-hit by steel layoffs). People did expect it, however, to show that it realized how much symbolic violence was contained in the substitution of the emblem "Lorraine Coeur d'Acier" (Lorraine heart of steel) by "Lorraine Coeur de Schtroumpf" (Lorraine heart of Smurf).

Indeed, it is on the symbolic level that the left failed. The vulgar materialism of a socialism converted to the imperatives of business defeated the imaginary and the desires for a broader definition of the future.

With the rise of instrumental logics, the crisis of theoretical reflection, which had begun much earlier, has been consummated.

There was also, however, an unexpected side effect. France's reconciliation with the media had at least one positive consequence: it helped to liquidate a heritage of elitist indifference. The cultural left long believed it had divine rights over culture. Its adversaries were for many years thoroughly impotent to contest the hegemony of left-wing intellectuals and creators. It was this "natural hegemony" that the left seemed to enjoy (and that relegitimated its definition of high culture) that allowed it for years to avoid asking questions about the media.

Like the earlier audiovisual situation, this preponderance of the left and the illusions it created will soon be nothing more than a memory. But this is no time for regrets. If the pragmatic climate has had one virtue, it is to have finally swept away the normative approaches and the normalizing theories that had prevented recognition of reality and the identification of facts and objects. As provocative as it may sound, the triumph of pragmatism somehow indicates the failure of a conception of theory that was cut off from concrete subjects and from the issues of democracy in everyday life. The outcome seems a natural one.

This era marks the end of "heroes of theory." Theory can now start to show its true face—very simply, that of the critical distance that gives meaning and relief to the immediate, which is constantly being defined by the multiple mediations that characterize our relation to the world.

Without indulging in futurology, one may safely claim that the topic of communication has a long future ahead of it. Contrary to what one might believe, given its remarkable ascension in collective perceptions since the end of the seventies, discussion about communication is not merely the result of a fad or a conjuncture but is indeed a structural fact. Communication now occupies a central place in strategies whose object is to restructure our societies. Via electronic technologies, it is one of the master instruments in the conversion of the major industrialized countries. It accompanies the redeployment of powers (and counterpowers) in the home, the school, the factory, the office, the hospital, the neighborhood, the region, and the nation. And beyond this, it has become a key element in the internationalization of economies and cultures. It has thus become a stake in the relations between peoples, between nations, and between blocs.

Since concepts must not be confused with the things they represent, it is generally admitted that the concept of a dog does not bark and wag its tail and the concept of a rose does not prick. But in the case of "communication," this principle is much less certain! There is a tendency to define it with regard to its applications and its uses rather than engaging in the theoretical operation that would allow us critical distance from the ever more present technological objects in our daily environment.

While the topic of communication today generates a support that approaches consensus, it is far from achieving, in the area of theory and the definition of its concept, the unanimity it has gained in media practice. The decision to go back to theory is therefore an attempt to bring to light the contradictory character of this field of knowledge in order to try to reconstruct the network of meanings in which the ordinary dimension of communication practices is caught: practices of consumption, professional practices of production, militant practices of production, and so forth.

The analyses that follow are the fruit of our personal intellectual journeys, which have led us to encounter, inside and outside France, the multiple pathways of those men and women who have never stopped asking the question of the relation of intellectuals to society. May our many friends find here the expression of our gratitude. Our thanks go in particular to François Gèze who, on numerous occasions, helped us to deepen our reflection about certain of our questions.

Armand and Michèle Mattelart
Paris, March 1986

PART 1

The Varieties of Learned Discourse

Introduction to Part 1

The infatuation with technology that gripped France in the 1980s has imparted to the theme of communication an extraordinary aura of consensus.

There is a great contrast today between the mobilizing power of projects for expanding new communication technologies and the disarray, hesitations, and uncertainty that now more than ever surround the theoretical status of knowledge and practices associated with the notion of communication.

Caught as we are in the daily avalanche of revelations about the future of new technological networks, how can anyone deny that it is becoming more difficult for us to articulate questions of a general nature? The flood of media messages may very well inform us abundantly about the present history, produced on a daily basis, of technological expansion, but it complicates the endeavor of reflecting on these new technological objects and makes the task of defining the status of theory a more troublesome one.

Similar remarks have been made by many researchers and educators from various posts of observation. In his report entitled "Computer Knowledge and Know-How," submitted in 1983 to the French Ministries of National Education and Industry and Research, computer specialist Maurice Nivat brought to light certain obstacles to theoretical reflection in his discipline:

> In computer science, the voice of researchers is heard very little;
> it is covered by the noise that comes to us from America and
> Japan—a noise made up largely of more or less false advertising.
> (It should be noted that the absence of widely heeded computer

3

researchers is felt in those countries as well.) Computer science
thus appears as a very disorderly field; anything that has just
come from California is considered, *a priori*, to be interesting; all
questions are given equal importance, and research thus breaks
up into countless fragments. We will not overcome this situation
unless we establish some kind of hierarchy among the problems,
designating some of them as important or fundamental and
choosing priorities for action. . . . Theory provides a framework
and a support system for thought, and it is through theory that
knowledge is transmitted, particularly—and this is
fundamental—for young people.[1]

On the basis of his reflection on schools and new computer and audiovisual techniques, in his report entitled "Research on Education and
the Socialization of the Child" Roland Carraz asks why it is so difficult to
structure knowledge in a society where the media occupy such a predominant position in the transmission of knowledge.

There is no small danger that association of ideas will replace the
logical sequence of concepts and that the high value placed on
what is immediate, spontaneous, and close at hand will eclipse
the necessary time for the critical distance, work and effort
required for the objective elaboration of knowledge and cause
these things to be forgotten. If the civilization of the image,
computer technology, and electronics does not bring forth an
in-depth analysis of how these new languages can be managed,
and does not stimulate citizens to exploit new possibilities for
imagination, creation, and responsibility, we are in great danger
of unintentionally ending up in a society where it is impossible
for individuals to take distance from objects, and consequently,
from their own demand.[2]

For the majority of people, promotional and advertising discourse on
new products is the main mode of access to knowledge about the novel
dimensions of these technologies. For the minority who read daily papers
and news magazines, the abundantly documented and often penetrating
analyses presented by a new generation of journalists in the field of communication provide a more orderly frame of reference. But even so, although journalists partially make up for the absence of popularization in
the publications of researchers, their work remains subjected to the need
to quickly inform people about an extremely mobile reality, the very mobility of which fuels their writing with exuberance. Even if the present
moment tends to promote this new form of journalism as the expression,
in its developments and its limits, of the thought we need to apprehend
the new technological environment, time is not the same for journalistic
writing as for theoretical reflection. The borders between the two kinds

of knowledge grow fuzzier by the day, because the scientific milieu itself is tempted to think in terms of media dissemination. Many scientists no longer practice science as it was practiced ten years ago precisely because scientific knowledge is not disseminated in the same way.

But these factors are nothing compared to the weight of the historical legacy that has discouraged the recognition of theoretical inquiry in the disciplines of communication (or has conferred on such inquiry only parcels of legitimacy based on a few, hyperselective angles of analysis). This is a restrictive legacy. The theme of so-called mass communication has been given very little legitimacy in academic institutions. Many researchers have felt it necessary to apologize for the triviality of their concerns as compared with the nobility of literary canons or the aesthetics of *cinéma d'auteur*. This lack of legitimacy granted to communication as an area of study mirrors the lack of legitimacy granted, in the field of literary production, to popular novels ever since they first began to appear at the end of the nineteenth century. As Anne-Marie Thiesse has written:

> The principle of the incompatibility of art and money that underlies the dominant representation of the artistic universe has the effect of identifying popular production as commercial (in the most vulgar sense). Deciding to become a popular novelist is thus perceived as the deliberate choice of those who are repelled by the heavy demands of a disinterested vocation and motivated by the hope of easy riches.[3]

This old cleavage has found new expression in the field of audiovisual production, where there is an opposition, in dominant representations, between the legitimate status of the film director and the devalued status of the television producer. This sense of hierarchy has often been expressed in French television, where producers have insisted on claiming the status of *auteurs*. As the producer Serge Moati writes, "What fascinates me about film is its unique character, its magical aspect. What we do is a little like mass production, at its best *haute couture*, but serialized *haute couture* . . . and most often Monoprix-style merchandise** (Monoprix has its charm, by the way)."[4]

In the following chapters we have set out to trace some landmarks of the history of communication as a field of research. This history will show us which questions have acquired pertinence and which have not, thus providing an idea of how French society has conceived and spoken of itself through this field.[5]

The exercise in which we have engaged in this first section of the book should not be misinterpreted. One obviously cannot deduce, from the state of academic research about communication, the problems that cause concern in the different components of civil society. The academic institution cannot reflect the full spectrum of questions the various social actors are asking. The disparity between the research themes that have mobilized scholarly institutions and the concerns of civil society has been especially noticeable in the area of practices of social intervention, and more noticeable still in local communication. Many independent researchers or research groups, engaged in a combined perspective of research and action and taking a direct part in new social movements, for a long time have helped fill the gaps left by institutional research and have opened new fields of investigation.[6]

Once this important proviso has been made, we must express our conviction that scientific production is not, after all, so independent from production in society as a whole that it could be considered nothing more than the expression of the obsessions of the intellectual class . . .

1

On the Difficulty of Reflecting on Communication

Import/Export

France has traditionally been an important center for the production and export of concepts. Just how important it has been is all the more evident now that its source of concepts seems to be drying up and many are rallying to an excessively technical discourse—a certain form of thought characteristic of cosmopolitan modernity. This development is deplored in many intellectual circles outside France; it is feared that the rich wealth of ideas accumulated in the past, particularly in the areas of culture, ideology, and the state, may fail to be renewed at a time when new transformations are bringing forth new challenges.

We are faced with a paradox: although the theoretical production of the French intellectual class has stimulated a great deal of research throughout the world, the conceptual systems it has established in the areas noted above—culture, ideology, and the state, which are the strong points of its theoretical preponderance—have scarcely been reinvested, *intra muros*, into the study of communication and information systems in France. One may remember, for example, how the Althusserian theory of ideological state apparatuses influenced research in Latin America on the press and television as well as religion, or how it left its mark on analyses of media production in Great Britain.[1] (Many other examples could be cited.) After Althusser, one could mention the French school of structural linguistics, which included figures such as Greimas, Barthes, and Metz; and more recently, Foucault's theories of the microphysics of power, the ideas of Deleuze and Guattari, and of course the Lacanian approach. All these theories have contributed greatly to raising new questions about popular culture, the interaction of subject and text, the pro-

7

cesses by which meaning is produced, and the analysis of powers and counterpowers.

It goes without saying that in intellectual circles outside France, these theoretical contributions have undergone the alchemy of reappropriation and reinterpretation; they have even, in some cases, been critically refuted and superseded. The Althusserian phenomenon as experienced in Latin America should remind us of the unpredictable effects of theoretical exchange, ranging from widespread infatuation to severe critical refutation. These exchanges have been by no means synchronous; that is, they have not taken place at the same time that the aforementioned currents of thought were establishing their intellectual hegemony in France. Linguist Michel Pêcheux has pointed out the curious contradiction between the rising influence of French structural linguistics in a number of other countries among specialists in the "science of texts" (including media texts), and its simultaneous crisis at home. "The paradox of the early 1980s," wrote Pêcheux in 1983,

> is that the bogging down of French political structuralism, its breakdown as a "royal science" (that nevertheless continues to produce effects, notably in Latin America), coincides with the growing acknowledgement of the works of Lévi-Strauss, Lacan, Barthes, Derrida, and Foucault in the Anglo-Saxon countries — in England, West Germany, as well as in the United States. By a strange seesaw effect, at the precise moment that America discovers structuralism, the French intelligentsia "turns the page" by developing a massive *ressentiment* against the theories suspected of having spoken in the name of the masses, while producing a long series of inefficient symbolic acts and unhappy political performances.[2]

A Latin American scholar points to the very same phenomenon when he describes the influences felt in the sciences of communication in that area of the world in the 1960s.

> We must realize the importance of French and Italian [theoretical] production when the "boom" in new types of studies on mass communication was beginning to occur. Among the Italians, Umberto Eco and Gillo Dorfles were already exercising their influence on Latin America, while in Germany and the United States, to take two well-informed countries, they were still unknown. Something similar, and no doubt more intense, happened with French intellectual production, especially certain representatives of the multidimensional structuralist school. We can mention, in particular, Roland Barthes, and the perhaps more original contribution of Jean Baudrillard. At that time we were deeply marked by outside influences. The European influence

was notorious and took effect even before translations were published. With the exception of a few individuals, it was only in the seventies that we began to produce a more autonomous current of thought.[3]

Until very recently, France had many exports but few imports in the area of critical theory of communication.[4] The French have simply ignored as flourishing a school of thought as the Birmingham school, led by Stuart Hall,[5] which has made considerable innovations in the study of popular culture after having appropriated the works of Althusser and Barthes. Similarly, the works of the Frankfurt School were translated only partially, and much later than in most other countries. It was not until a work by Edgar Morin introduced the concept of "cultural industry" that Adorno and Horkheimer, who invented the concept, became known in France.

How is it that concepts created in France could produce effects in the study of cultural production in other European countries and other continents, while they were rarely reinvested into communication research in France itself?

The Limits of the National

If any apparatus of socialization has been the privileged object of French critical analysis of the mechanisms of the production of signs, values, and norms relating to power, it is certainly the educational system. Any number of currents of thought—from the sociology of culture, including the works of Pierre Bourdieu and Jean-Claude Passeron, to the Althusserian current represented by Baudelot and Establet—have investigated this particular domain of social reproduction. In contrast with the accumulation of knowledge about schools, one can only be struck by the relative scarcity and the extreme fragmentation of scientific concern with critique of the media. One is especially struck by the fact that there has been so little conceptual exchange between these two fields of research on social reproduction.

One might speculate that this theoretical primacy of the educational sphere only confirms the real historical importance schools have had in the formation and the national cohesion of France. There is no doubt that the school system has for a long time competed successfully with the means of mass communication in the production of consensus and knowledge. After all, only as late as 1979 did a theoretician of the state as prolific as Nicos Poulantzas acknowledge the displacement of the major role in the formation of ideology from schools, the university, and literary culture to the audiovisual media.[6] But the claim of primacy for the educational system in the actual political and cultural formation of French society may well seem a bit thin as an explanation. Is the importance of schools really so particular to France?

The primacy of the educational system, and a second idea often presented as an explanation of the first, that is, the late arrival of technological progress in the French media, do not fully account for the very Althusserian tendency to classify both schools and the apparatuses of mass information and cultural dissemination in the category of "ideological state apparatuses," without specifying whether they are public or private. Althusser wrote: "It is unimportant whether the institutions in which they [ideological state apparatuses] are realized are 'public' or 'private.' What matters is how they function. Private institutions can perfectly well function as ideological state apparatuses."[7] To Althusser, the unity of the apparently disparate set of ideological state apparatuses is constituted by the very way in which they function. The state turns out to be everything because there is nothing that is not more or less immersed in dominant ideology.

This was without a doubt an ahistorical conception because, the primacy of the educational system having been engraved into theory, there was no way to raise questions about the possible shifts in hegemony among the various components of state ideological apparatuses, or the possible significance of the process of privatization of public services. Worse still, Althusserian theoricism, locked into the rationality of social reproduction, perceived "structure" as a self-sufficient, self-sustaining machine. This was a new version of left functionalism; it did not account for social contradictions that penetrated the state as well as civil society.

A number of social movements in civil society at the time suggested that there was a renewal, in social struggles, of reference to popular experience, popular memory, and popular cultures. These movements, in search of new forms of communication, felt a strong need to find a new approach to reality and to invent new ways of mobilizing collective knowledge.

We might add that Althusserian theoricism fit in very well with the role assigned to intellectuals by the French Communist Party—a role that allowed them to "produce concepts," thereby leading them to believe that they were changing the world. On the one hand the Party promoted corporatist strategies placed under the sign of economic demands raised by the large trade-union and political organizations; on the other hand, it promoted the idealism of theoretical production. The consequences of this gap were particularly serious for the evolution of public services. This schizophrenic approach was not the least of the obstacles to the development of critical thought on the necessary evolution of the notion of public service in the areas of education, culture, and communication.

And yet the moment when the theory of ideological state apparatuses first came into vogue was not so far removed in time from the first challenge to public service by the commercial logic stimulated by the breaking up of the state broadcasting corporation ORTF[8] in 1974.

We shall leave it to historians, or even to anthropologists, to develop a hierarchy of reasons French society as a whole—and not just the Marxist left—was so obsessed by education. However, we can suggest a hypothesis to explain this: Might there not be a link between this focus on education and the tendency to confine the analysis of the mechanisms of social reproduction within a problematic that does not transcend the borders of the nation-state? In one way or another, the rise of industrialized cultural production projects a national society into the process of internationalization of cultures and subcultures. Further, we suspect that the focus on education corresponds to the avoidance of a question that has only gradually emerged as a central one: the implication of forms of production and dissemination of knowledge in the changes in commercial and industrial systems, and more generally, the intervention of technology in cultural production.

Without claiming that there is a mechanical cause-and-effect relationship in these simultaneous focuses on education and the national level, we must note a particular feature of research on communication in France: the lack of questions raised about the process of internationalization. This was such a crying lack that in 1979, Jacques Rigaud, in a report submitted to the minister of foreign affairs under President Giscard d'Estaing, wrote:

> The interdependence of cultures is no longer a subject of philosophical reflection but an experienced reality. Dominant models promoted by ideological or economic imperialism, or simply by the uniformization of customs, are creating planetwide references and values. As a result, there is a twofold tendency, visible throughout the world, which consists of exalting the cultural identity of nations, local communities, and minorities of all sorts, while acknowledging the universal civilization emerging from this process. A country like France, more than others, should be conscious of this notion of interdependence, for its culture has both given a lot and received a lot. . . . Unfortunately this is not always the case. One might even be tempted to say that France is moving rapidly away from its tradition of cultural internationalism. . . . We are retreating back into our hexagon while believing that we are still casting a brilliant aura throughout the world.[9]

For the first time in an official report, the author (who was soon to be in charge of the multinational radio and TV group CLT-RTL) observed how little importance was accorded, by the French diplomatic apparatus and by French society in general, to the rise of the new paradigm imposed by competition in international markets; the French were still fascinated by the idea of the sovereignty of national culture.

It is therefore easy to understand why in collective modes of perception the stakes of internationalization are hardly present at all or are very vaguely perceived.

It was not until the second half of the 1970s that one began to see research in France — and this was still very much the exception — on the internationalization of communication systems.[10]

The Limits of Centrality

The rootedness of the problematics of culture and communication in the national space (which corresponds, after all, to the centrality associated with the concept of the national as it has been historically experienced in France) has condemned reflection on subcultures and local and regional specificities to remain marginal.

As sociologist Louis Quéré noted in 1979:

In France, we are just beginning to become interested in these questions of local sociability and local communication, whereas they have been attracting attention for a long time in other countries, particularly Great Britain, where researchers have engaged in much observation of life-styles, neighborhood relations, participation in local associations and various practices of sociability. . . . However, when this question is raised, it is usually raised only from the point of view of the observation of interindividual relations or the measuring of the frequency of contacts among individuals. The entire symbolic dimension of social exchange, which constitutes a culture and a form of sociability, thus escapes analysis. It is therefore advisable to integrate this dimension into an observation of the mechanisms of local communication. . . . It should be noted that such an orientation requires attention to methodology: in particular, detailed knowledge of the social processes which constitute local sociality (socialité) and the economics of local power call for an anthropological style of observation which is incompatible with the sociological habit of crossing the territories under study on highways rather than on small country roads.[11]

Certain approaches used by geographers in France stressed the importance of local objects of study long before communication research did. With the rise of decentralization and projects for establishing local networks, these contributions now stand out in particular relief. Such is the point of view of geographer Armand Frémont:

> Communication today occupies an important place in geographical thought as it confronts the problem of analyzing the transformation of space and the ways in which collective groups construct and appropriate space.[12]

The despatializing and delocalizing action of the major audiovisual means of mass communication conflicts with the logic of relocalization borne by cable and local networks, and this gives rise to new criteria for appropriating and dividing up space. "Power," writes Frémont, "has always been associated with the idea of a center or a pole; could it be exercized in the future without reference to what was for a long time one of its main characteristics?"[13]

A similar cluster of questions has been raised by geographer Roger Brunet. He observes that a whole new category of research projects has begun to focus on the new social uses of space. They are examining not only the material transformation of spaces but also the relationships between inhabitants and their space: attitudes, representations, myths, and values.

> The promotion of "new spaces of solidarity," "regional pools of employment," and other "territories," as well as concepts and fantasies about local and regional cultural identity and the dialectic of local and central power, cannot leave geographers indifferent, especially those who have long resided in their areas of study and have observed their development. A whole series of debates about territory and territoriality, the idea of the "local," the management of the spaces of daily life and recreation, and finally decentralization, require the mobilization of the practical knowledge of geographers and the production of a theoretical corpus of which only the broad outlines have yet appeared.[14]

This invitation for geographers to investigate new transdisciplinary areas centering around communication has not yet been formulated, or at least not so clearly, by historians. And yet the new light shed by the "history of mentalities" approach on the relationship beween the formation of power arrangements and popular resistance to them would be very useful for tracing the genealogy of contemporary systems of communication, and for the analysis of modes of interaction of diverse social groups with media systems—with mass systems as well as with fragmented ones.[15]

The history of mentalities, which is a fertile rapprochement between philosophers, ethnologists, and historians, has seen a considerable upsurge as well as a profound methodological renewal in the past few years. New interrogations have forced historians to look for new sources or to reread already known materials in a different light, but most of all to widen their territory considerably to include ways of loving, living and dying, the structuring of space and time, the categories of systems of representation, the symbolic dimension of bodily gestures, and iconography. One area in particular appears fruitful: the examination of relationships beween high culture and popular culture. "Far from seeking to identify 'pure' popular cultures or religions and seeing them, so to speak, as 'original' and purged of the scoriae with which time has soiled them, historians have, on the contrary, tried to trace the strategic places of encounter in which exchanges and borrowings as well as conflicts and resistances have taken place."[16] In a different vein, the research by historians on the production and circulation of books and the practice of reading opens up new paths of reflection on the passage from limited literacy to generalized literacy — from oral culture to an overwhelmingly written one.

In a country like France, the historians of mentalities have shed light on the resistance to the passage from oral to written culture manifested by newly literate people of the popular classes during the Enlightenment era, and have done a better job at this than has the sociology of media in its effort to investigate the passage from written culture to audiovisual culture, not to mention from audiovisual to computerized culture.

A Conception of the Middle Classes

No state can exist without a middle class, or so said Hegel. Where Marx saw the bourgeoisie-proletariat opposition as the motor of history and predicted the end of the middle classes, Hegel considered the latter to be the center or the essential element of what he called "civil society."[17] In his view, tomorrow's society would be a society of the middle classes — with the whole package of connotations related to the term "middle" (*moyen*) corresponding to as many functions: mediation, intermediary, and means (*moyen*). But all this has been forgotten: those who created the concept of "consumer society," and poured all the "masses" into this mold during the period of growth of the sixties, considered the "silent majority" (another appellation for the middle class) to be an inert component of modern society, a formless common denominator with no other identity than being a representation of average aspirations and average purchasing power — in short, the statistical profile of the consumer-citizen. Where Hegel saw the locus of cultivated intelligence and juridical consciousness of the mass of people, and a universal class that would serve as a mediator between the production of things and sociopolitical relations, critical sociology saw the group where mentalities were being molded by the "stupidity-inducing industry."

It had been forgotten, however, that this class also worked, so imposing were the ideologies of consumerism and leisure in defining it. This leisure was seen as corresponding to a "petty-bourgeois" taste, that is, a petty-bourgeois culture and ideology that Barthes characterized as "the residue of bourgeois culture, bourgeois truths which have become degraded, impoverished, commercialized, slightly archaic, or shall we say, out of date."[18] This characterization is reminiscent of Pierre Bourdieu's: "The petit bourgeois is a proletarian who makes himself small [*petit*] to become bourgeois."[19] Only the intellectual fraction of this class—preferably literary and philosophical intellectuals—could be saved from petty-bourgeois cultural banality, because this fraction was the bearer of high culture and noble forms of knowledge. This notion demarcated the territory and the content of the intellectual function, to the exclusion of other possible definitions of bearers of knowledge and culture: engineers, scientists, researchers, communication professionals, and all other "technicians of practical knowledge," as Sartre called them.

Today, uneasiness predominates. The concepts of middle class and petty bourgeoisie have been replaced by others that seek to account for a new reality: the new professional class, the "new petty bourgeoisie," the "third class," technocracy, technostructure, and so forth. The proliferation of approximate terms shows that we are still far from determining the nature of the new groups. All these expressions agree in acknowledging the rise of new social layers, the transformation of the labor process, and the increasing integration of intellectual labor into this process via technical knowledge, as well as through new configurations of power.

The heavy weight of received ideas is felt when it comes to giving the middle class an identity that no longer confines it to its consumer status, emblematic of the leisure activities of modern society. If the notion of entertainment as an area of freedom, pleasure, and enjoyment has made so much progress, it may be because from the start, analyses separated the notions of work and leisure, which in fact, as Brecht clearly saw, cannot be dissociated from one another.

Forgetting the Economy

The journal *Communications* represented a transdisciplinary alternative for French researchers in the sixties and seventies. When its first issue appeared in 1961, Henri Mercillon, one of the very few economists studying the film industry, lost no time in expressing to the editors his astonishment that economics had been left out of the journal's initial declaration of its aims. He wrote:

Without falling into the trap of a simplistic Marxist determinism, how astonished I am to see how the influence of economic reality has been neglected. There is no lack of film critics who are always ready to denounce, in their political professions of faith, "the influence of the infrastructure on the superstructure," but they compose their learned articles without ever making any reference to the problems posed by the economics of the seventh art [film]. Many sociologists, though experts in mass communications, are unattentive to changes in the structures of audiovisual broadcasting systems. This represents a striking inconsistency. . . . However, the cultural industries do not deserve to be treated with such silence (a silence which, one must add, suits their interests very well), when one thinks of the capital at stake, the complex economic and financial regime, the intense competition in which they engage among themselves, and the place they occupy in the general economic scheme of things.[20]

This type of observation had occasion to be repeated often in the course of the following twenty years. In 1976, a researcher taking stock of economic studies on art and culture observed the difficulty of legitimizing the economic approach:

One sometimes comes to doubt the usefulness of this kind of research: it is at best an alibi and at worst a danger, or simply subject to caution, or too costly with respect to other more "real" priorities, in particular taking stock of the heritage or preventing its death. Whereas, all too often, decisions of cultural policy still seem to refer to "the era of tastes and colors."[21]

By the second half of the seventies, however, a consciousness of the importance of economic research began to take hold. The urgency of retracing the evolution of cultural practices in the industrial and commercial context of mass cultural production came to be recognized by a handful of researchers.[22] Thus it was that the Center for the Sociology of Education and Culture, under the leadership of Pierre Bourdieu, sought to "vigorously attract economists to this new economics of symbolic goods."[23]

Ten years later, some would contest the Bourdieu school's borrowings from political economy. They criticized the members of this current for having, in their attempt to transcend the economism of economic theory, made a parody of economic language. Under the title "Economic Metaphor and Social Magic," Annie Cot and Bruno Lautier commented that

the exercise of borrowing a banal statement from economic discourse and conferring meaning on it by associating with every "market," "capital," or "profit" the qualifiers "linguistic," "symbolic," or "of distinction," is not so much a metaphor as it is a parody, according to the definition of Louis Marin—that is, a strategy of description and analysis involving the displacement of terminology and notions from the domain in which they were produced, their dissociation from the epistemological and methodological acts that gave birth to them, and their deployment on a different stage.[24]

Despite the limits of state policy in the area of research, in 1976-77 a pioneering study, financed by official agencies, was made of the economics of cultural industries. This work and those mentioned above on the problem of internationalization mark the rise of a new type of research. The genealogy of this approach is clearly expressed by the authors of *Capitalisme et industries culturelles* (Capitalism and culture industries):

> Our orientation is part of an approach that began several years ago and that had led us, on the basis of questions concretely raised for us by an increasing number of struggles on the cultural front, to analyze in terms of ideological state apparatuses the emergence and the institutionalization of structures that engage in cultural action. Wishing later on to understand the influence of cultural action on the forms and contents of commodity exchange, it appeared to us, upon reflection, that the study of exchange (that is, the realization of value) should not be made independently from that of production, thus taking into account capital in its unity. The result is this work, which is mainly dedicated to the economic analysis of cultural products and services.[25]

In the same period, another current of research emerged, focusing not on the problem of culture industries, but on telecommunication and "new networks," rapidly dubbed "thinking networks" (*réseaux pensants*). The theoretical inspiration and political traditions that fueled this line of research were very different from those that fueled the study of culture industries mentioned above: while the "culture industry" pole of research was initiated by economists and critical sociologists seeking to examine policies of cultural democratization and their growing dependence on the commodity circuit, the "network" pole was more closely bound to the preoccupations of industrial planning. Starting in 1975, it undertook research on communications systems for the benefit of the major technical and administrative bodies of the state, within the framework of a policy of modernization of the telephone system and strategies to promote a broad process of computerization in French society. Systems analysis and systems theory began to take form in the remodeled field of operational communication studies, amid numerous contradictions.

These contradictions had become apparent by April 1977 at a symposium organized by the French National Center for Telecommunications Studies, an event that marked the entry of social science into the area of telecommunications. For the first time, reference was made to the relation between technical innovation and social change. Several papers addressed the topic of "the informational economy," lending official recognition to the idea that economic development could be launched through information goods and services, in substitution for traditional energy sources. In an attempt to legitimize a vision marked by the determinisms of technological innovation, this approach took for granted the emergence of the "convivial society" of tomorrow, but it thereby avoided posing the problem of gaps or time lags between technical logics and social logics — between logics of innovation and symbolic and cultural logics. This criticism was formulated by Dominique Wolton and Jean-Louis Missika in a long conclusion they wrote for the published papers of the symposium.[26]

It was at this same symposium that sociologist Lucien Brams farsightedly pointed out the epistemological problems this new type of research, tied as it was to the needs and demands of state administration, was likely to encounter. Brams pointed to the lessons that could be learned from other fields of research that, since the beginning of France's Sixth Plan,[27] had brought together social scientists and state administrators as well as political-administrative and technical-administrative agents. He referred in particular to the urban research commissioned by the Ministry of Industrial Plants, Housing, and Transportation. These research programs, in his view, revealed confusion within the administration between means and ends, the means in fact becoming the ends. The logic of the engineer is founded upon a single postulate: it is necessary and sufficient to transform space in order to transform social life. "Let us build an agora, let us build a plaza, so that people may enter into relation with each other." In this perspective, commented Brams,

> the social sciences are considered as auxiliary disciplines contributing to the improvement and enrichment of the model-building activities of a certain number of engineer-researchers, by introducing into mathematical microeconomic and econometric models some sort of sociological dimension that makes the model more complex and helps it function better. In other words, these government ministries favored those social science research procedures that could be considered reassuring by the engineers; this was particularly true for the more technical ministries."[28]

It was not until a few years later, toward 1981, that another approach was to be formulated in communication research, challenging the logic of the engineer and the dominant status of "technological supply" and instead placing "social demand" at the heart of experimental practices and research on the uses of new technologies. The demand-oriented approach, unlike the other, begins with the analysis of individuals' needs and asks questions about the capacity of new technologies to meet them. This led to new contradictions, which we will examine in chapter 13.

At the same symposium, decidedly a paradigmatic one, there was also evidence of a historical approach to telecommunications and networks—in an open break from the monolithic theories about the state that continued to dominate critical references. Yves Stourdzé, in his study of the genesis of the telephone, clearly showed how the slow development of the telephone in France could not be explained by the shortcomings of the administration, but rather by the very nature of the French state and the particular mode of articulation and equilibrium between the different sectors of the state apparatus. He demonstrated, for example, how the development of the telephone had been sacrificed to that of postal services, an option that had favored the widespread distribution of the local press at low prices.[29]

At the threshold of the emergence of new information and communication technologies, this new type of analysis served as a reminder of the contradictory context in which the macrosocial uses of technological innovations took form. Other analyses of cultural industries at roughly the same time served as reminders of the sinuous paths followed by the formation of micro-uses in the economy of audiovisual technology.[30]

At the level of the state machine, rivalries progressively became apparent among the different ministries and organizations that shared responsibility for the management and maintenance of the apparatus of information and communication (in the broad sense): rivalries between the large cultural institutions and the Ministry of National Education; between the telecommunications apparatus and the audiovisual communications insitutions; between industrial policy-making bodies and security forces. In all these areas, there were perceptible differences in points of view and in strategic interests involving the control of the new networks and communications systems. The struggle over new technologies revealed how, in what was also a phase of the modernization of the state, hegemonies were pursued within the state apparatus itself. This silent conflict brought out the unequal degrees of development among different sectors of the state apparatus with respect to the question of technology. In other words, the search for hegemony could be explained by the uneven topography of the state, marked in particular by tensions among the major administrative and professional bodies.

2

The Quest for Transdisciplinarity

A French Project

If, in the questions addressed to communication theory in France, there has been a tendency to neglect economics, the problematics of language and discourse have by contrast benefited from an undeniable legitimacy. Roland Barthes's semiological project attests to this. In the founding document of his research group at the Ecole Pratique des Hautes Etudes, the author of *Mythologies* wrote in 1960, "To the extent that culture appears more and more as a system of symbols, in short, as a language, it is legitimate to envision, as Emile Benveniste did, the development of a true science of culture inspired by semiology."[1]

This project was conceived in an ambitious framework and given concrete form by the creation of the Center for the Study of Mass Communications (CECMAS). Barthes's project was one of three major axes of a larger project aimed at developing a French approach to mass communications in a resolutely transdisciplinary perspective. Several considerations justified the establishment, on the initiative of Georges Friedmann, of this center, which was the first serious attempt in France to constitute an environment and a research framework that went beyond the narrow field of traditional studies on the press and sought to examine "relations between the overall society and the mass communications that are functionally integrated into it."[2]

The first observation made was the tardiness of French research in exploring mass communications, defined as "the whole set of cultural phenomena that are inseparable from technical civilization: the mainstream press (dailies and weeklies), magazines, radio broadcasting, cinema, records, advertising, and the rapidly ascending medium of television."[3]

Violette Morin was to recall eighteen years later, upon Georges Friedmann's death, that in Friedmann's mind what was important was "to not allow the Americans the exclusive privilege of evaluating the importance of the audiovisual media and to refine the celebrated content analyses of which the Berelson school furnished the first models."[4]

The second observation was to point out the insufficiency of the founding idea of the center: "mass communication." The editorial of the first issue of *Communications* is clear on this point:

> The study of mass communications is still seeking its path; the expression itself is not very satisfactory; like its companions ("mass culture" and "mass media"), it provokes many reservations. . . . On these points the Center for the Study of Mass Communications does not want to choose its doctrine in an *a priori* fashion: *we hope that its work will serve to define things, not words.* [Our emphasis]

The third observation was on the necessity of setting this project in a transdisciplinary perspective. This requirement was embodied in the very structure of the center. Next to the semiological project of Roland Barthes, which brought together all the research on the symbolic status of cultural phenomena, there were two other research orientations, under the respective leadership of Georges Friedmann and Edgar Morin.

For Georges Friedmann, the study of mass communications was to be included in a perspective opened up by his previous studies on labor and technology — in particular, the appearance in Western societies of leisure time created and liberated by a technological civilization (nonlabor time). In a more encompassing way, it was to be integrated into his investigations on "massification": mass production, mass consumption, mass audiences. As he wrote, "Technological civilization and mass culture are organically linked."[5] As was reflected by his research on American, Soviet, and Latin American societies, the founder of the CECMAS was also someone for whom the international dimension of mass communication was ever present.

The research of Edgar Morin took place in the framework of what he called, in a neologism, "the sociology of the present." "The term 'sociology of the present,' " he wrote,

> does not designate a doctrine and does not circumscribe a field. Rather, it brings together a certain number of preoccupations. To what extent is an event occurring in the present not only a piece of historical data but also sociologically revealing information? To what extent can the sociologist consider that the field of social experience is also an unrefined field of experiment? To what extent can attention to phenomena of the present clinically

enrich sociological reflection? To what extent can our relation to the present claim a privileged status for understanding society's relations with the dimensions of time (past, future) and that of space?[6]

In 1974, the Center for the Study of Mass Communications became the Center for Transdisciplinary Studies: Sociology, Anthropology, and Semiology (CETSAS). In this new title, the recognition of the pluridisciplinary approach appeared to justify the original project, but in fact it masked a growing distance from the earlier object of research, which was mass communications. As the years went by, the number of studies in this area diminished. Only a few researchers, such as Christian Metz, Violette Morin, and Eliseo Verón (an Argentinian semiotician who was to leave the center at the end of the seventies) continued to pursue research that reflected the original project. Moreover, very few of the studies undertaken dared to explore the area of radio or television discourse.[7] The researchers preferred to remain in the area of theory and analysis of film, or literary texts more generally.[8]

It must be added that by the end of the sixties, the tools of structural linguistics had begun to produce effects in the practices of the advertising industry, lending decisive support to the first modern media revolution that French society had experienced: the marketing revolution.[9] Linguists and semiologists made key contributions by shedding light on the encoding and decoding of advertising discourse; the main contributions were lexicological analysis and semiotests. The research director of the large advertising firm Publicis was a student of Roland Barthes for a long time; this firm became the pioneer and promoter of what was then called "advertising semiology."[10]

In 1979, following the deaths of Georges Friedmann and Roland Barthes, the CETSAS was renamed the CETSAP. The reference to semiology was dropped and replaced by a reference to politics.

At the end of the seventies, paradox moved in to stay. At a time when mass communications had become a political and industrial stake of major importance for the restructuring of French society, when relations between intellectuals and the media were becoming a truly determinant question and when educational institutions were having to come to terms with media modes of production and dissemination of knowledge, this first collective project for the constitution of a field of research on communication was largely absent from theoretical and practical debates. The consequences of these important changes in society would be understood only through the isolated interventions and individual projects of researchers scattered throughout the universities, the media, the national research institute (CNRS), private research groups, or simply those who chose—or were forced—to find their orientations outside these institutions.

Toward Cybernetics

"To define things and not words." How and why did this objective, over time, metamorphose into its opposite? Henri Mercillon, whom we quoted earlier, has suggested the first element of an answer: the forgetting of economics. This is correct but does not explain everything. One should at least add the forgetting of history. Indeed, one finds very little trace of research on the genealogy of media systems, and few analyses attempting to answer questions as basic as: How are media linked to their historical and geographical areas? What are the relations between the different media? What are the economic and political determinants of the social functions and uses of communications technologies? What role does the realm of the imaginary play in the invention of these uses?

With the exception of a few studies launched by Georges Friedmann, the great majority of analyses were caught in a conceptual framework that rapidly became a dead end.

The theoretical corpus was buried in "universals" (as witnessed by the constant reiteration of themes such as "massification," "standardization," "uniformization," "passive consumption," etc.); the result was, naturally, an abstract and ecumenical language about media and their action on humankind. By not grasping communication through the material conditions of its functioning, through its history and through its links with other systems of socialization, this generation of researchers left the door wide open to all kinds of beliefs, illusions, and mythologies.

The vacuum created by the lack of historical questioning and by the resulting "culturalist lure" explains the failure, at the end of the sixties, to reflect on the progressive diversification of communication techniques; it explains the focus on consumer society and its manifestations (advertising, vacations, leisure), and finally the silence regarding the major issues appearing on the horizon of the coming decade. With the exception of an issue on cable television in 1974, the journal *Communications* broached none of the questions raised by the French policy of computerization pursued from the midseventies on. The field of the media continued to be treated as the field of leisure activity, even as technological evolution was turning communication and information into one of the major axes around which all the structures of French society and international relations were reorganizing themselves.

The absence of history and economics particularly manifested itself in the unfocused definition of the "source" (*émetteur*) of communication. The practical result of this lack of precision was the promotion of a conception of media power as perfectly unified and monolithic, unaffected by the action of the diverse components of civil society. This conception of unmediated power reigned without challenge throughout the sixties and the beginning of the seventies. It was just as visible in the Althusserian theory of ideological state apparatuses, as we have already noted, as in the studies on the reproduction of social relations of domination through the educational system.

The break with history did not occur only through the neglect of the genealogy of systems of communications. It also took place through more subtle channels: thus history was the absent party when structuralist research neglected questions about the nature of enunciators and the role of addressees, isolating contents in closed corpuses referred to as "messages."

From within the field of linguistics, however, certain voices, which were in the minority, risked suggesting approaches that broke with the analysis of closed and immobile corpuses. Borrowing the notion of "discursive formation" from the archaeology of Michel Foucault, linguists such as Michel Pêcheux attempted to escape from the internal, immanent logic of "processes of discourse," reinserting such processes into contexts that were both technologically and sociohistorically identified: within a given historical period, coherent discursive formations can be distinguished, each one defining a "regime of truth" ("what can and must be said, and what remains unspoken") and a set of positions accessible to individual subjects.

But even here, the idea of an origin-structure of enunciations could not succeed in locating with precision the position of the enunciator. As Michel Pêcheux would later write,

> Believing itself to be following Michel Foucault, discourse analysis continued in fact to credit overall historical visions that claimed to account for the complete gamut of texts. This deviation manifested itself in the systematic use, in discourse analysis, of expressions taking the following forms: the/a + adjective (designating category or subcategory) + discourse; the discourse of + (abstract nominal subject); the discourse of + (collective subject); or the discourse of + (plural nominal subject). For example, "the discourse of the bourgeoisie" or "the petty bourgeoisie."[11]

In 1965, at the colloquium of Royaumont, where scientists, engineers, and philosophers had been invited to reflect on the concept of information in contemporary society, sociologist Lucien Goldmann raised a provocative issue: the place of the addressee or receiver in the definition of information. "Information," he said, "is the transmission of a certain number of messages — true or false statements — to an individual who receives them, deforms them, accepts or refuses them, or remains completely deaf or refractory to any reception."[12]

This kind of thinking, involving notions such as Goldmann's category of "possible consciousness," was then in the minority. Structural analysis scarcely granted any place to the subject in the production of meaning. The few studies that considered the role of the enunciator or sender always gave the same image of the receiver, stressing the latter's passive nature and conceiving the sending apparatus exclusively as a machine for reproducing the system of social domination. How could there be any room for analysis of the uses receivers make of discourses? By definition, receiving subjects were subordinated to the imperative rationality of the structure. What else could they do, in their reading or viewing of messages, but obey the schema of stimulus and response?

Eviction of history also occurred when the cybernetic schema was clumsily imposed on the complexity of social relations of communication — an approach that could first be detected in 1971. Issue 18 of *Communications* reflected this development when it inaugurated the new definition of the transdisciplinary character of one of the center's lines of research: the sociology of the present.

The issue, which included a preface and a postface by Edgar Morin, was built around the notion of event. It included contributions by Henri Atlan, Jean-Pierre Changeux, Anthony Wilden, Emmanuel Le Roy-Ladurie, Abraham Moles, Henri Laborit, and others. It was followed by another issue, number 22, on "the nature of society."

In 1971, the project of a sociology of the present gave way to a project of a science of events: the idea was to "transform into an object of science what had remained up to now the irrational residue of objective research."[13] Although the contributions of other disciplines in the human sciences could not find their way into the research of the center, for the first time the life sciences made their appearance; they were called to the rescue and turned into the "hard core" around which Edgar Morin thought he could develop a new conception of transdisciplinarity.

> Like all creative novelties, the science of the event is emerging not in the heart of an already constituted discipline, but in a no-man's-land between several disciplines. It is being created at the crossroads of cybernetics and modern systems theory, at the point where a theory of self-organizing systems appears. . . . The relation between system and event becomes the central problem. Between structure and history, there has been an infinite and unfortunate vacuum. . . . This vacuum can and must be filled by the system (which encompasses the structure, which constitutes the invariant feature of the system) and the event. In fact,

consideration of the event brings us to pursue, indissociably, a systems approach (which has only been sketchily outlined here and there in systems theory) and a science of evolution.[14]

In 1974, the rapprochement between the life sciences and the human sciences took more precise form. The diagnosis is clear: the former had neglected what, in the *Homo*, is *sapiens, loquex, faber*, and *socius*; the latter had forgotten to inquire about the natural (biological) world. But new elements and new events had arrived in abundance, making urgent the destruction of barriers among disciplines: the discovery of sociability in the natural world; the discovery of a profound naturelike character in human society; the realization that sociological and anthropological theory were lacking in foundations; the possiblity of no longer seeing the distance between animal and man, nature and culture, as an absolute gap between two uncommunicating universes, but conceiving them rather as within an evolving, transformational phase. Thus communications theory, cybernetics, systems theory, and the theory of self-organization all had concepts and methods to offer, with equal applicability to biological organization and to social organization.

By 1974, Serge Moscovici, in his conclusion to the *Communications* issue on "the nature of society," while recognizing the necessity of a new episteme for redefining the contours of society and its relationship to nature, noted:

> Biology, molecular or otherwise, has acquired some unquestionable merits in our time. The failings of physics have, moreover, further enhanced its brilliance and that of cybernetics, and that is only right. But it is still true that sciences, when they gain in precision, seek to dominate one another; behind their democratic façade, they are internally autocratic, and always close to the comforts of power. Biology is no exception. The general character of social phenomena should nonetheless persuade it, contrary to what is actually happening, to seek to change its concepts and models, which were all formed on the basis of the individual organism and the animal locked into its cage at the zoo.[15]

Suggesting the possible broad lines of an equal exchange between the sciences of life and human sciences, he continued:

> It is by breaking with the pecking order and learning the lessons of sociology, anthropology, and social psychology that biology can better understand the significance of social phenomena and their repercussions at the organic and evolutionary levels. (Most research in ethnology, biology, and animal psychology manifests the poverty of their authors in these domains, to the detriment of

both observation and theory.) Failing this, it will relapse into a sort of zoomorphism that uses scientific jargon but is hardly better than the anthropomorphism that has been made fun of so much. This zoomorphism is a soil that nourishes diverse ideologies; it combines a claim of expertise with a hair-raising ignorance of the social and the historical; it shelters, beneath the shallow surface of its discourse of reason, a thick layer of badly clarified prejudices and badly settled emotional troubles.[16]

3

The Temptation of Metaphor

On the Difficulty of Extrapolating Models

The introduction of the life sciences into the conceptual framework of social communication is an indication of how much these sciences govern, in France, the development of the social use of the concept of communication and, even more so, that of information. It is no coincidence that for a long time molecular biology and linguistics, as well as mathematics and physics, have shared a single conceptual framework via the concepts of code, image, message, and information. Although French scientists were not the first to imagine the transposition of vocabulary from linguistics to biology, they have in one way or another greatly contributed to the exchange between the life sciences and certain areas of the social sciences. What can be learned from the writings of a number of French specialists in molecular biology is that it is possible to take an interest in the social without necessarily subscribing to the theses of sociobiology.

There is practically no way of understanding the trajectory of structural linguistics without taking into account the exchange between biology and linguistics in the sixties. It is enough to mention the parallels between the ideas of François Jacob, biologist and Nobel Prize winner in medicine, and the theories of Roman Jakobson, an influential figure in French linguistics. Jacob explained:

> The image that best describes our knowledge of heredity is that of a chemical message: a message written not with complex molecular structures as had long been believed, but through the combinatorial possibilities of four chemical bases. The four units repeat themselves millions of times all along the chromosomal fiber; they combine and permute infinitely like the letters of the

alphabet throughout a text. In the same way that a sentence constitutes a segment of a text, a gene constitutes the segment of a nucleic fiber. In both cases, an isolated symbol represents nothing; only the combination of signs acquires a "meaning." In both cases, a determined sequence, sentence or gene, begins and ends with specific "punctuation" signs. The translation of the nucleic sequence into a proteic sequence is comparable to the translation of a message that arrives in Morse code, and which does not acquire meaning until translated, into French for example. This occurs through a "code" that provides the equivalence of "signs" between the two "alphabets," nucleic and proteic.[1]

The linguist Roman Jakobson, stimulated by the research of geneticists, went beyond these analogical promenades and revealed other structural resemblances between the two systems of information studied, respectively, by linguists and geneticists: in both cases, there is a strictly linear character to the temporal sequence of coding and decoding; it is possible to reduce the relations between elements, phonemes or chemical bases, to a system of binary oppositions; the levels of construction are hierarchically ordered by the successive integration of units of inferior rank, and so on.[2]

It was very difficult to question the validity and the particularity of this type of interdisciplinary marriage in France in the sixties and seventies. Structuralism, then predominant, determined which questions were valid. And yet the attentive reader of certain texts by François Jacob could locate serious reservations on his part regarding the genetic-linguistic parallel applied as mechanically as Jakobson had done. If bridges could be built between the linguistic model and the genetic code, that was no reason, thought Jacob, to fall into promiscuity:

> The analogies of structure between the two systems must be sought, preferably, among analogies of function. In many regards, they do indeed play similar roles. Both function by accumulating information, preserving it, and transmitting it. But to establish a parallel is also to state its limits. Linguistics studies messages transmitted from a source to a receiver. In biology, however, there is nothing of the kind — neither source nor receiver.[3]

The Nobel laureate in medicine had also explained why genetics was so fond of models and why it borrowed them so freely from the human sciences. "For lack, perhaps, of being able to achieve true mathematically founded theories, biology functions most often with the aid of models. It is a fact that in biology, there are many generalizations whereas theories are very rare. . . . That is why there is a frequent tendency to confuse the model with an explanation and analogies with identities."[4]

In the sixties, structuralism was in search of a scientific status; the human sciences were attempting to escape from the impressionism of which they had often been accused. The rapprochement with the life sciences provided them with the security of an identity close to that of the "hard sciences." In a dialogue with François Jacob, Claude Lévi-Strauss expressed such a feeling:

> Yes, for imagine what is happening to us in the sciences referred to as human: we constantly sense that there are "true" sciences which are those of the physicist, the biologist, or the astronomer, and that we are usurping a title to which we have no right. You [of the natural sciences] achieve certainty, whereas we vegetate in the domain of conjectures and probabilities.[5]

The relations between the human sciences and the life sciences already have a long history. The example we have just mentioned constitutes merely the prehistoric phase. In the sixties, linguistics came to the rescue of biology, offering it a structured analysis. In the eighties, things have changed. According to an official report on the state of scientific research, "until now the human sciences have provided the specialists of the life sciences with only the foundations for an epistemological reflection. This relation—a rather one-sided one—is tending to reverse itself today, as certain sectors of the human sciences draw closer to the life sciences."[6]

The borrowings made in the sixties by molecular biology from linguistic models cause us to smile today, because so strict a symmetry is clearly no longer sought by anyone. What leaves us less indifferent is the movement in the other direction: the tendency of the life sciences to move toward discourse about humankind, society, and politics. Metaphors from the biological sciences are now being reinvested into social and political thought.

More than ever, the field of communication is being exposed to such transfers. The vocabulary of biology is so dense in certain interpretations of the social in the eighties that Antoine Danchin, in his book *L'Oeuf et la poule: Histoires du code génétique* (The chicken and the egg: Histories of the genetic code), does not hesitate to use the term "biologism" to designate a current of thought in which biology is indeed mobilized and recruited by force into conceptions of the totality and the thermodynamics of the social. In revolt against the recent vogue of identifying information with "entropy" and using other categories of thermodynamics, he writes:

> We have seen other abuses of the mechanical imposition of thermodynamic concepts on certain aspects of reality. In the

present case, these concepts, applied to the central nervous system, are particularly dangerous, because they carry with them an ideology of *order*, the political and moral connotations of which can severely alter our vision of this system.[7]

"Communication," in these discourses, often designates a regulatory function within a system or organism. The notion of system common to both biology and computer science can entail neglect of the basic differences that may exist between the nature of the living organisms studied by biologists and the nature of the society studied by anthropologists and sociologists.

Theories in the social sciences obtained by extrapolation from physical or biological models have become too numerous to count. It is possible, however, to observe the changes in viewpoint reflected by discourses that mobilize biology and cybernetics to reflect on the social. The novelty no doubt resides in the fact that in certain of these extrapolations, the life sciences, in raising the problem of human communication, start with a definition of this notion that has nothing to do with the human sciences. At another level, in their insistence on reflecting on the organization, the totality, and the social regulation in real time that would supposedly be assured by technologies of information and communication and their performances, it is clear that these schemas do not define communication by opposition to the notion of atomization so much as against the notions of conflict and contradiction. Hence the confusion generated by arbitrary rapprochements.

Through the mechanical transposition of models of this kind, the illusion is spreading of a society that is transparent because it is self-regulated, and which, like a living organism, supposedly finds mechanisms of retroaction and equilibrium within itself.

The danger here is pointed out by Antoine Danchin when he speaks of the conjunctural tendency to stress the totality of the living, and to "introduce totalitarian ideological principles into 'scientific' discourse."[8] This supernatural form of thought, which posits communication as a vital principle, takes into account neither the sending nor the receiving of messages, neither the carriers nor the receivers of information; it is also indifferent to meaning, taking an interest in return transmission only insofar as it signals regulation and constitutes a means of testing the effect obtained. It matters little what is circulating—and that is no doubt why "communication" seems to this form of thought a more usable notion than "language," "symbolic expression," "ideological discourse," or "exchange."

The emergence of the life sciences reflects the competition into which biological research has been violently propelled for the first time in its history. As Professor Jean-Paul Lévy noted in May 1984, "Research is undergoing a change in spirit because of the penetration of biology into industry and the rise of biotechnologies. What counts is no longer to participate but to win. Our competitors consider, alas, that all is fair, and this will be more and more the case. More and more, there will be war."[9]

From the Philosophy of Progress to the Philosophy of Communication

In 1979, we wrote, "It is no exaggeration to say that the philosophy of communication is in the process of assuming, through the voice of political power and electronics corporations, the role played by the philosophy of progress in the nineteenth century."[10] In the years that followed, this trend was confirmed. Today, communication's role of the heir to progress is no longer borne only by advertising discourse. More and more, communication in this role is at the heart of scientific discourse. It is thus quite interesting to return to certain pioneering texts in order to understand the success this notion has enjoyed through its almost unlimited extension in biology (at a time when biology is adopting a more and more integrated approach, turning more and more, after the success of molecular biology, toward the study of superior organisms).[11]

In *The Logic of Life*, François Jacob wrote,

> Every object that biology studies is a system of systems. Being part of a higher-order system itself, it sometimes obeys rules that cannot be deduced simply by analysing it. This means that each level of organization must be considered with reference to the adjacent levels. . . . At every level of integration, some new characteristics come to light. . . . Very often, concepts and techniques that apply at one level do not function either above or below it. The various levels of biological organization are united by the logic proper to reproduction. *They are distinguished by the means of communication, the regulatory circuits and the internal logic proper to each system.* [Our emphasis][12]

It would seem that it is precisely the specificity of "means of communication" and "regulatory circuits" that had been forgotten when such descriptions were interpreted to the letter in an effort to reflect on the organization of information systems in our societies. It would also seem that "the new characteristics," both of properties and of logic, have been passed over in silence—those original characteristics that Jacob saw appearing at each level of organization of living organisms. This shows to what extent certain people wished to retain only what allowed them to achieve the legitimation of "communication" through biology.

It is true that the limits set by Jacob were violated somewhat by the manner in which he presented biology's way of ridding itself of "metaphysics": "From particles to man, there is a whole series of integration, of levels, of discontinuities. But there is no breach either in the composition of the objects or in the reactions that take place in them; no change in 'essence,' "[13] From particles to man: the formula reminds one of the famous phrase of Jacques Monod: "What is true for the coli bacillus is also true for the elephant."[14]

Perhaps even more significant is the slide from the notion of *information*, linked to molecular genetics, to that of *communication*, in the effort to reflect theoretically on the growing complexity of living systems and also to define evolution in a different way; progress, progression, and perfection are all inadequate descriptives.

As is well known, an important place was accorded, in the ideology of progress, to the biological discourse identifying progress with evolution. Today, this same discourse states that evolution does not open a path to progress, but to communication. By substituting a link between evolution and communication for the older link between evolution and progress, progression, and perfection, biology has officially ratified our entry into a new way of representing the social. It is also, without a doubt, in the process of establishing ties with other social groups, according to other logics than those that, in the nineteenth century, assured the success of the notions of progress and perfection. The consequences of this recognition and promotion of communication by biology have not yet been fully felt; it will invoke first of all a new scientific paradigm—to remodel the frontiers between the sciences and to renew conceptual frameworks—but will also spur change in ways that will influence research. One finds, for example, that the association between the growth of freedoms and the growth of communication possibilities is accepted without challenge, as if it were obvious, even when it is applied far from its original terrain— that is, in most political and mercantile discourses.

Returning to the idea of the code, Jacob further noted, alluding to the structuralism of the time:

> From family organization to modern state, from ethnic group to coalition of nations, a whole series of integrations is based on a variety of cultural, moral, social, political, economic, military and religious codes. The history of mankind is more or less the history of these integrons and the way they form and change. There again appears a trend towards growing integration made possible by the development of new means of communication. As long as it is confined to speech, the transfer of information is limited in space and time. With writing, communication can break free of time and the past experience of each individual can

be stored in a collective memory. With electronics, with the means of preserving sound and image and transmitting them to any point on the globe at a moment's notice, all restrictions in time and space have disappeared.[15]

As the evolution reaches its momentary term, we discover today that we have succeeded in inventing modern technologies of communication, but we have also returned, with electronics, to the origin of the word "communication," and moved imperceptibly from *systems* to *means* of communication. Are these the same? Can the media or the new technologies of information be reduced to the "nervous system" of a society?

It is tempting for biologists in particular to draw relations between the different processes in question and to seek "analogies"—that is, to believe, in Jacob's words, that "the variation of societies and cultures comes to be based on evolution, like that of species," and that "all that has to be done, then, is to define the criteria of selection." "The trouble," concludes Jacob, "is that no one has yet succeeded. For with their codes, their regulations, their intersections, the objects that form cultural and social integrons transcend the explanatory schemas of biology."[16]

The problems raised by Jacob in his unified program for the science of man are most certainly at an early stage of formulation, and the interdisciplinarity he postulated allows us, at best, only to raise a certain number of questions and to envision the redefinition of boundaries. In the current state of interface among disciplines, any claim to go beyond this, any claim to do more than establish links among various elements, would be to fall victim to the analogies of which he spoke. And not everyone resists the temptation.

In 1977, for example, biologist Jacques Ruffié wrote the following comment about animal communication: "Almost all animals communicate among themselves. Communication thus appears as a very general phenomenon of the living world. It forms the 'cement' of the social bond; the more the means of communication are precise and rigorous, the better society will perform."[17] In a chapter entitled "Langage et communication," the author continues:

> Without an adequate means of integration, the human type of society would have disappeared long ago. Even more than in animals, the growing specialization of [human] individuals constitutes a powerful centrifugal force, the tension of which has increased throughout human history. . . . *Today, it is the audiovisual means of communication that, via the mass media, spread knowledge throughout the world. These constantly expanding means of communication are indispensable for the*

maintenance of equilibrium and harmony in the human group.
They ensure the cultural unity of mankind. [Our emphasis][18]

Jacob spoke of communication as the trend of evolution and as a process leading to greater openness. Ruffié seems to add a new dimension by speaking of media as the antennae of the successfully performing human race; consequently, there is an identification between evolution and the country with the highest level of development in communication equipment, no matter how wary Ruffié may claim to be of certain deformations of Darwinism. It is no doubt this natural philosophy of history, and this tendency to refer to animal societies, that provoked the following remarks by an anthropologist: "Men, contrary to other social animals, are not satisfied merely to live in society—they produce society in order to live. They manufacture their history, History itself."[19]

A Science Lacking an Epistemology

Forgetting the locus of production: this is a constant that can be found all along the paths of research in France toward the construction of the object known as "information and communication." The loci of historical, economic, and linguistic production have systematically been forgotten.

Furthermore, there is especially a tendency to forget the locus of intellectual production—the refusal of a real epistemology. This forgetfulness has taken on certain particular connotations in France today. Mathematician René Thom, in the debate that pitted him against certain biologists and against Edgar Morin, took a position against hasty syntheses that mix together thermodynamics, systems theory, cybernetics, and biology:

> The concepts brought into play in our framework (determinism, chance, uncertainty, order, disorder, complexity, information, etc.) all have one characteristic in common: they admit of no precise meaning except in the framework of an explicit (mathematical) formalism. If one does not bind these concepts to the formal framework that gives them precision, one is condemned to indulge in a discourse . . . that is so fluid and so ambiguous that they [the concepts] sink, almost inevitably, into mere verbosity.[20]

Observing the proliferation of what he calls "works of popular epistemology" (we leave him the responsibility for this label, which is far from satisfactory in our view)—a genre in which he includes Henri Atlan's *Entre le cristal et la fumée*, Jacques Monod's *Le Hasard et la nécessité*, and Edgar Morin's *La Méthode*, all of which have participated in the rise of cybernetic schemas—René Thom writes:

A question may be raised at the sociological level: What explains the flourishing of the relatively new genre, that so conspicuously cultivates the art of fuzziness and approximation? Why, in France, has the race of true epistemologists, such as Poincaré, Duhem, Meyerson, Cavaillès, Koyré, apparently died out? Why has French scientific philosophy not produced, like the Anglo-Saxons, a Popper, or, more recently, a Kuhn? Could it be the fundamentally subjectivistic and ascientific character of a university tradition growing out of Husserl and Heidegger, dominated too often by an atmosphere of political moralizing? A person comes to mind as being responsible for this situation: Could Bachelard, with his big smile, be the one at the source of this literary deviation of epistemology? I admit that I have fewer reservations about this latter type of production which, after all, does not so much claim to state what science must be as to draw from scientific metaphors a strongly literary resonance, for the pleasure of all. At least these authors do not speak *ex cathedra*, from the heights of their scientific reputations.[21]

Thom, who goes so far as to speak of "apostles of desertion," risks a hypothesis that coincides with some of our earlier questions. "Aside from the very lively tradition of Christian idealism in France, one must also evoke the case of the Marxist thinkers: contrary to their counterpart on the other side of the Rhine, the Frankfurt School, French Marxist thought has all too often been sterilized by political dogmatism."[22] This observation reinforces our idea that it is impossible to explain the deviations noted in the process of building the field of knowledge about communication without adopting an international and comparative perspective. This appears all the truer once the overly provincial character of French research has been observed.

PART 2

New Paradigms

Introduction to Part 2

Although their history is short, the sciences of information and communication have had breaks in their trajectory too numerous to count. The movement of revision began at the end of the seventies; since then, there has not been a year without journals and colloquia announcing the decline of certain paradigms and the rise of others. No geographical area has been spared by these challenges, not even — or especially not — the place consecrated by history as the birthplace of the first scientific analyses of modern means of communication, the United States. This was demonstrated by the publication in the summer of 1983 of a special issue of the *Journal of Communication*, one of the most representative journals of the American academic community in this discipline.[1] The issue, entitled "Ferment in the Field," not only undertook a discussion of the founding themes of functionalism but also invited dissenting approaches to express themselves.

A long path had been traveled from the disdain expressed in 1949 by Robert K. Merton, one of the fathers of American sociology, when he drew a contrast between the speculative approach of European sociology of knowledge (in which he included Marx alongside Mannheim and Durkheim) and American-style sociology of communication, which in his view was less marked by "metaphysical preoccupations." In this contrast he saw the expression of two different mentalities, two different world views, and two profoundly different cultures: the European one with its philosophical tradition, and the American one with its empirical orientation. Carried away by ethnocentric arrogance, he allowed himself to utter some terse judgments: "The American knows what he is talking about, and that is not much; the European knows not what he is talking about, and that is a great deal. . . . The European imagines and the American looks; the American investigates the short run, the European speculates on the long run."[2] There was no room for dialogue between the "objectivity" and the "veracity" that in his view characterized American sociology of communication and the value-judgment orientation that, according to him, affected what he called the "historical method of [European] sociology of knowledge."

In 1985, by contrast, the 35th Annual Conference of the International Communication Association (the largest professional association of researchers and practitioners of communication theory in the United States) chose as its title "Beyond Polemics: Paradigm Dialogues." American empiricism rediscovered the Frankfurt School, lent an ear to French linguistic structuralism, invited English Marxists to talk about the contributions of contemporary semiotic theories of representation, and accepted a confrontation between the conception of language underlying traditional forms of content analysis and new conceptions of "language space" introduced by Derrida, Barthes, and Foucault. One idea was omnipresent in the colloquium's publications and haunted its corridors: the crisis of the dominant paradigms.

But let us not be misled: if it is true that certain minority sectors in the social sciences in the United States are seeking resources in the philosophical traditions and in the history of European critical consciousness, others, and not the least influential, welcome the new paradigms in order to reinvigorate the old ones.[3]

This appeal by American empiricism to the European critical schools is quite paradoxical, especially considering that on the European side of the Atlantic, these schools are not immune to the crisis of paradigms.[4]

In Europe, theoreticians thought they had gripped certainty. Structuralism was such a certainty: with it, they thought they possessed a unified method applicable to all sciences, including the human sciences. In the quest for truly scientific status pursued by the latter since their origins, it was thought that structuralism had ushered in a new era. In spite of strong opposition from history and sociology, structural linguistics thought of itself as the royal science, "the science of sciences." The concept of communications system became central and was generalized by the structural approach. For Lévi-Strauss, communication was the unifying concept par excellence, and in his view it could explain the rules of kinship, language, and economic exchange.

During the structuralist apotheosis, although everyone invoked the concept of communication to the saturation point, in fact the communication process was what received the least attention. The height of absurdity was reached: linguistics saw fit to study languages in abstraction from the speaking subject and the referent. Language was studied, but not the language actually spoken by psychologically and sociologically situated subjects. Linguistics studied sentences and the system of rules and constraints underlying their forms, cutting them from their loci of production.[5]

4

The Theory of Information

Linearity

If structural linguistics and the schools of thought that claimed its mantle eliminated from their field of analysis all reference to context, postulating the neutrality of the sending and receiving instances, it was because some of their premises were borrowed from a theory with mathematical origins.

In his book *The Mathematical Theory of Communication* (1949), Claude Shannon put forward an outline of the "general system of communication."[1] He exposed the mathematical framework that allowed problems to be posed relating to the cost of a message, the cost of an act of communication between a transmitter ("the source") and a receiver in the presence of random disturbances, known as "noise." In order to minimize total expense, one will transmit the message using the least expensive agreed-upon signs. The conceptual framework he proposes is based on the following chain of elements: *the source of information*, which produces a message (the words spoken into a telephone); *the transmitter*, which transforms the message into signals (the telephone transforms the voice into electronic oscillations); *the channel*, which is the medium used to transport the signals (the telephone cable); *the receiver*, who reconstructs the message from the signals; and *the destination*, which is the person (or object) to whom the message is sent.

This theory, formulated by a mathematician working for Bell Telephone Company, obviously borrowed heavily from biology, in particular the study of the nervous system. Having passed through mathematics, it was to be used again shortly later by molecular biology in its search for new ways of understanding heredity. Biological specificity—the characteristics that make an individual unique—is explained by the genetic code and the ways in which segments of deoxyribonucleic acid (DNA) are arranged to transmit information, or the "order" of life.

At first, the mathematical theory of information became a rallying point for disciplines as diverse as physics, mathematics, sociology, psychology, molecular biology, and linguistics, all of which shared, in the fifties (as we have seen), a common analytical procedure using the concepts of code, image, message, and information.[2] Later, the famous schema proposed by Shannon would become a mandatory stopover for any neophyte in the sociology of the media; it was to serve as a founding reference.

In 1952, the linguist Roman Jakobson saw the theory of information as an essential tool for constituting the science of linguistics. In his view, this theory offered both linguists and anthropologists a model with which to build a theory of systems (linguistic systems, but also systems of kinship) and to better apprehend the synchronic dimension. In a paper entitled "Results of the Conference of Anthropologists and Linguists," Jakobson wrote in 1952:

> For the study of language in operation, linguistics has been strongly reinforced by the impressive achievement of two conjoined disciplines—the mathematical theory of communication and information theory. Although communication engineering was not on the program of our Conference, it is indeed symptomatic that there was almost not a single paper uninfluenced by the works of C. E. Shannon and W. Weaver, of N. Wiener and R. M. Fano, or of the excellent London group. We have involuntarily employed terms such as encoder, decoder, redundancy, and the like. What, precisely, is the relation between communication engineering and linguistics? Is there perhaps some conflict between these two approaches? Not at all! As a matter of fact, structural linguistics and the research of communication engineers converge in their destination. . . . We must confess that, in some respects, the exchange of information has found on the part of the engineers a more exact and unambiguous formulation, a more efficient control of the technique used, as well as promising possibilities for quantification.[3]

Nearly 30 years later, here is how American linguist Noam Chomsky described the historical context in which mathematical models of communication exercised such a strong attraction:

> In the late forties and the beginning of the fifties, we saw the development of a mathematical theory of communication, known as the theory of information. . . . It was usually assumed that

these models were well suited to the description of language. Jakobson made vague references to it. . . . These theories were very much in fashion and even stimulated euphoria. In intellectual circles such as Cambridge, the greater part of technological development was a result of World War II. Computers, electronic acoustics, the mathematical theory of communication—all these technological approaches to human behavior gained extraordinary favor. The human sciences were constituted from these concepts. . . . This group of ideas seemed to me to be closely linked to a political current in power. It was very authoritarian, very manipulative, and linked to behavioristic concepts of human nature.[4]

Needless to say, the transposition of the schema of the mathematical theory of information onto other disciplines was rapidly criticized by certain mathematicians. As one mathematician wrote:

The consequences of Shannon's theory of information, outside mathematics and theoretical physics, are, to date, practically nonexistent in the different domains of the real world; the ritual invocations of Shannon by linguists and biologists aim perhaps to gain the favor of the gods, but they are not taken seriously by the specialists.[5]

The Rehabilitation of Noise

At a time when the notion of performance is invading the industrial and commercial field and having an ever greater effect on scientific practices, it is being challenged from many different social and scientific standpoints. This paradox demonstrates the tension, particular to the eighties, between a voluntaristic project for resolving the economic crisis and a reality that inspires nothing but doubt.

When American mathematicians created the theory of information, their aim was to make telephone communication as effective as possible—to transmit the greatest amount of information with the smallest quantity of units. The notion of linearity was elevated to an ideal, while "noise" designated everything that constituted an "obstacle." This model was completely subordinated to a finality; the fate of the relation between sender and receiver can be functionally determined by reading one's light or telephone bill. Now, however, "noise," which had been seen as a "disturbance," is now seen as a "virtue."

This, at any rate, is what we are told by those who examine how user instructions are composed for documentary data banks and those who analyze the conditions for a plural use of new means of generating information. To quote one such specialist:

The printed word allows us to master time, which is essential for the construction of meaning by the reader. Books allow for shortcuts, . . . skimming the text, . . . all things foreign to the universe of hierarchically ordered systems of searching for information. Computer data banks, for example, exclude this type of semirandom (but not hazardous) access to information; more generally, complex systems exclude all approaches containing "noise"—in the sense that information theory attaches to this term—or resorting to chance. . . . We do not mean to plead for using candles instead of electricity, or for documentation by successive approximations as opposed to documentary rigor. But we cannot hierarchize these logics, or consider these uncontrolled practices to be prelogical residues that have to be fought—they must, on the contrary, be seen as full-fledged research approaches. . . . The danger would lie in making these new techniques not a supplementary tool of access to accumulated knowledge, but, in the name of efficiency, a tool for all kinds of access, and a substitute for the other forms of stocking and communicating information, which are judged to be outmoded.[6]

Is *groping* not a virtue when the problem at hand is to open the field of expressivity or, very economically, that of utilization? The tension between singularity—the specificity of practices and uses—and the project of an information strictly defined in order to avoid all losses in transmission is particularly marked when, for example, in research on the human-machine dialogue, respect for redundancy becomes a necessary condition in order for users (groups and individuals) to express themselves, although they experience a different temporality from that of the prescribed utilitary norm.

The idea that noise can be something other than a source of disturbance is emerging also through the wrenching revisions in one sector of linguistics. Take the following elementary observation: if noise is indeed a negative element when techniques such as isolation, correction, and recording are involved, it cannot be so when it is used in sound-effect and noise-making techniques. Furthermore, certain questions arising in language studies are having a direct influence on the way we approach "communication": we do not speak only to inform or to transmit a message. As Jacques Derrida explained in an interview in 1984:

The function of communication does not exhaust the essence of language. Naturally, language communicates, transmits, and transports meanings, messages, and contents. But the effects produced by an act of language or writing cannot necessarily be reduced to the transmission of a piece of information or knowledge. . . . When I say something to someone, it is not certain that my major preoccupation is to transmit knowledge or meaning; it is rather to enter into a certain type of relation with the other person, to attempt to seduce him or her, or give him or her something, or even to wage war. Thus, beyond the schemas of communication appear other possible finalities.[7]

In order to understand and evaluate this trend toward the rehabilitation of groping, of trial and error, we must restore this trend's broader context, which is that of a double crisis: first, the economic and social crisis, the pervasiveness of which diminishes our confidence in univocity; and then the crisis of models of rationality, of truth and norms, which affects the entire Western *logos*.

5

Postlinearity

The Mechanical and the Fluid

The "mechanical" and the "fluid" are two opposite modes of thought. The latter is perceived today as having definitively replaced the former.

The mechanical mode involved that which was "solid," and which had a top and a bottom, a before and an after, an infra and a supra; it was associated with the whole parade of metaphors that attempted to express the direction of history, of progress, of the disequilibrium of forces, and of the dynamics of social movement. The famous metaphor in the work of Marx of society as a building—the base/superstructure model—may be the best example of this type of thought.

To use a cinematic metaphor, the syncopated editing of the social, one shot cut to the next, was replaced by editing in a fade-over mode. The former established the before and the after, hierarchical orders, source and destination, cause and consequence, breaks and continuities. Between the two modes of thought, there is a frontal opposition of categories: force is counterposed to flow, rigidity to flexibility, verticality to horizontality, stabilization to perpetual change and renewal, linear causality to circular causality, closure to openness, sum and juxtaposition to cross-analysis.

It is very tempting to consider fluidity and transparence as equivalents. But to subscribe to this equivalence would be to miss, first of all, the contradictory genesis of this "fluid" mode of thought, and secondly, the equally contradictory functions that this mode of thought fills today in a society in a process of simultaneous disintegration and reintegration. This contradictory genesis reflects the concept of the fluid (and associated concepts) in different moments of the thinking about postindustrial society and postmodern society.

This debate has been oversimplified. In attempting to grasp the evolution of the large industrial societies, the concept of postindustrial society offered an organic framework for understanding changes in modes of thought. But as often happens with concepts that are accepted without being seriously evaluated, "postindustrial society" appeared as a smooth and homogeneous totality that brought about the fusion of historically antagonistic ideological families and redistributed modes of perception of the world according to an opposition between archaism and modernity.

The first formulations of the concept of postindustrial society date back to 1959, with sociologist Daniel Bell's contributions to the Salzburg seminar. It was in the Year 2000 Commission, of which Bell was the chairman, that the concept was launched. Its takeoff was contemporaneous with the rise of other, less tantalizing theses—the one about the end of ideology, for example, as developed by Bell in his book *The End of Ideology* (1960).[1] And at roughly the same time, political scientist Seymour Lipset sermonized—well before the workers' movement had entered its crisis in the large industrial countries—about the decline of the class struggle and its metamorphosis "into a struggle devoid of all ideology and without red flags."[2]

The first conception of postindustrial society was born under the aegis of engineers and specialists in the physical sciences, linked to large technocratic apparatuses whose members lived in cities and embodied the values of urban civilization.[3] Their mode of thought was closer to the mechanical than to the fluid. They used objective methods that involved linear projections employing quantitative techniques. It was precisely by applying linearity to the problem of extrapolating growth rates in the postwar period that they proposed a vision of postindustrial society and a society of abundance (with exponential growths in income); an essentially service (or tertiary-sector) society in which services would be overtaking industry; a society in which the work/leisure dichotomy persisted; and in which the continual pursuit of progress took place through the accumulation of goods, which, it was assumed, would create happiness. In its initial version, the concept reflected an inclination toward centralization (at the time, Bell defined "centrality" as "the source of innovation and of the formulation of political choices for society"—a centrality that gave the technostructure control over procedures of so-called rational decision making, and thus evaded the necessary debate about political choices). With centralization, size became a virtue, as did mass society, seen as homogeneous and uniform. Following economist W. W. Rostow and futurologist Herman Kahn, Bell indulged in a mystical belief in science and technology. Technology was supposed to resolve all problems engendered by technology. For the future, Bell foresaw a permanent role for technocratic bureaucracies, with the reinforcement of a new highly trained scientific elite, as well as the continuation of the welfare state and international "interdependence."

It was not so much debates among theoreticians as the crisis of the seventies that invalidated the optimistic view suggested by the linear projections from years of high growth. Of the first concept of postindustrial society, hardly anything remains but the notion of service society (which was to turn into the concept of information or communication society) and the belief in inevitable technological growth and international interdependence. What remained, above all, was the conviction that the new era of the service economy and the service society went hand in hand with the rise to power of the new class of masters of science and technology.

What the crisis destabilized first of all was not so much the idea of the formation of new technocratic elites as the mode of legitimation of their new type of competence. The fracture of the prevailing model of exponential growth revealed that the transmission of power from the industrial bourgeoisie to the "third class" would not take place according to a process of natural and metabolic evolution—contrary to what was believed by agents of the technostructure who were already in the wings of power and tightly linked to a state that provided large military contracts and administrative programs. In its tendency to conceive planning and decision making only from above, the first postindustrial model had neglected the existence of people on the receiving end of administration and development policy and who were thus the subject-objects of planning; and it especially neglected the diversity of new interests motivating other sectors of the "third class" in the wings of power.

A New Context

The second generation of the debate on the emergence of postindustrial society restored to the definition of the concept its full weight of social contradictions. The concept now designated ruptures rather than convergences, and it involved some truly radical challenges to the initial premises.

First of all, the new class, having lost the objective support of economic growth, which had made its ascension appear to be a natural phenomenon, was now forced to consider its access to power and its mode of legitimation in relation to other groups and classes in society. Moreover, the breakup of the consensus (first referred to by the Trilateral Commission[4] for all the industrial societies, and later by the Nora-Minc Report for French society in particular) served as a reminder that other groups and other social actors had different outlooks about how to resolve the crisis and different premises from which to draw lessons about the failure of the dominant model of growth, involving different alliances and different philosophies of life and development.

Centrality ceased to be the supreme reference, giving way to the recognition of differences—specificities of gender, social category, or locality. The schema of mechanical and linear thought was delegitimized by organicist thought (with the paradigms proposed by the life sciences becoming, as we have seen, mandatory references). The objective method was countered by the primacy of values; quantitative techniques were challenged by empirical qualitative techniques, the logical approach by the heuristic approach; the cognitive by the intuitive, and linear projection by the principle of multiple options.

The initiators of the postindustrial doctrine, in their haste to proclaim the end of ideologies, in fact consecrated the myth of a unified and omnipotent science, and especially that of a neutral science and technology, autonomous from their conditions of production. With the crisis of the linear mode of thought, the crisis of science became manifest. It was also a crisis of theory, which saw the rise of thought based on observation of facts (*la pensée du constat*), a style of thought that took more care to describe the ordinary, to adhere to experience, and to rely on common sense than to attempt theoretical elucidations that do not afford direct access to lived experience.

The first concept of postindustrial society had been born in the heart of the most advanced capitalist society, the United States. The second generation was characterized by its plural dimension. It gathered the contributions, interrogations, and specificities of heterodox and dissenting ideological families; it opened itself to different cultural territories. The centrality that characterized the first version gave way to the polyphony of the periphery. The Third World and Europe were now included in the questions regarding evaluations of social needs, the objectives of growth, and models of development. In reaction to the crisis, there reappeared a whole tradition of critique of industrialism—a critique that had been stifled until then, as much by theories of exponential growth as by the dominant practices of a workers' movement that had rallied to the productivist ideology, and to industrialization as the sole method of development. The utopian socialist currents sprang from this tradition, and were joined by new social movements such as the women's movement, ethnic movements, and all those forms of association that represented the quest for an alternative to the hegemonic form of the Bolshevik organization of labor, politics, and daily life, a model characterized by centrality. In France, this same tradition also produced the basic concepts of a humanitarian socialism, which had been kept from appearing on the political horizon by the rise of the vanguardist conception of the popular party.[5] In the field of popular culture, one cannot fail to notice that the renewed interest in serialized literature is irreverent in light of Marx's famous reading of Eugène Sue's *Mystères de Paris*, which, during the period of structuralist Marxism, served as a paradigm for analyzing the people's "false consciousness."[6]

This new phase of discussion about postindustrial society is plural in another way as well, thanks to the numerous disciplines involved in the interrogations provoked by postindustrialism: the life sciences, the environmental sciences, anthropology, sociology, economics, and philosophy, including ethics.

The first conception of postindustrial society consecrated the linear character of history and the continual pursuit of progress. The second one speaks of the discontinuity of history and even the possibility of regression. The celebration of possession and the accumulation of goods as guarantees of happiness is replaced by a confidence in being and in the quality of life. The dichotomy of work and leisure gives way to the unity of work and creation. Generalized urbanization gives way to a form of development that reconciles the city and rural life. Omnipresent public supervision gives way to autonomy from the state. Centralization gives way to decentralization, verticality to horizontality, hierarchies to networks, large to small, macro to micro, "masses" to "affinity networks," and homogeneity to differences. The megamachines of the first postindustrial society, built to adapt to state-industrial and military demand, find their counterpart in "appropriate" technologies, adapted to the environment and designed to save energy and matter and be useful and comprehensible to the majority of citizens. In response to the Western ethnocentrism of the first version, incapable of proposing other models of growth than those that reproduce the phases of development of advanced capitalism (Rostow is the best example here), emerges the idea of a development supported by local resources and the self-reliance of groups and countries (this idea of development does not, however, fall into the myth of autarky). And most significantly, the representative democracy of the first model, in which science and technology take matters increasingly out of the "public sphere" or the "sphere of public interaction" (in Jürgen Habermas's terms) and place them in the hands of experts and professionals, is confronted with the demand for forms of direct democracy.

To reveal, even in schematic form as we have just done, the double face of postindustrial thought is an important conceptual operation. In the new "regime of truth" where causality itself is cast into doubt, there is a paradoxical tendency to put the cart before the horse (if we may use a distinctly preindustrial image). That is, social and cultural transformations, and the most profound changes of the total episteme, are often interpreted as being the corollaries of technological changes. When we examine the paradigms that underlie the new approaches, we observe that to attribute too much importance to technology is to credit the technological revolution with the capacity to produce nothing less than a new social bond. If there is one important insight in today's epistemological trend, it is surely the rise of a new thought in which the social and the technological are no longer separated and isolated worlds—in other words, the awareness that material artefacts contain within them social relations and representations of them. Thus we can say that the engineer puts into his artefact his own representation of a social use; this representation confronts the user, who can respond either by conforming to this prescribed use or by avoiding it or putting a distinctive stamp on it.

The Deviations of the Paradigm of Fluidity

It would of course be ingenuous to think that the two paradigms are mutually exclusive. If the first indeed preceded the second historically, today they both have an effect on society, in a largely synchronic manner. It is possible, for example, to speak about decentralization while actually having centralization in mind. To think of the two paradigms as two catalogues, the second of which has rendered the first obsolete, would be to apprehend what is moving with a rationality adapted only to what is frozen. Far from excluding each other, the static and the dynamic coexist, and contaminate each other and interfere with each other in a multitude of ways.

The rise of information technologies and networks corresponds to the decline of the first paradigm and the rise of the second. The so-called information society manifests itself in the passage from one phase to the other, and takes part in the new set of modes of legitimation of the second.

The new paradigm of the fluid can only be interpreted with ambivalence—ambivalently and in an open manner, just as we perceive the formation of micro-and macro-uses of communication technologies. This process takes place through adaptations, transitions, individual and collective resistance, and especially through contradictory pathways in which different imaginary conceptions, interests, and social projects conflict with each other. The ambivalence in interpretations reflects that of the conceptual tools (such as participation and decentralization, whose contradictory history has to be perpetually rewritten) designed to apprehend realities that are said to be new and that are open to multiple interpretations and uses.

Thus we can reduce the new paradigm to a purely formal model, if we forget the social logic(s) that inspired the radical challenge to linearity—a radical challenge representing no less than a model of society, a model of organization of social relations, and a model of development and growth. And this is precisely the reduction committed by those who, while celebrating the rise of fluid thought and joyously burying the "paradigm of mechanics," inadvertently bring back the linear schema of historicism by combining the promise of the fluidity of new networks with strategies for resolving the economic and political crisis, thereby reinstating the equation: progress = sophisticated technology. These crisis-resolution strategies are not credible unless they stipulate that all change is possible except that which questions the basic rules of the existing socioeconomic game. A paradigm rich in potential for the redefinition of the social thereby serves to legitimate a technocratic project in which technology is called upon to justify and mask the absence of a social project meeting the demands underlying the new modes of thinking and acting in society. On the social side, the paradigm of fluidity runs the risk of turning into a mirage, concentrating all its efforts in fact on displays of high technological performance.

Perhaps the best symbolic expression of this lure are the temples being built to science and technology in the form of huge museum exhibits in the advanced industrial countries. A similar trend can be perceived in the ways of interpreting social demand in order to guide technological choices. A notion of social demand inspired by the concern for establishing a link between new technological possibilities and social actors, with a redistribution of power and more democracy, is answered by a project for managing solvent demand in the framework of "experimentation" controlled by social engineers.

These phase differences explain why the ground is so fertile for the blossoming of new systems approaches and ideologies that excel in dissecting interactions, mobilities, flows, circularity, and the continual renewal of the elements of a system—while neglecting the rules governing the overall system in which it is included. In this conception of "dynamic stability" of complex systems,[7] what is offered as the broadest set of alternatives and the greatest number of choices in fact entails a closing of the field of possibilities, because the basic axiom is the determinism of science and technology.

All these developments can be understood and experienced only with reference to the reconciliation with pragmatic humankind and the happiness of pragmatic humankind spoken of by Kant, and which signifies, no doubt, the recognition of the needs of concrete individuals, but also the beginning of infinite negotiations—not only endless but without finality, because they are born just at the point where utopias end.

The paradigm of fluidity is tending to become one of the most widely shared references in the world. It is easy to understand why the approach it suggests may explode into a multitude of tendencies which, while sharing a number of common features, also display considerable and sometimes insurmountable divergences. To be convinced of this we need only consider the debates over the micro versus macro choice, decentralization versus centralization, civil society versus the state, democracy versus hierarchy, local versus national versus international, as they appear not only in movements of thought but in social movements, strategies, and state policies (in both the First and Third Worlds). One perceives that the paradigm is suited just as well to nourishing new networks of solidarity as to legitimating the logics of atomization of the social movement.[8] Some seek shelter under the paradigm of fluidity in order to proclaim the end of the class struggle (seen as peculiar to the age of machines and mechanics), the end of conflict, and the rise of convivial society. Others, recognizing a plurality of determinations, move critical theory forward by stressing that the class struggle and economic history, while remaining components of reality, are no longer the only factors that determine the history of dominant power and countervailing power.[9]

What becomes of social cleavages? The different conceptions of the fluid are split over this question. This paradigm, both as seen in contemporary thought and as a prospective scenario, cannot be understood independently of the challenges from different strategies for moving beyond the crisis. The more the danger of a dual society becomes concrete, the more the fluid is called upon to serve as a legitimating reference by acting as an ideology of consensus for a profoundly segregated society, and this in two ways. First, it assures the strata that participate in the benefits of the crisis economy of a transition from a hierarchical society to a corporatist society, in which power relations are conceived exclusively from the perspective of harmony between capital and labor. Secondly, to the excluded layers it offers the adventurous spirit of the unofficial economy and the daily struggle for self-sufficiency.

The idea of the disappearance of social cleavages and the decline of social struggles masks at least two phenomena: first, the fact that "fluidity" has two parallel circuits, meaning that between the sphere of the excluded strata and that of the integrated strata there is no easy mobility. And this is precisely the context in which the ideology of communication—the new egalitarianism through communication—comes to fulfill a legitimation function. Secondly, the idea of the disappearance of social cleavages abrogates the idea of the necessity of social alliances, since fluidity, which becomes a fetish (to use the term that would have been employed not only by Marx but also by the early Barthes, in *Mythologies*), maintains communication among all individuals. The necessity of such an abrogation is all the clearer in these times when the utopia of social mobility, development and growth for all is tending to lose its credibility, and when, among the integrated strata, the idea is gaining currency that only strategies of security can contain the psychological and social violence of those excluded from society.

6
Negotiated Power

The Uses of Ambiguity

With the paradigm of the fluid, something was fractured: the image of power located at a single point in society, visible and unambiguous — the image of a central power perfectly articulated with its periphery. The emerging image is one of complex networks of places, whose very entanglement makes decision making complex. This complexity brings with it a corresponding plurality of instruments of interpretation.

The importance of this break cannot be overstated. It represents without a doubt an advance in our understanding of reality.

For a long time critical theory was dominated by a strict distribution of the true and the false, which corresponded, on the political level, to the opposition between the "correct line" and the "deviant line" — the good and the bad, truth and error. These modes of interpretation delayed or even blocked the recognition of the specific status of subjective consciousness, culture, and the symbolic. Take, for example, the obstacle posed by the infrastructure-superstructure paradigm for the development of critical and practical knowledge about cultural production. The theoretical question of the determinations and primacies of one "instance" or another (be it economic or ideological) were related to political strategies in which they were conceived as phases in the space and time of linear change: one "before" and the other "after" (an "after" that was constantly being postponed). The deferment of the "culture question" and the question of symbolic production expressed the tendency to reify concepts and void them of their concrete social content and lived experience, on the pretext of adhering to their *material* concreteness. What a multitude of contortions were performed in the history of critical theory of culture and the media (semiology, political economy, anthropology, and philosophy) in order to escape from vulgar materialism or conform to it! And what a multitude of contortions were performed in order to retreat from the primacy of economics and conclude that, in spite of everything, the base was only the base "in the last instance"; that the superstructure was more or less out of line with the base or that it could become "relatively autonomous" with regard to the conditions of material life. What contortions there were before it was finally allowed that ideology is not first of all a repertoire of contents (opinions, attitudes, representations) but the signifying dimension of all practice, a "grammar for generating meaning and investing meaning in signifying matters," to borrow the phrase of semiologist Eliseo Verón.

The great contribution of the new paradigm of the fluid is precisely to have challenged the smooth and unilateral certainty of the categories and paradigms that had long dominated critical thought. Along with its merit, however, we must point out the ambiguities of the progress thereby made possible. And we must also be quick to recognize that the ambiguity itself has some merit, because it allows us to gain a better grasp of the polysemic character of reality and the actors who embody it.

The Metamorphoses of Structuralism

One cannot move from a Manichean conception of the social to the idea of a multipolar, widely distributed set of social relations without a significant evolution of one's conception of power, the forms by which it is exercised and the modes of resistance to it. We have reached a new conception of power via a twisted and contradictory path.

One of the great contributions of structuralist literary criticism was, as we know, the break with idealist historicism and a certain version of Marxism. By stressing the necessity of determining the specific structure of the text, it challenged the assumptions of a tautological approach that, in order to understand a work, referred back to history and society, thus ignoring the contours of the object under examination. The criticism of texts that was inspired by this historicist current had taught us to separate positive heroes from negative ones, and progressive contents from reactionary contents, while elevating the nature of the author's commitment to the rank of an essential question for the understanding of that author's work.

The questioning of the historicist approaches to literary criticism represented primarily by Lukács expressed a questioning of an entire conception of history and historical movement. In the historicist perpsective, the notion of revolutionary change in the area of culture was seen as being tied up with the rationalist, secular, and democratic heritage of the bourgeoisie, so much so that it was demanded of the bourgeoisie to remain faithful to itself by avoiding the traps of irrationalism and decadence. As an Italian critic wrote in 1967, the problem consisted of

> studying the cultural manifestations [of the bourgeoisie], taking care to reveal their progressive aspects that socialist culture should appropriate for itself (hence the necessity of following the lessons nineteenth-century realism of the Balzacian type) since the revolution is defined, in the final analysis, in a perspective of substantial (historicist) continuity of bourgeois development (given that the proletariat must pick up, in the cultural field as well, the flags that the bourgeoisie has let fall).[1]

In setting out his hypothesis about the microphysics of power, Michel Foucault moved the debate forward by destabilizing, in his own way, the cleavage between positive and negative heroes, by breaking up their traditional polarity. In postulating that power is not the acquired or conserved privilege of the dominant class, but rather the overall effect of its strategic positions, he also questioned the position of the dominated in the system of power: "This power is not exercised simply as an obligation or a prohibitive on those who 'do not have it': it invests them, is transmitted by them and through them; it exerts pressure upon them, just as they themselves, in their struggle against it, resist the grip it has on them."[2] To the great entities recognized by Marxism (the state, classes, dominant ideologies), and to the conception of ideological instances as manipulative by definition, he opposed a theory of discontinuous power centers diffused throughout the social body in such a way that it is impossible to detect the slightest overarching mechanism.

At the opposite end of the huge amalgam united under the label of structuralism, Louis Althusser was forging his concept of "ideological state apparatuses," which was much better suited to account for the way media work in authoritarian regimes than in societies where a long-standing democratic tradition had allowed a proliferation of the sites of production of power—and not simply its reproduction. As the philosopher Henri Lefebvre noted in 1976, "Insofar as it has any scope, [the Althusserian system of thought] can better explain what is happening in Eastern Europe (with its ideologized Marxism, transformed into apology for production, productivism, material labor and the manual laborer) than what is happening in the capitalist countries."[3]

From the very dawn of structuralism (in its different variants), everything possible was said about its contributions, but also about its limits. Everything was said in particular about the way it marked the passage from one philosophy to another. As one virulent critic wrote in 1972,

Until the end of the Algerian war, existentialism was the dominant ideology among the immense majority of the French intelligentsia. Existentialism corresponds, roughly, to a *continuous and visible crisis of capitalism*, whereas structuralism appeared, in the 1960s, at a moment of relative *stabilization of the system*. . . . The attack launched against Sartre came from two directions: from the avowed partisans of technocratic society (Lévi-Strauss, etc.) and from the avowed partisans of technocratization of theory (Althusser, etc.). . . . While with Sartre there was *too much* history, with Lévi-Strauss, Foucault, Althusser, and Lacan, there is *no more* history.[4]

Sartre's judgment is well known: "The target of structuralism is Marxism. . . . The idea is to constitute a new ideology, the last barrier that the bourgeoisie can erect against Marx."[5] Herbert Marcuse's attacks against structuralism are perhaps less well remembered; Marcuse saw in the structuralist approach the demystification of the old ideology, while asking nonetheless whether this demystifying approach might not be a part of the new ideology, and might not correspond, in turn, to the structural needs of the redefinition of the system. In *One-Dimensional Man*, Marcuse wrote, "What is involved is the spread of a new ideology which undertakes to describe what is happening (and meant) by eliminating the concepts capable of understanding what is happening (and meant)."[6] In the same period, Lucien Goldmann stressed what appeared to him to be a fundamental characteristic of the structuralist position: its implicit link with what he called "the new phase of capitalism: organized capitalism."[7]

Marcuse wrote his critique before 1968, at a time when structuralism was still a rising force. He could certainly not yet have predicted the contradictory influences the structural approach was to have in the social sciences in the following years. Nor could it be otherwise. After all, Marcuse himself drew inspiration from Barthes, who can hardly be dissociated from structuralism!

Today structuralism seems like ancient history. The amalgam it made possible between bodies of thought as different as those of Barthes, Lévi-Strauss, Althusser, and Foucault has today lost much of its force of cohesion. The social effects of the hypotheses launched by the different thinkers associated with structuralism have been quite divergent. It goes practically without saying that, beyond its internal diversity, structuralism did indeed inaugurate a fundamental movement in thought, which continued to gain depth and had a major influence on society in spite of the discredit to which it fell victim in the beginning of the 1980s.

Although structuralism was, for certain of its representatives, a radical investigation of power structures, it nonetheless entertained ambiguous relations with the notion of power. Even Foucault was unable to escape from this ambiguity. Refusing to identify the major instances of power, he returned, paradoxically, to a metaphysical conception of power: power is everywhere and therefore intangible and anonymous. His theory had two opposite facets, which explains why the approaches claiming to draw inspiration from him were often mutually antagonistic. Because of Foucault's refusal to consider state power and his tendency to perceive the production of power only as spontaneous generation, certain approaches to the study of popular practices used arguments of his in order to claim the irrelevance of analyzing the overall field of social relations — in which experiences actually find their context, even if one considers them autonomous. Other approaches, drawing support from the Foucaldian idea that all power is both power and counterpower, or negotiation and subjection, broke the theoretical dichotomy separating the sphere of action of civil society from that of the state, thereby suggesting new questions about the relationship between democracy and the organization of information.

The ambiguity of structuralism with regard to power reflects the ambivalence of the vigorous movements in thought and in society that had a profound impact on France starting at the end of the sixties. If, in the short run, new analyses and practices, theories and forms of action, played a role in the destabilization of existing social hierarchies, in the somewhat longer term it could be said that they prepared the way for the constitution of a new hierarchy on other bases than those of the chain-of-command model of hierarchy.

From this standpoint, we may note the contribution of structuralism to the consecration of the status of the specialist. Scientific discourse was promoted as the only objective discourse. Harking back to the old myth according to which the mission of the intellectual is to enlighten the masses about their fate, this conception of science was contradicted by the questionings astir within French society — questions about the social division of labor as source of social domination and about the validity of the role of intellectuals and their monopoly of expertise in the revelation of meaning.

The Gramscian Contribution

Foucault's changing moods were well known: sometimes he acknowledged his debt to Marxism, which had become "common sense" for a great portion of the intellectual class involved in developing structuralism; but at other times he declared Marxism obsolete on the grounds that it was an ideology produced by the society of machine production at the end of the nineteenth century. These were pithy statements that were never backed up by the argumentation that might have been hoped for; pithy statements that of course evade mention of the diverse contributions that prepared the way for new paradigms of power. Indeed, they made light of an entire tradition of philosophical and sociological thought informed by Marxism but far removed from the dualistic visions of class versus class, proletariat versus bourgeoisie, and "formal democracy" versus the "dictatorship of the proletariat."

In the second half of the 1970s, no analyses had a greater influence on new ways of apprehending the organization of media production and forms of popular culture than those of Italian Marxist Antonio Gramsci (1891-1937). The French intellectual milieu, absorbed in theories of social reproduction, remained in fact at the margin of the Gramscian contribution in this precise area of research in culture and communication. The contrast is great between the widespread influence enjoyed by Gramsci in his own country of birth,[8] in the Anglo-Saxon countries, and in Latin America, and the rare references to his work in French circles.[9] This is true in spite of the fact that certain French philosophers had written veritable treatises on Gramscian thought.[10] Most ironically, in the late seventies certain representatives in France of what was called the New Right were the ones to claim the inspiration of Gramsci on the problems of the state, power, culture, and the intellectuals.

If we had to sum up briefly the Gramscian contribution to the new paradigm of power, we would have to lay emphasis on the notion of hegemony. Gramsci defined "hegemony" as the ability of a social group to exercise intellectual and moral leadership over society and build around its own project a new system of social alliances, a new "historic bloc."

The contemporary importance of Gramscian thought lies perhaps in the fact that it stands at the center of the debate about the state and civil society; it considers democracy as a construction process rather than as a given, already existing condition. This approach raises the question of the organization of multiple social actors in the construction of a popular hegemony, defined not as an endeavor to do away with differences through a process of "normalization," but rather as an articulation of all the new forms of consciousness that arise along with new social movements.

Here, doubtless, is where the greatest cleavage occurs between Gramsci's thought and the conceptions associated with the Foucaldian approach, which suggest a complete autonomy of social movement and see such movements as simply promoters of microresistance and of fragmentary experiences.

The notion of hegemony breaks with the idea of vertical power—a power that is never negotiated and is above all nonnegotiable. It breaks as well with the tendency to neglect questions about the basis of the intellectual's power as mediator of the production of intellectual and moral leadership, otherwise known as "consensus." Finally, it breaks with the currents of thought that have limited the question of popular cultures to the practices of "people's" political parties, in the name of representation.

But in the seventies the reappropriation of Gramscian thought was to be invested above all in the question of the state. Thus the dualistic conceptions of the state as a monolithic structure faced with passively and completely dominated citizens—a locus outside the contradictions of the social movement—gave way to approaches that attempted to grasp the places of consensus production (in particular the media and schools) as places where the expressions of civil society do manage to penetrate and create a balance of forces. These were no longer terrains where power was mechanically reproduced, but rather where it produced itself through mediations between classes, groups, and individuals. By exploding the "compact" Althusserian conception of the state, the reappropriation of Gramsci made possible a conception of power both as co-optation of the multiple interests of the different classes, groups, and individuals and as the negation and exclusion of vast zones of interests of subaltern groups and classes.

This theoretical breakthrough was achieved, however, in a context where the question of the state was at the center of contradictory debates. First of all, the new synergies between the state, industry, the university, and civil society (consumers of goods and users of services) were related to the conception of a flexible state, ready to stay in the background and cede to negotiations with civil society. This conception represented a break from the other one that had long galvanized a workers' movement oriented entirely toward the seizure of state power. This conception of a flexible state sheds light on the co-opting facet of the state, leaving in the shadows its other, very real, face, that of coercion and exclusion of subaltern groups and classes. At the other end of the spectrum, the theses of neoliberalism, which sought to rehabilitate the image of the state as Leviathan, were also gaining an audience. By opposing civil society to the state in order to galvanize citizens dominated by this huge blind and deaf machine, this theory legitimated the populism of the ideologues of the market (all tendencies included).

The Actor and the System

Gramsci said that "hegemony is born in the factory" and saw in Fordism the culture that sought to provide ideological cement for society at labor.[11]

If there is a topic forgotten by those who have examined the forms of ideological and cultural subjection, it is indeed that of labor, and its site, the company. Neither Althusser nor Foucault (to name only them) escape this reproach. For Althusser, ideology apparently stops at the factory gate. As one of his critics notes,

> Having excluded ideology from the immediate production process, all Althusser has to do is put the label of "ideological state apparatus" on all bourgeois institutions that are not corporations; not because, according to Althusser, ideology has nothing to do with corporations, but because ideology is injected into them by the ideological state apparatuses, which reproduce the relations of production. In other words, the division of society into classes and the relations of the exploited to the exploiters are reproduced outside the corporation by ideology; this reproduction of the classes by ideology, or more exactly, by superstructures, is the beginning of the negation of classes.[12]

For Michel Foucault, the most important means of confinement the state has succeeded in accomplishing is the prison. Henri Lefebvre disagrees, arguing as follows:

> This is a valid approach provided that it does not stop along the way. The formation of capitalism in the West is characterized not by locking people up, but by putting them to work. . . . Starting in the seventeenth century, the producers, dispossessed of their means of production, were thrown into *abstract* labor. This labor was mediated by tools and machines and executed in abstract locations (workshops, factories, companies) for a faraway market. . . . The admirable and astounding thing is that this operation succeeded. The dominant class brought the workers to like their (abstract) labor.[13]

How could the emergence of the themes of power and counterpower and those of negotiation, transaction, and contradiction have been seen as nothing more than an intuition whose only use was to subvert power in everyday life and political society? It is well to remember that at about the same time, new modes of grasping the overall problems of integration between workers and management arose — theories of scientific organization of labor, inspired by games theory — and that these theories have their own ways of conceiving the microphysics of power, particularly at the workplace.[14]

Fordism is in crisis. This form of organization of labor, in conjunction with a model of regulation that had enabled an unprecedented rationalization of production, is giving way to a restructuring of labor tasks that better satisfies aspirations toward autonomy. New modes of command

and communication are appearing, allowing the organization to adapt to circumstances and pressures. The old notion of class struggle, recognized implicitly by a management that attempted to counter its effects, is being replaced by the idea that it is necessary to seek an optimal equilibrium among actors, each of whom has an open or tacit strategy and margins of maneuver and moves in a field of power and counterpower relations, in the interstices of which conflictive dynamics may manifest themselves. What counts therefore is not so much the established structure as the way of elaborating strategies and organizing transactions among competing groups and individuals.[15]

With systems analysis, which emphasizes the role of the self-regulation of actors, new scenarios of communication within the company have begun to flourish. This qualitative leap in the management of resources is spoken of revealingly in the declaration of the president of the Conseil National du Patronat Français[16] before the European Congress of the Corporate Press in 1974.

> There is no participation in the strongest and fullest sense of the term if one does not have the feeling of being an integral part of a social group with its raison d'être and its vocation, its particular style, its traditions and its objectives—if one does not have the feeling of belonging to a community. . . . Information and communication will be called upon to play a decisive role here. The company that does not inform its personnel is like a world populated with stateless persons.[17]

In that same year, the Union des Journaux et Journalistes d'Entreprise de France,[18] an organization quite clearly on the side of management, adopted a new set of statutes. These were introduced with a preamble that read as follows: "Since information and communication are part of the given conditions of the life of the company, they must be conceived as a function of management." Here is how the trade-union journal *Cadres CFDT* summarized this implacable logic: "Community + Information + Communication + Leadership = Participation."

7

The Return of the Subject

The Rehabilitation of the Subject

Do periods of growth and the ideologies that accompany them cause the receiver, the consumer, and the citizen to be forgotten? Do they help to entertain the illusion that citizens can be done without and that their demands can be planned according to the available benefits of redistribution?

Based on what is happening today, one is tempted to believe so. It was not until we entered a crisis that legitimacy was at last granted to the quite elementary idea that the process of communication is forged through the active intervention of very diverse social actors. The need to identify the Other is tending to be recognized as a crucial problem.

Certain logics, often in contradiction with each other, explain the return to theory of the consumer of services, which is the particular identity assumed by the generic subject today in the field of communication, with the rise of new networks. The main such networks are the new synergies induced by industrial strategies for overcoming the economic crisis. Industry is projected into a new type of relation with society as a whole. The necessity of achieving maximum "levels of acceptability" for new communication products brings together the inventors, the distributors, and potential users and leads them to seek the modes of interaction that most favor exploration of how social uses of the product are formed. This type of cooperation appears all the more desirable because, according to all estimations, the users are the only people able to finance the considerable investments required by new communications infrastructures. New synergies are also emerging from the politics of decentralization: the role that has fallen to local authorities in the administration of new cable

networks is one of the numerous manifestations of how redefining the
state-citizen relationship has become an essential stake in the reconstitu-
tion of an endangered political consensus. But beyond the logics of the
restructuring of power, a vast questioning of the role of civil society in the
daily construction of democracy is gaining importance again after having
long been pursued only by a small minority. At the same time, there is a
greater and greater challenge to modes of organizing resistance founded
on a conception of collective action that has historically neglected to take
the individual—the subject—into account.

These developments in social reality are related to developments occurring in science that are also an integral part of reality. In the structural
approach, the desire to abolish the psychological sciences' obsession with
a subject isolated from all structures or social organization manifested itself by a turning away from the subject. But the cycle is returning to its
earlier phase: in the eighties, particular subjects are at the forefront.

As the subject is given greater value, the study of daily life and the "ordinary dimension of meaning" (l'ordinaire du sens), according to Michel
de Certeau's excellent expression, acquires new relevance. How does ordinary communication constitute itself among ordinary people in in-
frastate contexts? How does the individual subject negotiate, on an everyday basis, his relation to power and to institutions? As Georges
Balandier has written:

> The most important thing (perhaps) in the new vogue of research
> on daily life is the recent tendency to bring the subject into view
> against the background of structures and systems—quality as
> against quantity, lived experience as against what is established in
> institutions. This strong tendency affects much more than the
> social sciences alone, but this is where it has its main effect.
> From this point of view, it is interesting to observe that the
> sociology of daily life (which considers the relation of the
> individual to durable, repetitive, imposed social phenomena)
> makes significant connections with two disciplines that have been
> celebrated in the past twenty years: anthropology (social,
> cultural, and historical), which considers relations with the
> "Other," and psychoanalysis, which considers the relation of the
> individual to his or her personal history. In all three cases, the
> point of view of the subject is privileged—without necessarily
> conferring some exceptional significance on the subject;
> considering [the subject], rather, as "ordinary" or
> "commonplace."[1]

And this, precisely, is what the history of mentalities has devoted itself
to studying in the past few years. As one historian of mentalities puts it,
"We plead here for the rehabilitation of the ordinary event. Not so as to

squeeze out of it a scandal or an anecdote intended to satisfy the taste of a public for whom 'story' and 'novel' are synonyms, but in order to analyze the social logics the event reveals — no matter how minimal it might be, nor how trivial or insignificant it may appear."[2]

Linguistics did not stay on the sidelines when the subject made its comeback. "Communicational linguistics" challenged the structural and generative approach, rediscovering the sociality and historicity of written as well as oral messages. By upsetting the premises of information theory, the so-called enunciative and pragmatic theories of linguistics helped to restore the enunciator and the addressee, the speaker and the receiver.

These new currents of thought coincide, in some of their concerns, with a school formed in the United States in reaction to the linear conceptions of information theory and communication theory in the 1940s. For indeed, it was during a period when the mathematical theory of communication was exercising its hegemony that researchers such as Bateson, Birdwhistell, Hall, and Goffman, who came from disciplinary horizons as diverse as anthropology, linguistics, mathematics, sociology, and psychiatry, resolutely turned away from the linear model of communication in Shannon's work and espoused a circular, retroactive model, as proposed by one of Shannon's former professors, Norbert Wiener. They considered that since Shannon's theory had been conceived by and for telecommunications engineers, to them it should be left; communication should be studied in the human sciences according to a model of its own. In his excellent introduction to *La Nouvelle Communication* in which he presents the work of these researchers, Yves Winkin clearly summarizes the antagonism: "In their view, the complexity of even the slightest situation of interaction is such that it is fruitless to try to reduce it to two or several 'variables' operating in linear fashion. Research in communication should be conceived in terms of levels of complexity, multiple contexts and circular systems."[3] The notion of the isolated act of communication, such as a verbal utterance, is challenged by the idea of communication as a permanent social process integrating many modes of behavior: speech, gesture, look, interindividual space, and the like. Birdwhistell and Hall thus introduced into the traditional field of communication the notion of body motion (kinesics) and interpersonal space (proxemics), while sociologist Erving Goffmann tried to show how the accidents or mishaps of human behavior reveal the pattern of the social environment. The content analysis privileged in Shannon's model is abandoned in favor of context analysis. Since communication is conceived as a permanent process occurring at several different levels, the analyst, in order to grasp the emergence of meaning, must describe the functioning of different modes of behavior in a given context.

The history of the group identified as "the invisible college" or "the Palo Alto school" began in 1942 under the decisive stimulus of Bateson. Forty years later, among all the new paths opened in the analysis of processes of communication, the one traced by Goffman seems remarkably close to the contemporary sensibility which, having tired of theories of great totalities, has returned to the spaces of proximity.

The Traces of a Memory

It cannot be denied that the upsurge of currents and problematics featuring the return of the subject has broken the conceptual barriers of the sixties. But this is occurring in a context in which, as new systems of communication are being introduced, the majority of theoreticians are once again espousing neofunctionalist conceptions, reflecting a rampant cybernetic bent. Moreover, the advances that have occurred as a result of theoretical challenges are subject to a double interpretation.

There is after all no denying the contradictory genesis that brought the subject, in the eighties, to the center of common sense. Nor can one deny the ambiguous consequences of this process of rehabilitation of the subject in the large industrial societies. It is especially hard to deny these when one notes that the return to the subject for some becomes the return, for others, to the ethic of "every man for himself."

This is why the emphasis on *the event, daily life, and the ordinary dimension of meaning* can be accompanied by a tendency to neglect the largest power apparatuses. The refusal to overevaluate "structure" may have as its obverse side a utopian vision of the autonomy of "resistance." The analysis of ordinary events can lead not only to a rethinking of the role of silent actors in history but also to the focusing of a cybernetic schema intended to legitimate an authoritarian order.

These ambivalences may favor a "narcissism of the subject" that takes the place of the "narcissism of structure," as Michel Pêcheux has commented; and Pêcheux sees in this trend "the risk of a tremendous regression toward positivism and the philosophies of consciousness."[4]

The striking comeback of expressions of moralizing or religious types of humanism claiming to be "systems of thought" already attests that these fears are not unfounded. The same can be said about the refusal to consider the unconscious or the symbolic dimension, observable in certain currents of biology and the neurological sciences. The break with ego psychology and behavioral psychology that structuralism had tried to carry out through its alliance of Freud, Marx, and Saussure is in danger of being forgotten. Furthermore, we are in danger of being increasingly separated from history and social relations, particularly since, in this realignment, other sciences close to the life sciences have appeared and announced their hegemonic objectives.

Why should this not be acknowledged? The malaise currently provoked by the upsetting of the paradigms makes it all the more difficult to evaluate the contributions and the limits of the new approaches and new theories emphasizing spaces of proximity, interaction, and interpersonal relations.[5] The attention they give to the dimension of daily life, lived experience and corporal expression, and the fact that they have inspired therapeutic methods for improving *hic et nunc* the well-being of the individual within the family or the small group, is not unrelated to the sense of "security" these theories procure, giving science the image of an activity that reconciles mind and body and liberates the potential for communication. The contribution of such integrative, humanistic approaches seems so apparent that one is tempted to adhere to them right away. More than in any other situation, it is difficult to observe, with respect to these approaches, the epistemological distance that continues to be necessary.

And yet, in spite of the great number of determinations, rules, and constraints that the disciples of "new communication" choose to analyze, there are certain troubling absences. It is not very gratifying to appear as a *trouble-fête*, but it is after all necessary, with regard to these theories of the return to proximity and interpersonal relations, to practice the same multidimensional reading that these theories themselves recommend in their approach to social phenomena today.

Anthropologist Gérard Althabe, reflecting on the soaring frequency of studies in France inspired by ethnomethodology and symbolic interactionism, as practiced by the "new communication" current in the United States, has written:

> Such projects are rather lacking in critical distance with regard to the research orientations they claim as their own; they ought to give greater emphasis to their origins (G. Simmel, G. H. Mead) and the significance of their emergence and current development (in the past fifteen years) in the social sciences and in American society. One should also raise the question of the meaning of such orientations in the social sciences in France (in certain respects, they represent a break with the Durkheimian sociological tradition); the authors of these studies ought to make explicit the evolution that led them to adhere to such perspectives. The disappearance of critical distance often gives the impression that these studies proceed from a simple imitative practice.[6]

Althabe's remarks are all the more judicious in that we have seen, in the past few years, a proliferation of ethnographic studies on practices of interaction between media and their audiences. These studies are conducted as if the interaction between radio (for example) and its audiences did not require a genetic and historical approach. The evolution of the "field of communication" (for example, the changes in models of advertising) is grasped only in terms of this interaction. True, adopting another type of approach would multiply the difficulties in the choice of methodology: interviews in people's homes are not a sufficient basis for carrying out studies of a historical order.[7] This methodology claims to adhere to lived experience in order to analyze and reconstruct the microphysics of interaction practices between public and sender. It makes no other claim than to describe the basic data of a reality that the theories of manipulation, because of their premises, had kept out of sight. It is a great deal and at the same time it is very little, particularly in view of the general tendency for research objects to shrink in size.

Much has obviously changed since the time when the notion of "interaction" could have the connotation of critical participation in a project of society. We have returned in fact to the original sense of the concept as it had been elaborated by the cybernetic theories, in which it is a synonym for a relation between elements of a system, given that exchanges take part in a mechanism of system autoregulation. The problem is that in real situations, like that in France, where the notion of participation has continued to weigh a great deal on people's definition of political, social, and cultural relations, this new notion of interaction (whose origin in cybernetics is forgotten) operates at two levels. It allows new managers of social engineering projects to move smoothly and discreetly from one mode of administering public affairs to another, while still keeping in touch with the old "discursive formation" of militant sociocultural activity.

It cannot be denied, indeed, that the socialization of new technologies in countries such as France seeks its way forward between two paths acting as boundaries: first, the path of marketing and solvent demand, that is, the promotional approach to material exchanges; and second, the path of communication-as-emancipation, which continues the tradition of militant sociocultural activity, whose traces persist in the notions of social demand, appropriation, and participation in technological choices.[8] There is thus a need to analyze how the imaginary dimension (*l'imaginaire*) inherited from a recent period of social struggles and victories is invested in a new one that presides over the formation of social uses of new technologies. This was in fact the wish expressed in one of the conclusions formulated by the convention of the French Society for the Sciences of Information and Communication, held in Paris in 1984.

8

The Procedures of Consumption

Worst-Case Functionalism

If there is a shadowy zone in critical knowledge, it is definitely that of the procedures of consumption and reception of the media. These two terms, "consumption" and "reception," are both quite unsatisfactory because they are based on the postulate of a decisive break between the sending pole and the receiving pole. This break introduces the idea of a passive attitude on the part of the receivers, or even their fusion with the receptacle; it also introduces the idea that the instance of consumption is reducible to a phenomenon rather than having to be comprehended as a process.

Many factors contributed to the freezing of this paradigm: among them, the weighty pedagogical heritage of the Enlightenment, which not only made it difficult to imagine the resistance of educated majorities to the school system organized by the nation-state but also made it difficult to conceive of the resistance of television viewers to the action of the enlightened minorities presiding over the production of public discourse. This heritage is particularly well preserved—and what a perverse turn of events this is!—in countries that have cultivated a philosophy of public service inseparable from an idea of "high culture" as a level to which all citizens should be raised.

Another equally cumbersome heritage is the conception of the role of the political party as enlightener and vanguard in the countries where the major historical organizations of the left have played an important role in defining the notion of legitimate and official culture. The trace of this heritage, which is linked to the older heritage of the conception of the missionary role of the church (the pastor and his flock) as responsible for

72

revealing the Good Word, may be found in the design of a good many policies of cultural action.

Equally present is the obverse of this same heritage: the tendency, on the left as well as the right, to cling to certain explanatory and interpretive schemas that subscribe to the theory of manipulation and thus promote the idea of an active minority (the elites, capital, or the party) molding an amorphous and inert society.

The traces of all these realities are found, in one way or another, in the representations established by the different schools of critical thought throughout the world.

Indeed, for a long time, the critical schools—the Frankfurt School and the currents inspired by Althusser—accepted as an implicit postulate the omnipotence of the mass media.

This problem had been clearly exposed at the beginning of the sixties by Bourdieu and Passeron. They were the only ones, at the time, who rejected what they called "worst-case functionalism" (le fonctionnalisme du pire), and refused to believe in the Machiavellian designs of the media-as-Leviathan. It is particularly important to provide this reminder because, as Jacques Rancière and his Révoltes Logiques group saw clearly, these same authors were not able to avoid basing their analyses of the educational system on a logic of social reproduction seen as inevitable. "If the study of the mass media has not achieved its proclaimed ambitions," wrote Bourdieu and Passeron in 1963,

> it is at least reaching the unavowed goal that all its methods betray, that is, of evading the simple, down-to-earth questions that challenge its own existence. Does not each means of communication divide up the "mass" into groups that are as many temporary publics? . . . Why, for example, prior to any experience, grant the false face-to-face television relationship an unequaled power of persuasion, while affecting to ignore the all-too-evident effectiveness of direct human presence? . . . There are a thousand ways to read, to see, and to listen. Why seek to determine the "influence" of the mass media by the strangely bureaucratic procedure of measuring the quantity of information emitted or the analysis of the "structure" of the message? . . . Should it be recalled that meaning does not exist as such in the object read, but rather—here as elsewhere—has the modality of the intentional consciousness that constitutes it? Superficial reading perhaps carries within it its own defense and absent-minded watching or listening transforms the discourse of the speaker into mere noise, which can, from that point on, be measured in decibels. And why ignore the protective mechanisms with which the masses arm themselves against the mass-media invasion?[1]

The essential point had thus been raised: social uses of media do not necessarily reproduce the logics that emerge from the analysis of the structure of the media. And even that which is supposedly conceived to do so does not necessarily induce the expected effect. Any hypothesis that does not accept this principle of discontinuity is condemned to belong more to science fiction than to serious analysis of the media. At a time (1957) when in France a cause-and-effect relation between the structure of the message and the structuring of its reception was predominant (with the exception of the two sociologists of culture quoted above), a British ethnologist of daily life, Richard Hoggart, published a seminal work of critical sociology of mass culture in his country: *The Uses of Literacy*. In this book he studied the practices of exchange and complementarity between traditional and industrial forms of culture in the practices of different groups of the urban working class.[2]

In Latin America in the early seventies, when for the first time a left-wing government was confronted with the necessity of offering an alternative in programming and production, some pioneer studies considered receiving publics as producers of meaning; for example, they analyzed the unintended uses of serial television shows by the different groups of the Chilean working classes.[3] In this period, semiological studies in France retained, out of the Saussurian distinction between language (*langue*) and speech (*parole*), only the path opened by the linguistics of language, neglecting the second path opened by Saussure, that of speech. As Yves Winkin astutely remarks about Barthes's *The Fashion System*:[4] "A famous semiological analysis of fashion considered as a system analogous to that offered by language was carried out on the basis of fashion catalogues, not on the basis of the clothes actually worn, which could have been considered acts of speech."[5]

One can understand why, in a context dominated by the tendency of structuralists to isolate senders and messages, which assumed that the media had some great, mysterious power, the analyses of an author like Jean Baudrillard were a welcome leap into novelty. By emphasizing nonreciprocity in the process of "communication," he had the merit of refuting the idea of communication as an exchange always successfully carried out. Communication exists, and where it cannot be found, there is noise: this idea was the postulate of all mass media studies that were too neglectful of detail. Baudrillard reversed the equation: because of nonreciprocity, and because of the break in exchanges, the media function in a noncommunication mode, producing communication only as the simulacrum of itself. This hypothesis certainly appears more fertile than the first one, which takes communication to be given *a priori*; at the very least, it renders the object "communication" more ambiguous.

However, its error is to interpret the failure of the media's injunction as a sort of self-dilution of meaning under the effect of causes purely internal to the technological media, without ever introducing the action of the "dominated people" as a factor. In this sense it is perfectly coherent with its underlying thesis, that of "the end of the social." Michel Pêcheux pinpointed the problem when he wrote,

> What is effective in this travesty is that "the masses" remain just as invisible to themselves and as impossible to represent as concepts . . . And this phantomlike phantasmagoria works so well, apparently, that certain thinkers have come to declare that reality is only a mirage, a network of simulacra, a self-production of discourses of seduction. . . . "Power does not exist," says Baudrillard in his effort to "forget Foucault"! Is there any better way to fall back into the maternal lap of contemporary state power?[6]

From Mass to Differentiation

Positioning his work on "the invention of daily life" with respect to Michel Foucault's, Michel de Certeau described in the following way what he called practices of resistance:

> These "ways to do things" constitute the thousand practices through which the users reappropriate the space set up by techniques of sociocultural production. They raise similar questions [to those of Foucault], since it is a matter of perceiving the minute operations that proliferate inside technocratic structures and divert the way they function through a large number of "tactics" aimed at the everyday details; they raise opposing questions as well, since it is no longer a matter of pointing out how the violence of the order turns into disciplinary technology, but rather of digging out the surreptitious forms taken by the scattered, tactical and "do-it-yourself" creativity of groups and individuals who are henceforth caught in the nets of "surveillance." These user's procedures and tricks make up the pattern of an antidiscipline.[7]

The insight about reading as "poaching" is in fact an old one, and Michel de Certeau had the merit of putting it into theoretical perspective. When Goethe read Spinoza, he stopped only at the passages that stimulated his curiosity and which he sensed would strengthen his thought and make it more fruitful. He had also grasped that "with the same words, no one thinks the same thing as his neighbor; reading stimulates different chains of ideas in different individuals."[8] This observation, which seemed commonplace to Goethe, took a long time to impose itself as a commonly accepted truth, as is the case today.

What the sociology of the media long neglected, historians of the printed word and literacy, as well as historians of mentalities, had patiently gleaned from their study of the resistance of worker and peasant subcultures to the first wave of cultural "normalization" — that is, the entry of the written word into the oral tradition and that of the printed word into the tradition of the manuscript.[9] That is what the American author Jack Goody called "the domestication of the savage mind."

While the sociology of the media had a striking tendency to totalize the field of new technical means of communication and to apprehend the media environment in a uniform light, the historians of the printed word were able to discern the complementary relationships, the levels of rivalry, and the reciprocal influences between the written word and oral expression and between texts reserved for elites and popular stories. They were able to understand, in particular, how the Biblical scriptures were received and understood according to the lesser or greater richness of the oral tradition of the reader.

The prevailing theory on the left as well as the right to explain the functioning of modern means of mass dissemination fixated on the stereotype of "the mass," linked to that of "mass society." Where historians of popular cultures saw differences, theoreticians of mass society saw an atomized, amorphous whole, with no capacity to resist. This theoretical stance concerning the massifying action of the means of mass communication (notice the tautology) brought together very diverse and even antagonistic philosophical traditions (Riesman had little to do with Ortega y Gasset, who in turn did not speak of massification in the same way as Adorno or Friedmann). From this perspective, "modern society" was the result of the general disappearance of elements of differentiation that had characterized the societies of the past, and of the resulting loss of the sense of the sacred; technology, economic abundance, and political equality had brought forth a homogeneous society. Prior to modern society, there had been communities and "peoples," whereas now, the majority was identified with the mass, and man with mass man.

The Catalonian author Salvador Giner, in his work *Sociedad Masa* (Mass society, subtitled Critique of conservative thought),[10] has demonstrated that a deeply antipopular connotation has always been attached to the concept of mass, from Herodotus, who placed the confusion between people and mass in the mouth of an enemy of democracy, to Saint Augustine, who spoke of the *massa damnata*, since the chosen were by definition few in number. Closer to our subject, we must not forget the famous Roman formula *panem et circenses*, the first coordinated organization of mass diversion.

It is interesting to note that the very fertile school of the history of mentalities, which reinvigorated the study of popular practices, stopped research just where the modernization of French society started after 1945, thereby missing out on the field of observation opened by the new technological environment and the pursuit of the history of resistance.

Michel de Certeau's great merit is precisely to have regarded popular culture as a culture of the present. He fulfills the wish of anthropologists who are opposed to the narrow, past-oriented understanding of popular and ethnic cultures as "paradises lost," original cultures pitted against modern "homogenization."

There are, indeed, many ways to organize the defense against cultural homogenization. And it should be recalled, following Michel de Certeau, that when the occasion arises to mount this defense, salvation through "popular culture" or "cultural identity" may hide many ambiguities. A dubious obsession with the past or a rampant racism may stain either or both of these notions. This is what certain anthropologists remind us when they point out that the absence of debate about popular culture can only favor the confining of the latter to nostalgia. This nostalgia is encouraged by many—as much by ethnologists (including recently Claude Lévi-Strauss)[11] who manifest nostalgia with respect to "ethnic cultures" far removed from developed societies (ours in particular), as by a number of discourses or works about popular culture within our own societies. As Henri Giordan has written:

> This way of approaching relations between cultures raises some troubling prospects: if, as Claude Lévi-Strauss claims, cultural homogenization flows from the multiplication of cultural contacts, should we therefore attempt to reduce these? How could this be possible without adopting xenophobic behaviors? The defense of "cultural identities" currently risks giving way to the establishment of cultural ghettos in the very midst of our societies ("regional" cultures, immigrant communities' cultures, and cultures of subordinate classes). This trend has the danger of encouraging attitudes that prepare the way for a resurgence of racist behavior.[12]

Passive/Active

The questioning of hypotheses based on the idea of the inevitable passivity of consumers has not only opened to reflection the field of consumers' specific practices but also broken down the barriers that had blinded theory to the alternatives. For a long time, there was the image of the passive consumer up against the active media, which was related to a fetishistic opposition between passive media and active media that pitted the sad past against a promising future. For a long time this idea lurked behind all alternative conceptions of the media.

Accustomed to conceiving this opposition from the perspective of an autonomous territory, people were long tempted to reduce the alternative to an opposition between light media, the ideal terrain for self-management, and heavy, centralized media, the image of concentrated power. This vision of the alternative reflected a dominant tendency within the left: to consider its confinement in civil society as the autonomous framework within which it could conceive its transitional place in bourgeois society and elaborate its alternative. The prevailing idea was that the space occupied by the left was a nonporous space next to another nonporous space. In one way or another, this conception of a left separated from the general terrain of society underlay the dilemma of separatism versus integration, as if society began at the precise point where the actions of the militant social movement began. This compartmentalization was infinitely reproduced in the multiple sects of the extraparliamentary left.

This opposition was latent in many discussions about the emerging new technologies (militant film and video, community television, free radio stations),[13] as if these constituted the remedy to the central media. The resulting conception of alternative communication was devoid of any analysis of the balance of forces within the overall field of communication. The alternative communication movements tended thus to avoid questions about the evolution of central media apparatuses or about the pluralism that had been at the origin of public service.[14]

The question of social uses of the media exercised a powerful corrective influence to this way of thinking. It uncovered, indeed, a new space for progressive reflection on the media. It became less important to draw an opposition between active and passive media than to think about the social uses of each. To avoid posing these problems was to avoid thinking about the ways in which alternative experience could get caught in the game of prospecting for innovation, practiced both by media merchants and by those in political power. Given the reality of the balance of forces, the perspective of creating "new spaces of communication" drifts easily toward a perspective of "new spaces of consumption."

This type of questioning beginning with the consumer was thus at the origin of a new conceptual matrix which, by refusing to apprehend the media as an instrument of power, in fact apprehended media as a field of power relations. With this conceptual matrix, there was a refusal to grasp a mode of communication as a mere collection of technologies; it was considered rather as a set of social practices, a mode of articulation between social groups and actors. In this perspective, ideology ceased to be conceived as a coherent system of ideas or of discourses, and instead became, in Nicos Poulantzas's expression, a "set of material practices." Thus a mode of communication included practices of information collecting, practices of drafting texts, of writing, of viewing through a lens, of editing and so forth, in addition to practices of consumption.

Certain elements of the movement for free radio stations in Europe took up this new way of seeing the media, which broke with an idea dear to the traditional left, for which the main problem was posed at the level of ownership; according to this traditional conception, in order to change meanings, all one had to do was change owners.

The major problem thus became the places of different subjects in the process of media production. It was no doubt the debates that took place about Radio Alice in Bologna that best formalized the epistemological break in the very apprehension of the media. One reads in a manifesto of the Autonomia Movement that

> the problem of communication has not yet been broached in a specific way by the movement. Exclusive attention was paid to the content of communication — what was to be said — to the detriment of the relation between the content and the form of communication, and without seeking to deepen reflection about the idea that if the speaking subject transforms itself, then the form — the instrument, the mode of production, circulation, and reception of the message — must also change. The hypothesis according to which the structure of the means is the single factor conditioning the meaning of communication is false, but it is equally false to suppose that the content of the message can change without any transformation of its listener. It is necessary to break with the idealistic ideology of form and content: if the communicating subject is transformed, the material and ideological conditions of communication are transformed as well.[15]

But the evolution of media reality has proven more complex. Recent history is full of instances of debate on this question. Notions such as technology, technicity, and professionalism have given rise to one of the most important social questions at stake in the process of technological expansion: the challenging of powers and hierarchies. The history-in-the-making of local media is there as a reminder of this. The slogan "return expression to the people" gave way to fears that an excessively open radio station might become boring and unprofessional. The norm of technical perfection took over from the concern for liberating new social uses for the media and forging new relations with the audience.

In liberal democracies, the social practices of communication have tended to become confused with professional practices. From this professional definition of practice in communication, constructed with heavy recourse to laws, philosophical doctrines, and scientific arguments, has flowed a series of postulates that has linked to the means of mass communication the norm par excellence of what constitutes freedom of opinion and expression. Far be it from us to claim that freedom of expression thus defined is not (and has not been) a real guarantee of democracy and a barrier against impulsive intervention by political and financial powers. But more and more, freedom of expression defined according to this exclusively professional norm is showing its limits regarding the further blossoming of democracy. While technological expansion seems to promise nearly unlimited participation of the multiple social actors, professional codes, which regulate communication practices and have created habits and reflexes in the public, intervene and risk defeating other social actors who wish to express themselves through the new media. They also risk blocking the expression of professionals from other fields or disciplines who seek to communicate within the framework of this professionalism.

Two obstacles stand today in the way of groups in search of new options. First, there is the sacralization of a certain idea of professionalism put forward by the corporatist ideology, according to which one's profession involves know-how and a set of techniques that are codified for all time and thus not open to challenge. This sacralization is quite consistent with the strengthening of the positions of communications professionals. There is also the cumbersome heritage of a culture of activist communication concerned with returning expression to ordinary people and which considers lack of professionalism to be the very guarantee of liberated expression. Faced with the crisis of what militant communication practices became—a closed discourse for a captive audience—many have been tempted to transfer their faith, without the slightest critical distance, to the existing body of media techniques, and even to the logic of marketing. However, the multiplication of technical mediations in communication today has made necessary both the desacralization of the corporatist idea of professionalism and the abandonment of the "morality of inefficacy" that was present in the practice of activist communication and in the practice of the left in media in general. Professionalism is to be considered a field of innovation for the practices of social intervention. This is what certain sectors of the associative movement and the workers' movement have begun to understand when they observe that it is time to leave aside a certain "morose and boring image of social life," because their very "cultural identity" is at stake. It is at this point that the new paradigms help to find answers to the question: Which images? The search for new forms and new contents is indeed inseparable from the new emerging trends: the search for the individual within the mass, the right for everyone to cultivate sensitivity, to enjoy fiction, and to develop the imaginary.[16]

The Freedom of the Subject

There must be no misunderstanding about the conceptual framework in which media consumption is apprehended as a set of social practices. The temptation is great to seize this conceptual renewal regarding active consumption and emphasis on the possibility for unusual or surprising interpretations in order to support theses that minimize the strategic role occupied by the means of communication in reproducing social relations — and thus to delegitimize the necessity of continuing to develop a political economy of media production, itself inseparable from an "economy" of the procedures of consumption.

There is a great risk of denying the existence of a structure, in favor of a free and timeless subjectivity or a subject that plays with and makes light of the rules of domination. (From this point of view, the notion of intentional consciousness used by Bourdieu and Passeron has an odor of subjectivism.) Even if one refuses the determinism of structure, this is no reason to endorse a point of view in which the consumer is autonomous with respect to all social determinations. And this tendency can be observed in a current of studies that has gained momentum in the past several years. This current recommends moving beyond the "rational-empirical" school and affirms its preference for the "intuitive" as opposed to the "discursive."[17] Recent thought produced in a variety of contexts shows the extent to which analyses based on the freedom of the subject in the activity of reception are being generalized. We endorse the remark of a Scandinavian researcher who, in his comments on certain studies conducted in the United States and the Netherlands, observed:

> What is essential in journalism is not only the relation of the audience to the senders [of messages] but also their relations to some third phenomenon: what the messages refer to. If this "third factor" is eliminated we are only reproducing the main idea of the mathematical information theory, static in character, and neglecting the semantic information theory. This journalistic starting point would be acceptable if the audience were omnipotent and had created the social reality with its will and consciousness without any restrictions. But the audience is not omnipotent — it only may have an *illusion of omnipotence* — and misleading journalism may strengthen this voluntaristic illusion. It is necessary of course to increase the audience's capacity for acting but not without raising its consciousness of the objective conditions in social reality.[18]

If pragmatic linguistics and semiology have clearly shown the historical contextuality of enunciation and reception acts, they have also sought to pinpoint how each media institution has its own specific way of positioning the viewer, regulating certain aspects of the production of meaning and production of emotional responses, and so forth.

It is within this same framework that Jürgen Habermas extends the notion of competence to the universe of communication in his attempt to articulate the premises of a universal pragmatics which would succeed in demonstrating that even the pragmatic rules for the uses of sentences are rational. Certain French researchers have become interested in testing this notion. As one of them writes:

> The viewer perceives messages at two levels and mobilizes two different competences. Thus, for example, the expectation (which will be satisfied or frustrated) of ulterior narrative developments according to the characteristics of a sequence of a detective movie (music, images, narrative, etc.) brings into play a first-level competence. This competence results from familiarity with the genre or subgenre to which the product being consumed belongs. The viewer has internalized the codes and subcodes that structure it. By contrast, perception of the overall situation of communication of which he is a part, and of strategies of seduction, manipulation, and influence that take him as an object, arises from a second-level competence. This "communicative competence" also constructs itself on the basis of an accumulation of experiences, but this accumulation is only partially individual, for it is social experience that becomes crystallized in practices and in languages of objectification that the subject-consumer can put to use.[19]

It is precisely this negation of social experience, crystallized in a myriad of tricks and popular practices of "poaching," that characterizes a current systems-theory drift from a microphysics of power to a micropsychologism of the interstitial freedoms of the individual being.

In this drift, the social factor (*le social*) loses its value as a stake in the infinity of microscenarios and individual microconflicts. In the meantime, this same systems-theory trend, which helps in reflecting scientifically about the deployment of microsituations, also helps in scientific thinking about the reorganization of the totality. "The being in the reality of the vital flow": that is how Abraham Moles, the founder of a new autonomous discipline, micropsychology, locates his subject of observation. Society is a labyrinth, the archetype of constrained space. In the labyrinths of lived experience, he says, "there is indeed a freedom but the modes of exercising it are foreseeable by the constructors of the labyrinth, and it is all the greater and richer that the wandering individual masters through his thought the topological structure of the labyrinth."[20] But the constructor and the administrator of the labyrinth are always classified among the "universals."

The return of the consumer is no doubt the one most common theme of a variety of different currents of thought. With free trade, is not the freedom to consume assumed to be the corollary of free enterprise? And it is in the name of both of these—the freedom to consume being nonetheless more popular than the other—that the elimination of state interventionism is called for.

It should be noted, however, that with the increasing importance of the function of programming, action and knowledge appear more and more tightly linked on the sender's side in the effort to optimize control over the environment. And if Taylorism is on the decline in the factory—in production—may we not venture to speak of a Taylorization in the field of consumption? This is a paradox if ever there was one. Taylorism, from its origins, has been associated with the notion of discipline, disciplined bodies, disciplinary apparatus, and the like. Today, with the proliferation of knowledge about the movements of the consumer, and with the contribution of the sciences of functional and affective integration, the body is produced and programmed in its desires and its motivation by other "disciplines" based on the the organization-valorization form—disciplines that no longer act through disciplinary codes, but through codes of seduction.

However, one might wonder whether this logic is not too well thought out not to be illusory. The answer may be found, without a doubt, in the irony introduced by the subject in its comeback.

PART 3

Intellectuals and Media Culture
Redefining the Relationship

Introduction to Part 3

The industrial order, as it has developed under capitalism, proclaimed very early within its symbolic terrain the end of the reign of necessity and the rise of the reign of freedom. This liberty is no longer measured according to constitutional freedoms or closed into the dismal greyness of legal and political institutions; rather, it is a freedom that, as the market of goods extends itself and becomes diversified and the number and quality of its beneficiaries grows, becomes linked to the pleasure of the consumer. In the face of this euphoric mode of living the present and the future, those who persisted in believing that this reign of freedom was not for them could only experience a feeling of strangeness.

In the sixties, Umberto Eco characterized this position astutely by calling it "apocalyptic" and opposing it to that of the "integrated" people. The apocalyptics were the intellectuals who denounced the market-induced degeneration of culture, and the integrated were those who subscribed unconditionally to the democratizing virtues of so-called mass culture. For the latter, technological progress necessarily brought social progress and liberated a new way of conceiving citizenship. For the apocalyptics, the fact that capital had taken over culture deprived the consumer of any possibility for liberation and authentic experience.[1]

One may remember the virulence with which Pier Paolo Pasolini, in his daily contributions to Italian newspapers (compiled in *Scritti corsari* after his death), railed at the new "unifying cultural phenomenon" that he dubbed "mass hedonism."

> The fever of consumption is a fever of obedience to an unstated order. Everyone in Italy feels the degrading anxiety of being like all the others in the act of consuming, being happy or being free,

because such is the order that each person has unconsciously received and which he "must" obey if he feels different. Never has difference been such a terrifying fault as in this period of tolerance. Equality, in fact, has not been conquered; it is, on the contrary, a "false" equality received as a gift. . . . Of this equality, one of the main characteristics that expresses itself in life is sadness. The physical sadness of which I speak is profoundly neurotic; it is based on a social frustration.[2]

No one else has denounced with such force the centralism of what he called "this interclass culture of consumption" of which television was the emblematic vector. As we know, he even went so far as to say, under the influence of the Manichean rages that seized him (as he himself admitted), that the culture of television was more destructive to the soul of the Italian people than Mussolinian Fascism itself, since, unlike the latter with its monumental character, television culture was able to penetrate into the interstices of daily life and the new values that underlie it have have been adopted in everyday experience.

Well before Pasolini, at the dawn of consumer capitalism, many American sociologists had expressed worry over the new modalities of hedonistic modernity. A number of works appeared under the sign of Leo Lowenthal's famous phrase: "The hero of production has been replaced by the hero of consumption." It was at this time that David Riesman invented the expression "the lonely crowd" (1950). Later, in 1964, the same author asked in the subtitle of another book (*Leisure and Work*): "Abundance for What?" and analyzed the disarray provoked by a change in the system of values, one of whose main expressions, in his view, was "the illusion of a new hedonism." We may add as a reminder that this critique of consumer hedonism was to play a founding role in many analyses produced by the women's movement.[3]

All this has been said before. Everything has been written, both in the heat of the moment and with cold distance, about the tension between two models of freedom, two conceptions of liberation, two modes of realizing cultural democracy, that exist both in the countries spoiled by consumption and stimulated by the contestation of that kind of happiness, and in those which found themselves, at the dawn of their political or economic liberation, attracted by the promise of this "revolution of rising expectations."

These states of consciousness have inspired theories, given rise to a multitude of books, provoked street demonstrations, structured new social movements, justified strategies, unleashed tactics of cultural intervention, counterinformation, counterculture, alternative culture, activist culture, and more.

The 1980s were born under other another sign. We observe, in many areas of the world, the multiple pulsations of a single malaise.

9

Popular Pleasure as a Revelation

An Epistemological Shudder

The battery of hypotheses, tools of analysis, and theories that have helped intellectuals to examine the mechanisms of media discourses and to deconstruct the rationality of mass communication has suddenly revealed itself to be too sketchy to account for the concrete, lived reality of the public's relation to spectacles.

To pose the problem from the standpoint of the public is becoming an imperative that imposes itself with such a force of evidence that one may ask how it was ever possible to ignore it for so long, and on such a large scale, since it is, after all, the most precious resource of the entertainment industry.

English critic Michael Poole, in a review of two books about the audience for American television serials, wrote in 1984:

> In their different ways, both these books place a new emphasis
> on the TV audience. This contrasts sharply with how most critics
> write about TV. Yet it's clear that only such an approach can
> even begin to do justice to the peculiarly contradictory and
> ambivalent pleasures of "Dallas," the series most of us love to
> hate, hate to love, but go on watching anyway.[1]

Martin Barbero, professor at the University of Cali, Colombia, who has worked a great deal on popular cultures, shared with us in 1984 the discomfort he experienced with his students in a movie theater in an outlying district of Cali where a Mexican melodrama was being shown. Attendance of this film was meant to be a working session for his students, allowing them to test their frameworks of analysis for popular stories, but it was disturbed by a malaise when the students realized that what was appearing on the screen was moving the audience to tears. "What happened that day I dare call an epistemological shudder," wrote Barbero.

> After twenty minutes of viewing, we had begun to feel such great boredom—the film was so elementary and stereotypical—that we began to laugh loudly. The people around us (the theater was full, mostly with men; this film was breaking records in Colombia and that is why we were there) became angry, shouted insults at us and wanted to force us to leave. For the rest of the projection, I watched these men, moved to tears, as they "lived" the drama with remarkable pleasure . . . and when leaving I asked myself: "What does the film I saw have to do with the film they saw?" because what brought me such boredom induced such pleasure in them. What had they seen in it that I had not? And of what use was my "ideological reading," even if I manage to translate it into their words, since that reading will always be of the film I saw, not the one they saw? At that time I was under the spell of semiology and the paths it was opening . . . but here was where the spell ended. I wrote hundreds of pages that I dare not publish, in which I do nothing more, in the end, than ask and re-ask in every form a question that Dufrenne helped me to formulate: Why do the popular classes "invest desire and extract pleasure" from a culture that denies them as a subject? It is the very same question you ask [in the form]: "What enormous masochism, what suicidal class attitude could explain that fascination?" And today this question leads me to conclude that it is an inescapable necessity to interpret mass culture from a different standpoint that allows one to formulate another question: What, in mass culture, responds not to the logic of capital but to other logics?[2]

To be sure, in the course of the past thirty years, certain very isolated studies have used an approach involving structures of taste and habit, disturbing the prevailing trend of criticism, which was to perceive products of mass culture, too hastily, only from the angle of ideological injunction. But today new questions are changing approaches to mass cultural production: the gulf between the message sent and the one received; the practices of receivers and their roles in the production of meanings and uses in individual, family, and collective contexts; the way in which the institution represents public taste and the role of these representations in orienting audiovisual production.

The work of a researcher like Michel Maffesoli allows us to measure the long distance covered by a portion of the intellectual class in bringing the analysis of popular lived experience to the center of the "sociology of the present"; intellectuals are invited to reconcile themselves to observing the ordinary, everyday practices of the people. The television serial is one of these rituals that are attracting new attention. "Instead of always denouncing alienation," Maffesoli writes,

> maybe we should be watching how, in small touches, through the mediation of television sets, at a given hour, a community is created. . . . Television is a new household god which makes possible both a cult of the family and a feeling of universal belonging. This is no doubt a rather overly conclusive analysis . . . but after all, it does bring out the fact that, beyond the intellectual lamentations we hear all too often, people have a sense of the present. They take advantage of the present and see the good side of life: that is what any analyst who is not too disconnected from daily life may observe in all situations and occurrences that punctuate the life of our societies. There is a popular hedonism which, in its more or less vulgar and trivial expressions, does not fail to shock many delicate souls.[3]

Pleasure has become a key element of a paradigm that is revitalizing approaches to media culture. It defies the clear division proposed by Umberto Eco between integrated intellectuals and apocalyptic ones. It is the notion that attests to the changes that have occurred in the perception of the relation between media culture and its "users." In this sense, it also invites us to see the relation between civil society and culture in a different way, in our so-called postindustrial age.

The Traces of a Heritage

We know of the opposition, on more than one point, between the thought of Walter Benjamin and that of Theodor Adorno and Max Horkheimer within the Frankfurt School, when it came to evaluating the change in the significance of culture provoked by the advent of mechanical reproduction of works of art. Contrary to his two colleagues, Benjamin believed that the cult value of a work of art had been replaced by its entertainment value. Where Adorno and Horkheimer saw the degradation of free time into a very different entity, the commodity of leisure, Benjamin celebrated the opportunity offered by the show to reconcile criticism, the attitude of the connoisseur, and pleasure.

> Mechanical reproduction of art changes the reaction of the masses toward art. The reactionary attitude toward a Picasso painting changes into the progressive reaction toward a Chaplin movie. The progressive reaction is characterized by the direct, intimate fusion of visual and emotional enjoyment with the

orientation of the expert. Such fusion is of great social
significance. The greater the decrease in the social significance of
an art form, the sharper the distinction between criticism and
enjoyment by the public. The conventional is uncritically enjoyed,
and the truly new is criticized with aversion. With regard to the
screen, the critical and the receptive attitudes of the public
coincide.[4]

It is nonetheless true that Benjamin was one of the rare critics who at
that time raised the question of pleasure by broaching the subject of entertainment.

Where others saw "bad taste," "vacuousness," "low quality," "sopo-
rific consciousness," and the like, he claimed legitimacy for other cultural
forms than those enshrined by the classic tradition of aesthetics—opera,
ballet, art, and literature. He reproached Adorno and Horkheimer for
their sacralization of art and their nostalgia for a cultural experience free
of any ties to technology. He brilliantly took a contrary attitude to the
notion of cultural heritage, defending the notion of movement, which
seemed to him to be characteristic of the emergence of new forms of communication as well as new cultural forms. As an illustration, we may take
a passage, quoted in an anthology of detective fiction, in which Benjamin
refers to the perfect fit between the rhythm of train wheels on the tracks
and the suspenseful action of the plot, stressing the entertainment value
procured by the reader of a detective novel in a moving train. And oddly,
in her article "Transports of Pleasure," T. Davies of England, who does
not seem to know this text by Benjamin, demonstrated the concordance
that existed between the new pleasures of escape promised by a literature
intended for sale in train stations (bought and consumed quickly) and the
horizons opened to exchange with the world by that new mode of communication, the railway.[5]

Whereas Adorno required of the spectator or the listener a certain concentration and even an attitude of tension—he insisted on the importance
of a praxis of the authentic relationship with the work of art—Benjamin
accorded value to "the positive implications of distraction." "The tasks
which face the human apparatus of perception at the turning points of
history cannot be solved . . . by contemplation alone. They are mastered
gradually by habit. . . . The ability to master certain tasks in a state of
distraction proves that their solution has become a matter of habit."[6]

Once Benjamin had disappeared, this "relative optimism" (as Martin
Jay, historian of the Frankfurt School, characterizes it) was no longer
present in the analyses of this critical current. Indeed, this optimism re-
appears only through distant echoes like those of Hans Magnus Enzensberger at the end of the sixties in "Constituents of a Theory of the Me-

dia." Enzensberger sees Benjamin as the only theoretician apart from Brecht who can be of use in constructing an aesthetics adapted to a new historical situation, and the only one to have suspected the "emancipatory potential" of the new media. In revolt against a left that has remained a prisoner of the norms of the Gutenberg era and that, in his view, is incapable of making the transition to the audiovisual era, Enzensberger writes:

> George Orwell's bogey of a monolithic consciousness industry derives from a view of the media which is undialectical and obsolete. The possibility of total control of such a system at a central point belongs not to the future but to the past. . . . The New Left of the sixties has reduced the development of the media to a single concept—that of manipulation. This concept was originally extremely useful for heuristic purposes and has made possible a great many individual analytical investigations, but it now threatens to degenerate into a mere slogan which conceals more than it is able to illuminate, and therefore itself requires analysis. The current theory of manipulation on the Left is essentially defensive; its effects can lead the movement into defeatism. Subjectively speaking, behind the tendency to go on the defensive lies a sense of impotence. Objectively, it corresponds to the absolutely correct view that the decisive means of production are in enemy hands. But to react to this state of affairs with moral indignation is naïve. . . . To cast the enemy in the role of the devil is to conceal the weakness and lack of perspective in one's own agitation. If the latter leads to self-isolation instead of mobilizing the masses, then its failure is attributed holus-bolus to the overwhelming power of the media. . . . The fear of handling shit is a luxury a sewer-man cannot necessarily afford.[7]

The main thrust of Enzensberger's message is to give new life to Benjamin's intuition that technological reproducibility introduces a new tension into the social experience of culture. Benjamin would certainly not have disavowed the way Enzensberger plays in his essay on the words "mobile," "mobility," and "mobilization," seeing in the mobility of the media—their mobile character—their capacity to mobilize the public.

10

Negative Culture, Affirmative Culture

The Idea of Happiness

We should take care not to think of Adorno and Horkheimer as having only anathematized the culture industry, and as not having been able to make a dialectical evaluation of the new situation created by the industrialization of cultural production, despite the fact that dialectics were their strong point. There is a tendency to distinguish the Adorno-Horkheimer position from Benjamin's (and some of their texts, such as those on the criticism of jazz, would justify this), as if they opposed each other across a positive-negative divide. Indeed, we know how much Adorno and Horkheimer despised what they called "affirmative culture," which for them stripped the very idea of culture of what constituted its value — namely, its "negative resonance," which they linked to the experience of anxiety. Culture, in their view, must carry something negative, the experience of rupture.

The stress on the negative led them to stigmatize the inability of orthodox Marxism to go beyond affirmative culture because it reduced the idea of happiness to that of material satisfaction. The concept of real happiness, which occupies a central place in the Frankfurt School's critical theory — a happiness they refuse to identify with economic well-being — is the criterion by which they denounce the imposture of affirmative art's "false happiness." At the center of their critique of affirmative culture is the idea that "the promise of happiness" and the vision of a different society were systematically excluded from what had increasingly become a culture of the status quo. For Adorno and Horkheimer, art in an age of mechanized reproduction serves to reconcile the mass public to the existing order.

Adorno's article about the work of the first theoretician of leisure, the American Thorstein Veblen, who published *The Theory of the Leisure Class* in 1899, clarifies this idea of happiness that market capitalism has generalized. In his doctrine of conspicuous consumption, Veblen maintains that the consumption of goods serves less to satisfy real needs or to guarantee what he calls "the fullness of life" than to sustain social prestige and status.[1] In 1941, Adorno retorts that in fact

> the happiness that man actually finds cannot be separated from conspicuous consumption. There is no happiness which does not promise to fulfill a socially constituted desire, but there is also none which does not promise something qualitatively different in this fulfillment. Abstract utopian thinking which deludes itself about this sabotages happiness and plays into the hands of that which it seeks to negate. For, although it strives to purge happiness of the social stigma, it is forced to renounce every concrete claim to happiness and to reduce human beings to a mere function of their own work.[2]

From our standpoint there are two things worth noting about this analysis: first, that pleasure is a subjective historical experience, conditioned by social fact. Second, contrary to what we would call the sociologies of assent, or consent, the Adornian approach refuses to restrict the idea of happiness to that of adaptation; it refuses to reduce the definition of happiness to a technical fact—as does the pragmatist Veblen in recommending that mankind adapt to this development of technological productive forces. Adorno refuses to make of happiness the basis for individuals' rallying to the world as it is, for affirming its constraints and the dynamics of its developments. "The concept of adaptation," he writes, "is the *deus ex machina* with which Veblen tries to bridge the gap between what is and what should be." He sees a contradiction between Veblen's attacks on the existing order and his concept of individual adaptation, which weighs overwhelmingly in favor of the existing reality. "Today, adjusting to what is possible no longer means adjustment; it means making the possible real." With this sentence, Adorno ends his essay. In reaction to the rationalization of social constraints that makes Veblen resemble Darwin in calling for men to "identify themselves with the process of life," and in reaction to the notion of adaptation by which simple existence becomes the yardstick for measuring truth, Adorno returns to the essential Kantian question: How is anything new possible? This is an eminently contemporary question, at a time when an antiphilosophical sociology, while analyzing cultural and ideological forms of human subjection, demystifies the illusions of liberation.

Benjamin's death ended his epistolary exchange with Adorno about the revolutionary potential of cinema. They had agreed on the danger presented by cinema's jump from silent to talkies, Benjamin sharing with Adorno his fears that the progressive potential of cinema might be destroyed with the advent of sound. These thoughts show that it would be erroneous to overestimate Benjamin's anticipatory side and his progressive vision relative to Adorno's entrenched position on the evolution of the techniques of cultural production. We must not try to make the Frankfurt School say more than it was able as it groped its way forward.

In the lead article of an issue of the British journal *Formations* on the subject of pleasure, American literary historian and critic Fredric Jameson very rightly points out that the positions taken by the Frankfurt School were advanced at a time when, on both sides of the Atlantic, the reigning concept of culture was that of European "high culture."[3] After reminding us of the historical context of the school's theses, Jameson locates today's new sense of pleasure, its images and functions, within the "peremptory reality" of the international rise of commodification, which sanctions the displacement of cultural hegemony as much on a geographical as a conceptual level. The cultural pride of a central Europe conscious of its values and strengthened by its dialectical imagination is displaced by a diminished Europe in a world scene dominated by the massive expansion of the North American image industry bringing together all the signs of pleasure, from industrious New York to the Californian counterculture.

On Spontaneity

But we should not take the Frankfurt School's heritage too lightly. The paradigms it constructed continue to inspire many analyses of the public's relationship to cultural commodities: for instance, the studies by Dieter Prokopp in the seventies based on the concepts of fascination and spontaneity. By opening up new territory to the Frankfurt School's postulates, these concepts prove particularly useful for those trying to correlate pleasure and media culture.

Prokopp, inspired in particular by the analyses of Herbert Marcuse (another illustrious representative of the Frankfurt School), uses a diachronic analysis of the output of the American film industry to record the further narrowing of what Marcuse, following Roland Barthes, called "closed discourse." His analysis is based on two categories, integrated spontaneity and productive spontaneity, which he uses to characterize two modes of interaction between the public and the products of mass culture. The concept of integrated spontaneity seeks to account for the internalization of the constraints of the system of domination; productive spontaneity describes the desire to resist that domination. Prokopp, adopting Benjamin's innovative stance, sees the field of industrialized cultural production as a contradictory one, where different logics, needs, and aims coexist and confront each other. His analysis focuses on the dominant trends of production by large media conglomerates and studies the products of mass culture, as determined by monopoly conditions in production and distribution; that is, the products evaluated as those best adapted to the demands of a mass market. "Even if the monopolists who reign over the mass media market only respond to needs that are integrated and integratable *a priori*," he writes, "there are nonetheless moments of spontaneity, needs or desires that are only half conscious, nonexplicit. It is not an innocent mirror game. The products of mass culture constitute a battlefield where the constraints of the dominant system collide with desires seeking to express themselves."[4]

The concept of the integration of needs, desires, and spontaneity lies at the basis of Prokopp's analysis of the evolution of the ways in which the public interacts with mass culture. At the dawn of the industrialization of culture, burlesque films stimulated active spontaneity in the spectator: they offered the broad public a vision of reality in which solutions could be found in the realm of fantasy, allowing the individual to live out his revenge. Set against this analysis of the burlesque is an interpretation of the disaster movies that were particularly successful in the seventies. There, spontaneity is integrated under new conditions, and the individual becomes no more than a powerless participant.

To counter a conception of pleasure defined without reference to the historical time and place where its images and functions took shape, Jeremy Bentham's catalogue of pleasures may also provide a provocative reminder. Bentham is well known for his Panopticon (celebrated by Foucault) but less well known for the catalogue that he drew up at the end of the eighteenth century.

Bentham's project constitutes the first step toward introducing individualized pleasure into the field of social knowledge and regulation. Bentham's idea was to conceive a consensual network of regulation by establishing a thoroughly transparent link among individuals, pleasure, community, calculation, and legislation. The most striking and modern element of this imaginary construction is above all its individualization of pleasure (which refers us, as British author Colin Mercer has observed, to the famous Panopticon).[5]

Only in the new era of information was it possible to see this idea take shape in the future consensual networks that would preserve the principle of individualization. As one advertising executive has written:

From mass advertising inherited from soap merchants and

postwar consumer utopia we moved on to a more qualitative, adapted, personalized form of communication. To each the key to his own dreams. . . . With greater and greater sophistication, the media reaching a broad public will be accompanied by "targeted" media with a high qualitative imagination value added. In terms of media planning, this represents the victory of useful contact over multiple contact. Advertising, an echo of society's imaginary dimension, in this way will contribute powerfully to accelerating the passage from mass society to a segmented, multipolar society; from mass culture toward diversified culture; from messages addressed to the lowest common denominator to the personalized message. Advertising will guarantee a feedback that will be all the greater the more that the products of the future will themselves shape their consumers' motivation.[6]

Without adopting the theory of manipulation that Enzensberger discusses, and without inferring from the intentions of the sender the meaning registered by the consumer, we will remind readers, in all ingenuousness, that the notions of pleasure and desire are central to the strategies of those who are still thinking today in terms of conquering mass audiences and industrializing program content, and who tomorrow will be thinking more in terms of individualized pleasure.

The Cult of Didacticism

The ambiguity involved in the return to pleasure runs, in one way or another, through the numerous currents of research seeking a reconciliation with desire, emotional response, and the subjective dimension — all those shadowy zones though which critical theories of culture have passed. The outcomes of these theories cannot be foreseen and the definition of their epistemological status is also in debate. But one thing is already clear: through its discovery of ordinary pleasure, critical theory can at last resume its exploration of the true nature of the social environment of media culture.

There is something very odd about the mystification of pleasure. How could this essential aspect of reality have been so massively ignored?

Notwithstanding the insights brought to us by some nonconformist spirits, one cannot stress enough the difficulties critical theory has had in freeing itself from a banalized opposition between infrastructure and superstructure, and its decisive variant, the matrix of the question of pleasure, the mind-body dichotomy. Nor can one stress enough the heritage of the definitive split between the tradition of militant culture and the idea of pleasure. As a German Marxist philosopher points out, "Marxism has traditionally a split relationship to pleasure. 'Theoretically' it approves of the worldly life but in practice and in 'practical ideology' pleasure is suspect. Pleasure appears to be counter to effort, to the sacrifice we are called upon to make, to renunciation."[7]

In its obsession with the eve of the revolution, its dreams of a democratic society of tomorrow, and in its historicist optimism that claimed the victory of socialism to be inescapable, the left tended to scorn the persistent effort by which democracy is brought down to the level of everyday life and the incessant negotiation for the balance of power, considering these endeavors too modest and not flamboyant enough. Since we were too convinced that we were living in some sort of suspended dimension, or between parentheses, within the narrow confines of a so-called formal democracy, we could not but reject the questions posed by an idea of democracy in the here and now and no longer postponed until tomorrow. The corollary of this idea of the eve of the revolution was the ethic of effort, the sacrifice of the present and the conviction that no victories were possible until the Great Victory.

The obsession with the eve of the revolution is in itself only conceivable in a culture profoundly marked by Judeo-Christian tradition. This religious aspect of Marxism in fact concurs with the idea of individual sacrifice that motivates the church, in which the sacrifices we make in this "valley of tears" are justified by the hope of Paradise.

The idea of culture as it has been experienced and understood by most people in the West (on the left as well as on the right) is divorced from the idea of ordinary pleasure. For those who cannot reach culture so defined, be they individuals, social groups, or entire nations, it is a source of tension. As Venezuelan philosopher L. Silva writes:

> In underdeveloped countries, the ordinary citizen believes that "culture" is and should continue to be a sublime product, a spiritual blessing, a mental delight, created by privileged beings. He feels that to approach "culture" he must make a big effort, "reach the level," and ultimately stop being what he is in ordinary life. Culture seems to him to be a foreign body, the ultimate *alienum*.[8]

In their own time, and each in its own way, the surrealist and situationist movements challenged this dogmatic conception. Each in its own way, because in answer to the still male-elitist aura of the former, the latter replied, on the very terrain of ordinary pleasure, with its deconstructive explosion of the society of the spectacle — an effort which to this day remains one of the few in-depth interrogations about the raison d'être of the media.

The numerous problems faced by the left when it has been obliged to face the question of the media in the prerevolutionary process, outside the agit-prop schema, have provided equally numerous opportunities to measure the endemic bankruptcy of a way of thinking marked by the cult of didacticism, and which has always tended to consider the media as no more than tools to pursue its pedagogical vocation.[9]

Reflecting in the thirties about the conditions under which a national popular culture could emerge, Gramsci called attention to the pitfalls of this excessively rationalistic conception. He saw in it the possible source of a bureaucratic degeneration in relations between the party, intellectuals, and the people. To counter this threat he emphasized the importance of an organic relationship between popular feeling and intellectual knowledge, between one group's practice and the other's theory, between the party as the collective intellectual and the sensitivity of the people.[10]

Today, as the rationality of the media becomes more and more engulfing, these repressed ideas are making a comeback. They are doing so at a time when the relationship between intellectuals and other social groups — the "people" — is in deep crisis. The time is long gone when social responsibility could motivate generations of intellectuals — coinciding, for many, with the unhappy consciousness that they were only intellectuals within a movement carried forward by an idea and an image of the working class (an unhappy consciousness not unrelated to Judeo-Christian guilt feelings). And paradoxically it is precisely now that a debate about the relationship between intellectuals and the people is particularly urgent; *a fortiori* if one suspects that this new fusion with the people in delighting in media entertainment may be hiding more confusion than meets the eye.

Subjective Time

It is difficult to dissociate the emergence of the theme of ordinary pleasure from the demands and analyses put forward by the women's movement in the sixties. By criticizing the moral order of an orthodox left claiming to be progressive, the movement reappropriated for critical thought the dimension of the body, everyday life, and subjective experience. Although the influence of the women's movement in this sphere is widely recognized in the Anglo-Saxon countries,[11] this is certainly not the case in France, where theories of social reproduction have barely begun to analyze the epistemological breakthroughs induced by the emergence of this new sensibility.[12]

This sensibility brings us back to some themes we have already touched on when we spoke, in chapter 5, about fluid thought. What this way of thinking instills in the heart of the new episteme is a different conception of time. Time is no longer linear, but circular. It is a form of time that is strangely compatible with "feminine temporality." In "The Myth of Modernity" (1971), we wrote:

> This antagonism between the concepts woman/change essentially goes back to the fact that, in all cultures, myths associate the image of the woman with the life-giving elements: earth and water, elements of fertility and permanence. The image of woman is linked to the idea of continuity, perpetuation, timelessness. Against the transient nature of upheavals, crises, and chaos, corresponding to the concept of change, is played and contrasted the cyclic timing of woman, which traces concentric lines leading forever back to the starting point, unifying past, present, and future. This is a time that flows, in which the eternal roles are performed: marriage, home, motherhood. The pattern of woman's life is portrayed as the antithetical justification of, and compensation for, the pattern of a man's life, whose action is inscribed in the dialectic of a reality of struggle and domination of the world.[13]

The specific pace that feminine subjectivity imparts to time can be defined as both repetition and eternity at the same time: the return of the Same, the eternal return, and the cycle binding feminine subjectivity to cosmic time, which is an occasion for delight in oneness with the rhythm of nature; also, the matrix dimension, the myth of permanence and duration.

This idea of subjective time can help clarify the problem of ordinary pleasure. The notion of specific temporality can serve as a leading theme in explaining the enjoyment caused, for example, by the televion sagas studied by Barbero and Maffesoli, referred to above. What is difficult to understand is the fascination these stories continue to evoke in the women who watch them and who are, moreover, perfectly capable of seeing through them and criticizing their structural features. Indeed, we can append to this theory of subjective time the hypothesis that both "below" and "beyond" the content of these stories, with their chains of meaning drawn out over long periods of time in regular daily episodes, we encounter the experience of repetition and eternity; that these voluminous sagas, delivered in daily fragments and repeated every day, satisfy, through their stereotypical character and their rhythm, the need for feminine subjective time, which corresponds to psychic structures not incorporated in prospective time, the time of change. By cultivating enjoyment of this non-prospective time they delay women's access to the time of history-in-the-making, to the time of active undertakings.

This hypothesis would need to be tested in the light of recent research in the area of subjectivity and the unconscious structures of personality.

One thing is certain, however: in examining how media texts operate, we have been too satisfied with a focus on the units of discourse of images and words. But the power of the culture industries also lies outside the stories they tell; the latter, it might be said, remain the epiphenomena of what is communicated. The culture industries also occupy the psychic structures of the popular audience, which are as much elements of nature as they are of culture. Their ideological function also consists of administering this perpetual refueling of the deep structures of a collective unconscious.

The notion of time that women as a subordinate group possess can be read in two ways. On the one hand, there is a reading that brings out what we would venture to call its alienated aspect; on the other, a reading that draws out its alternative—and, we would also venture to say, positive—side, that of resistance to the hegemonic conception of time as productivist time.

When, in *Jeanne Dielman*, filmmaker Chantal Ackerman used real time to film the trivial daily movements of a woman, she did two things that amounted to one: she tried to give a language and an expressive form to her subjective woman's experience, left without a voice by earlier culture; and in so doing, she produced a shock—a creative shock—which made possible, by contrast, an understanding of the usual norm of time in entertainment products.

Beyond the equal status that they have sometimes achieved in the area of production, women are seeking to assert their irreducible difference in the realm of subjective experience and symbolic realization. This diffuse quest leads them to explore their archaic memory, which is bound up with the time-space of reproduction and where even today part of their sensitivity is still shaped and part of their difference is defined. The difference is irreducible because it is linked to their psychological, biological, and sexual difference, which has traditionally been used to alienate and subjugate them. It is a difference that today is expressed as an alternative in meaning and in symbol.

It is fascinating to note that this quest seems to find parallels in the exploration of the time of dominated peoples and the memory of marginal continents, as practiced, for example, in Latin American literature. This literature allows us to envision something similar to the feminine internalization of a double dimension of time: repetition and eternity. Novels like Gabriel García Márquez's *One Hundred Years of Solitude* or José Donoso's *The Obscene Bird of Night* are immense narratives made up of cyclical advances and monumental time which manage to satisfy magnificently the latent demand of the unconscious and to offer it democratic and liberating outlets.

One could speculate that the symbolic demands expressed by these temporalities of difference might be given increasing value to the extent that linear models of growth and development are called into question and the benefits of a society ruled by the principle of quantitative production are reduced to their true value. But by making people believe that the culture industries are already reconciled to popular demands (and that in fact—as the *mea culpa* of numerous intellectuals would have us understand—they always have been), certain sociological approaches tend on the contrary to seal off this perspective. At the very least, they simplify the problem of popular demand by retaining only its consensual side, the side that fits into the order of things, and a way of imagining pleasure that represses its subversive potential.

Although today we can see greater open-mindedness compared with earlier conceptions of alienation and earlier ideological injunctions, there is nonetheless an insidious risk of prematurely closing the debate and seeing what could be the beginnings of a new epistemological approach be led astray into a new ideology of assent. Though it attests to a change of mood and sensitivity, the notion of pleasure now current indeed runs the risk of realizing only half its potential, if we are satisfied to see it only as the sign of a reconciliation with the emotions and experiences of everyday life, or as a break with the elitism, contempt, and indifference that up until recently characterized the attitude of intellectuals. If we hold to the notion of pleasure as an essential new category in the field of criticism, we must explode the almost ecumenical aura that it is acquiring, and restore its conflictual dimension.

11

The Heavy and the Light

The Theoretical Order of Deregulation

The rising wave that at present is carrying forward certain conceptions of ordinary pleasure is far from being an innocent, unpolitical development. For beyond the theme of pleasure itself, what should be observed is its function in the mode of legitimation of a system of communication.

The context in which this great wave is rising is that of deregulation. If one keeps one's nose glued to the display window of new technological artifacts, one cannot perceive deregulation with the proper perspective. It is a conflict between the public sector and the private sector — a conflict which, if resolved competently, could give rise to a better adaptation to technological evolution. Beyond the disputes and debates over the future of public service, and beyond its possible disappearance as the structuring framework of television and telecommunications, it indeed prefigures a new conception of the social. This is why deregulation operates also on the theoretical plane and in the field of production of knowledge about the media, contributing to the destabilization of paradigms that have legitimated the institutions and practices embodied in the philosophy of public service and public interest. These paradigms have accompanied, for better or for worse, a certain relationship between creators and the state, between creators and industrial production, between creators and the market, between intellectuals and media production, and above all, between the sender and the receiver, the media institution and the citizen-consumer.

In countries that were only recently ferociously defending their heritages against the order of marketing, mentalities have evolved at a far more rapid pace than the advertising industry ever hoped for. And since a new legitimacy never arrives alone, others followed it.

With new legitimacy granted to the world of advertising, the link between culture and business, rejected by the Eco's apocalyptics, gained its place in the sun. In certain areas of research, the question is no longer to distinguish what is true from what is false in the Adornian paradigm: certain young intellectuals are joyously casting away the doubts that, in their view, inhibited their predecessors.

At a conference in London in 1984 that brought together researchers of all nationalities working on the subject of international television studies, one could note that this new attention accorded to the notion of pleasure stimulated much interest. Some of the papers read were particularly representative of the new trend and the new sensibility (which claims to be attached to a critical tradition).

Ien Ang, a young researcher from Holland, attracted much attention at this conference by making the notion of pleasure—the pleasure stimulated by commercial television—the starting point for a confrontation between the heritage of public-service television and that of market television.[1] This confrontation turned into a plea against public service and a celebration of commercial television, seen as much more liberating because it was attentive to popular expectations in entertainment.

This remarkable shift, made possible by the contemporary sensitivity toward ordinary pleasure, may be associated for some with Walter Benjamin's idea of enjoyment in consumption. The new sensibility is far removed from Benjamin's idea, however, because the current acquiescence to the "media-that-be" is incompatible with the philosophy of the Frankfurt School (all its members taken together). It will no doubt be remembered that in what Benjamin called his progressive conception of history, he saw in the new, highly technified culture a new field of cultural struggle, in tension with a social utopia that transcended bourgeois culture.

Pleasure, desire, and the spirit of play are mentioned as much in ordinary conversation about the daily experience of the media as they are in formal discourse. Through them, theoretical references oppose each other, each representing a different way of conceiving the appropriation of the new technological environment. This could be seen recently in France during the discussion on the social uses of new technologies (videotext, teletext, cable, etc.) and on the possible accompanying roles of social science research in managing the new networks of communication democratically. Particularly memorable was the opening speech at a debate held in 1980 by a specialist in advertising research, on the new perspectives opened to marketing by the new media. In the course of this debate, he vigorously criticized those sociologists present who, in the name of an improved conception of public service, saw social experimentation as one of the most democratic ways of incorporating citizens into technological choices because—so the argument ran—experimentation made it possible to understand their demands and thus to escape from the determinism of the manufacturers' logic of supply. "When I look at what is now happening outside France," declared this specialist,

> what particularly strikes me in Silicon Valley, California, is that what we see is not so much experimentation, but rather a flowering process. In all the talks I have heard [here], one major figure is absent: desire. What is currently happening with these technologies is a formidable upheaval in desire, a great vacuum cleaner sucking up desire. What is happening in California is that people are doing what they want to. When I say "people," I mean the word in its largest sense: it may be advertising agents, young entrepreneurs, consumer associations, etc. The idea is much more to create the conditions in which people want to play with [the new products]. . . . New Japanese or American products will be coming to us [in France] because they will have succeeded in creating the conditions in which people can let their desire run free and invent new products and uses.[2]

Against the cumbersome heritage of a public service whose thought about social relations is assimilated to the archaic forms of technocratic control, we can observe the legitimation of the rise of new technologies as a "natural" phenomenon because it corresponds to the (also natural) dynamic of desires: in the words of the person quoted above, "the desire to buy, the desire to communicate, the desire to use new means."[3] Let us recall how the authors of *Anti-Oedipus* reply to this desire, confined to what they call "lack" (*manque*) and reduced to the dimension of the contract:

> Lack is created, planned, and organized in and through social production. . . . The deliberate creation of lack as a function of market economy is the art of a dominant class; making all of desire teeter and fall victim to the great fear of not having one's needs satisfied; and making the object dependent upon a real production that is supposedly exterior to desire (the demands of rationality), while at the same time the production of desire is categorized as fantasy and nothing but fantasy.[4]

Civil Society versus the State?

In order to believe in the idea of desire-pleasure-play as a natural expression of individual spontaneity and free choice, it is clearly also necessary to subscribe to the idea that any attempt to take critical distance from the technological dynamics is an attempt at restoring order, and therefore an ideology. However, one certainty remains, and it is one established by the philosophers and sociologists of "the negative": what does not refer to a moment, a particular historical and philosophical place, does in any case refer to the naturalness of a system that in the final analysis governs its meaning; a system that owes to its having having dubbed itself natural the faculty to make one forget that it is also a field of balance of forces, with its mechanisms of social regulation; a system in which certain groups can pursue their interests at the expense of others. It structures a society in which, supposedly, contradictory interests harmonize with each other and have always done so spontaneously. This explanation by desire, which is considered to spontaneously shape the harmonious definition of the uses of the new technological instruments, is profoundly consistent with this idea of a natural order, in which the different forms of freedom are supposedly immanent in society. In order to achieve the best result for all, it suffices to allow private initiatives to sprout and multiply. However, the actual history of the constitution of the uses of technologies and systems of communication shows that, like history in general, conflicts among groups and interests are what determine its evolution.

If one does not recognize where certain discourses about pleasure come from, one is in danger of allowing a new populist discourse to gain currency insidiously—a discourse that, in spite of its comfortable and conformist tones, legitimates the emergence of the new "organic intellectual" of privatization, an intellectual who is functional with respect to the rules of the marketplace.

The danger consists of moving from one simplistic conception to another: from the simplistic idea of being closed into polar opposites such as didacticism and pleasure, to the simplistic idea of a new Manicheanism, in which the choices are reduced to two: being dominated by the laws of the market or dwelling on an ideal type of what public service never was. Discussions colonized either by a one-sided point of view of the market or by an outdated idea of public service mask the complexity of the relationship between public service and the market. The sentiment of being fed up with one corresponds to the outlook of total liberation thanks to the other.

The rising tide of the antistate current provides a growing legitimacy to such a vision of things. It is fueled by a simplistic and asociological idea of an abstract state, divorced from society and contrasted with the idea of a market articulated on the bustling activity of civil society, the flowering of the spontaneity of particular subjects. This idea of state abstracted from society is also reflected in the classifications of television systems according to the categories "state television" and "civil-society television," depending on whether they belong to public service or the market.[5] As if the state were not itself just as much part of society as the market!

The perverse effect of such an argumentation can already be seen. The opposition between state and society is at the root of populist modes of legitimation that are fond of appealing to the emotions of the people. A malevolent state, whose social origins have somehow evaporated, is opposed to a concrete people, defined as a community of free, useful, and responsible individuals who possess initiative. As Pierre-André Taguieff has noted in his analysis of the rise of neoliberal ideologies in France, the idea of struggle between the state and the people is a necessary ingredient of neopopulist ideologies: "The Manichean model can be found, in similar form, in its successive ideological versions, which finally become syncretic: the individual versus the state, the people versus the fat cats, civil society versus its Other, the enterprising capitalist versus the stagnant bureaucracy."[6]

The Central Planet: Entertainment

What is tending to disappear today is not only the idea that the media in every society assume functions other than that of entertainment, but also that the role of entertainment is not limited to providing distraction.

Yet the fact that the media assume, in every society, functions other than that of distraction is something that American functionalist sociology had already taught us well. Although this variety of sociology was quite prompt in allying itself with the advertising and public-relations industries, it recognized four major fields of activity in which the means of communication engaged: surveillance, correlation, cultural transmission, and entertainment. As for the different critical schools, they emphasized the historical character of the communication system as it was shaped by the rise of industrial capitalism and the liberal-democratic state. As we have written elsewhere,

> The system of communication and mass culture as the expression
> of a relation between sender and receiver, between producer and
> consumer and as the cement of consensus is the extension of a
> concrete political system, that of liberal democracy. It
> corresponded to the bourgeoisie's need to open itself to other
> classes, and it continues to be tied to the vicissitudes of the
> project of social co-optation.[7]

To borrow the terms of Jürgen Habermas, a disciple of the Frankfurt School, the means of mass communication are the latest element in the constitution of the bourgeois "public sphere" which began in the eighteenth century and which made possible rational discussion of the normative rules of social action—rules whose legitimacy is thus no longer based on their sacred character but on a consensus achieved by reasoning subjects.[8]

The divergent premises and epistemologies of these two major theoretical currents influencing thought on the media have not succeeded in challenging the idea, which both consider a certainty, that systems of communication are above all systems of consensus, whether the latter be defined as socialization, cultural consensus, political consensus, or social consensus. But the resemblance stops there. For the first current, the problem is to examine the laws of conservation of the social system; for the second, it is to criticize the production and reproduction of the means of social control.

The polarization on the question of entertainment today corresponds to the economic stake of capital in the cultural field. It is stimulated by the growing internationalization of new cultural commodities. With the breakup of national systems of communication and the explosion in demand thereby generated for programs, the internationalization of these commodities is entering a new phase. As has already been shown in the countries where television undergoes competition on its national territory from foreign broadcasts (Quebec and Belgium are exemplary cases here), it is the entertainment programs that cause national systems to internationalize. News and cultural and educational programming constitute pockets of resistance.

The informational function in society is a divisive factor because it is pregnant with the reality of conflicts that mark the daily experience of social groups. The idea of entertainment contains, on the other hand, a potential for consensus, interclass communion, universality, and popularity—things to which education cannot aspire, unless, of course, it undergoes a radical change in nature. School failure will always haunt education, since it is the sanction of a social system and as such stubbornly reminds people of social inequality.

The spectacular rise of entertainment has made it the "central planet" of communication systems, to such a degree that the very idea of communication itself tends, in collective perception, to fuse with it. The vitality of entertainment is, moreover, guaranteed by the fact that it has become a mandatory criterion for all forms of transmission of knowledge outside the school, as technologies increasingly penetrate the interstices of daily life. The great modern crusades against school failure have attempted to remedy the school crisis with an intravenous solution of pleasurable pedagogy—recently with television and today with electronic games and microcomputers (as is witnessed by the evolution of American systems of computer-assisted teaching toward game or entertainment form).[9]

In a context in which labor as a social value is severely challenged and the finality of effort tends to lose track of its object, the dullness of pedagogy in the schools is confronted with the seductiveness of leisure as it has been naturalized by media culture. This observation has become a commonplace. The technological leap of recent years has provided an opportunity to measure the extent to which these two modes of socialization of children are allergic to one another. The pedagogical bias in the training of the child as citizen serves as a repellent to the seductive appeal to the child as future consumer. This devaluation of a mode of socialization has not occurred alone: it mirrors other delegitimations. The didacticism of public service media programming has also suffered the effects of the same conflict.

The Temptation of Disinvolvement

For years, the outlook of analyses, denunciations, and critiques of mass culture (otherwise known as consumer culture or the society of the spectacle) was characterized by the perception of a connection between mass communication and the subjection of society. By denouncing the myth-building enterprise in which media culture indulged, Roland Barthes forged, at the end of the fifties, the paradigm of modernity as the new mode of social domination: the "dilution" of the social conflict. In *Mythologies*, he brilliantly demonstrated how myth empties social phenomena of their reality and thus acquits the system by purifying it. It deprives phenomena of their historical meaning and integrates them into "the nature of things." Myth domesticates reality and annexes it, to the benefit of a pseudo reality—that imposed by the system, which could only be considered real if the base on which dominant ideology was built were validated; that is, if one admitted as the parameter of objectivity and universality the particular point of view of a class of proprietors of "legitimate culture."

Barthes wrote,

> What the world supplies to myth is an historical reality, defined, even if this goes back quite a while, by the way in which men have produced or used it; and what myth gives in return is a *natural* image of this reality. And just as bourgeois ideology is defined by the abandonment of the name "bourgeois," myth is constituted by the loss of the historical quality of things: in it, things lose the memory that they once were made.[10]

This approach, while identifying myth, also revealed how mass culture accomplished its labor upon social data—how it seized hold of the social movement and processed it in its own manner. In the same perspective of demystification, the notions of co-optation and dilution of the forms of social contestation were shaped; they showed how the new ideal of advertising took shape in the movement of exchange and the incessant appropriation by the semantic field of the multiple processes of liberation that act on society. At that time, technological modernity made the ideal of the modern woman—symbol of a society of growth and consumption— the primary objective of its mercantile strategies. This version of modernity shielded itself behind the smile of femininity and fueled itself with the impulses of the women's liberation movement.[11]

Today, as the strategy of reindustrialization claims to be identified with modernity, its intellectuals are already in the era of postmodernity.[12] The era of the "look," the era of appearances, is beginning. We are witnessing the loss of the social bond. The necessity, recognized by Barthes, of identifying the social bond that unifies mass culture and publicity strategies with social movements, is no longer perceived. Form is sovereign. In the enjoyment of form and its explosions, content is no longer of any importance.

For decades, a mechanical sequence of reasoning characterized apprehension of media culture: the media was the vector of ideology, therefore it produced an effect on the experience of individuals and groups. Today, this idea is nothing more than the trace of a way of thinking that is rejected—just as the primacy of the question over the answer, the conclusion over the premise, have been rejected. The idea that everything manifests itself at once, in the instant, has upset the orders and hierarchies that presided over the determination of what was important and what was not, the essential and the nonessential, the entry and the exit, the first instance and the last instance, the preamble and the dénouement. Back to obscurity for the Barthesian science of demystification: after having spent years submitting all sorts of discourses (political, religious, literary, advertising, etc.) to an ideological interpretation, this approach, which had worn a scientific label and claimed to be above ideologies, is seeing its own argumentation turned against it: the opposition between science and ideology had been taken for the antagonism between truth and error. This discourse had been thought objective, immune to ideology—the same ideology that, on the other hand, discredited all the other discourses. But this was not the case. The theories and practices of demystification, which stripped naked the discourse of order, are now accused of having set up new decors on the old stage of rationalism.

Today, the emperor has no clothes. The questioning of the break between science and ideology reveals the foundation on which ideological interpretation was based: the idea that there are owners and proprietors of knowledge. A handful of people have the keys to the code, while the masses are condemned either to submit to the painful process of intellectual mediation and receive the magic words passed down to them, or to remain in a predestined narcosis.

The only problem here is that the representatives of what is called postmodernism, with very little concern for procedure, throw out the baby with the bathwater: according to them, the social and the political are nothing but illusions, or semblances (*semblants*) as Baudrillard would call them. The dominant empiricity is helpful in reconstructing a paradigm of submission to the prevailing order, the order of compromise, which tends to turn into an "unequivocal rejection of any collective projections into projects of broad scope."[13] From an ideology of demystification and unmasking of latent meanings, we move to ideologies of transparence.

And in this passage, the reflection undertaken since the Frankfurt School disappears; that is, the link existing between mass culture and a social bond marked by profound segregation, which caused Adorno and Horkheimer to say that they did not detest mass culture because it is democratic, but precisely because it is not.[14]

These new ideologies have their own new mediators. In the postmodern context, it is certainly no longer traditional intellectuals who are called upon to occupy the central position. The loss of the social bond, which affects this type of intellectual, also signifies the loss of the link between theory and practice, and consequently the loss of their field of competence and intervention in society. The new professional sectors that treat knowledge about the different social categories are now becoming the conceivers and administrators of the social bond, in the very name of its disappearance and the "evaporation" of politics.

For those who want to survive in this new force field, it is considered wise to observe the rules of media staging, even if this entails ignoring any troubling questions about the stakes of intellectual labor. One must occupy the terrain, taking care to define the best image that can be offered to the public, just as one must define the type of writing that produces the best performance. As novelist Annie Ernaux has observed,

> A certain language has appeared in literary circles: one now speaks of "career" instead of one's works, and of the "public" instead of readers. . . . There is a gradual and nearly generalized renunciation of questions that literature has always, more or less, raised about its role, its finality, its relationship to the real and to society, even if it be to deny [such a relationship]. . . . Could it be that through a strange sense of its limits, latent underneath the ambient derision, literature is renouncing all its powers other than those of pleasure and distraction?[15]

The philosophies of negativity, of which the Frankfurt School was a representative, established the role of the dialectic in the constitution of personal and social identity. They saw these identities as an acclimation of individuality to change, to otherness, and to development marked by conflict. Beyond the procedure of construction, enrichment, and socialization of individuality, dialectical thought promoted the ideas of development, contradiction, and history oriented toward an end to be achieved. Brecht expressed this ideal when he spoke of thought as intervention: "The dialectic as a manner of dividing up, ordering, and envisioning the world which, by revealing its revolutionary contradictions, makes intervention possible."[16] Today, the epistemological field of the philosophies of negativity has grown hazy, and with it, the distinction between the positive and the negative, power and counterpower.

Our earlier developments on culture as experience of anxiety, and on cognitive ascetic experience as opposed to the culture of ordinary pleasure, may be understood in the context of this crisis of dialectical thought. One may imagine the resonance of this crisis when one knows how important negative consciousness was in the formation of most of the European intellectual class; to quote Michel Foucault's remark concerning France: "Intellectual and left-wing intellectual: that's almost the same thing."[17]

PART 4

The Decline of Macrosubjects?

Introduction to Part 4

In the excellent January 1985 issue of the journal *Critique*, devoted to the new currents in Italian philosophy, one of the contributors clearly identified the conceptual categories most directly affected by the crisis of critical thought, or the crisis of the link between the critical function assumed by intellectuals and society in the modern history of Western thought and culture. R. Bodel wrote:

> At its origin, the dialectic was the expression of a phase of individual and collective identity linked to the emergence of macrosubjects such as the state or class. In certain countries and in certain social layers, this acquisition has already been achieved and metabolized: in these cases the problems have changed and taken another form. Very often, interest in these collective partners in dialogue, these "ethical authorities" or substances of the individual have completely faded. . . . In reaction to an excessively harsh loss of self within the collective group, cultures of subjectivity pushed to the extreme limits of narcissism have reappeared and flourished, along with ethics based on subjective preferences and the refusal of any form of "alienation" or cession of individual or community rights and the repudiation of the public sphere insofar as it goes beyond the radius of small groups.[1]

There is, in short, a crisis of identification of macrosubjects. Since the end of the sixties, the analysis of cultural practices, and among these the practices of communication, has carried with it the question of macro- and microsubjects, macro- and microstructures. At a time when, in an internationalized context, changes are occurring in the very structures of national and local systems of communication, the real stakes of this theoretical debate are becoming apparent.

12

The State as Macrosubject

A Very French Tradition

"Less state, more freedom." Only yesterday the decline of the state as macrosubject was a mere matter of intellectual speculation, but in the 1980s, thanks to the rise of neoliberal ideologies, it has become an everyday reference. One cannot help thinking that a moribund body has risen to life again.

Beyond deep divergences regarding the nature of the state or the means of changing it, a real consensus on the legitimacy of this macrosubject united the most diverse political and ideological families. It was, after all, in the name of the integrity of the state that the liberal right interpreted the free radio movement in 1981 as a criminal activity.

"Less state, more freedom." The narrowing of the space in which the evolution of the state can be discussed contrasts sharply with the knowledge accumulated over the past several decades in France. It also seems to be inversely proportional to the rise of passion invested in the debate.

Everything predisposed the French intellectual and political classes to focus on the question of the state. We may recall, for example, de Gaulle's remark before the Council of State: "There is no France except thanks to the state. France can maintain itself only through [the state]." It was by taking hold of the state that the French bourgeoisie established its hegemony in a society that was still agrarian. As Henri Lefebvre has noted, "In France, bourgeois hegemony preceded industrial expansion and capitalism, whereas in England, it flowed from these."[1]

It is doubtless this original stamp that explains why there was a rejection — sometimes latent, at other times explicit — of the doctrines and theories that gave primacy to the economic base over the superstructure.

And this is no doubt the underlying anthropological reason the French cultural milieu—"legitimate" French culture—finds it so difficult to recognize the necessity of analyzing the conditions of production of ideas, and why the problem of contents, discourses, and language occupies such a preponderant place. Finally, this is the reason it took so many years for the idea of a link between the economy and culture to gain acceptance.

The central character of the state as a reference has deeply influenced the behavior of the French left; the left has paid heavy dues to the fetishization of state power, for in state power it has too often seen the exclusive lever for the revolutionary transformation of capitalism. This fetishist tradition ill prepared the French left to react to the rise of ideologies of return to civil society, as opposed to the state, and the ideology of the market as the privileged expression of civil society.

These roots in a long tradition of state-centered culture fully explain the difference between the Althusserian theory of state ideological apparatuses and the Gramscian theory of hegemony. While the former remains prisoner of a mechanical vision of an intangible state structure affected only marginally by the contradictions of civil society, the latter is attentive to the incessant exchanges between the state and civil society, to the fluidity of expressions of differences in popular cultures, and to the movement of civil society. Whereas in Gramsci subaltern groups and classes are present as historical subjects in struggles for the construction of hegemony, for Althusser those who are subjected to the processes of social reproduction are deprived of a status in a "theater without subjects."

Conceptual Thought versus Experience

The narrowing of the field in which the evolution of the state is discussed presents a number of disadvantages. The first is that this narrowing gives rise to a perception of the state almost solely in terms of the scaffolding of its administrative and political apparatuses. The state is that, of course, but it is above all the keystone of a mode of thought. As Henri Lefebvre notes, following Hegel, the state is "the concept of concepts." It reigns over abstract thought and refers back to the opposition between the natural and the abstract. The crisis of the state is contemporaneous with the crisis of the concept and that of the abstract mode of thought within which the state exercised its rule.

When this secular abstract reference develops cracks, experience reoccupies the terrain and the approach it implies gathers more and more legitimacy, while the other faces considerable challenge.

In the old debate between naturalness and rationality (or custom versus law, habit versus code), which had earlier been decided in favor of the latter term, the former now triumphs as the mode of apprehending reality. This is a positive development in that it casts doubt on the philosophies of history (Hegel, Comte, Marx and Engels, Spencer, and so on) — bodies of thought that François Châtelet defined as "those systematic discourses with a totalizing vocation and which aim to present, under the sign of knowledge, the essence of the evolution of humanity (*res gestae*)."[2] In the field of politics, the philosophies of history, as expressions of the metaphysical will to unify thought around a primordial body of knowledge, had precisely the effect of legitimating centralizing powers with scientific pretensions and accrediting their ideology of progress.

The questioning of these philosophies today is without a doubt positive, for it allows us to discard the basic opposition between body and spirit at the center of Western thought and the Western logos, and to effect a recentering of the self with respect to the world. But this challenge is not without ambiguities, because it carries with it the risk of masking the emergence of the new macrosubjects which are now taking over from the action of the state, while continuing to uphold a model of development that remains within the framework of the same philosophy of progress.

This dazzling return to experience may indeed lead us to overlook the way in which the macrosubjects — considered by some as belonging to the prehistory of "class struggle" — are redefined in the national and international context.

It need hardly be said that in the relations between nations and peoples, this return to "lived experience" (*le vécu*) stands in contrast to the establishment of a new rationality, a conceptual thought (*conçu*) of a new type, which expresses itself in strategies. This is one of the characteristics of the passage from the national scale, that of the nation-state, to the world scale, that of the internationalization of economies. Henri Lefebvre wrote, in his treatise on the state:

> From the national to the worldwide scale, there is a leap, a
> political break, a rupture. The world scale no longer refers to
> historicity in the classical sense (causal chain, genesis, etc.). If one
> wishes to apply these classic terms — history, historicity — to the
> world scale, one must modify their meaning. Why? Because with
> the world scale, strategy dominates the determinisms and the
> accidents that have constituted historical time. The great
> strategies that confront each other take the entire planetary space
> into account and have at their disposal an enormous amount of
> information about practically every element of this space. And
> history? As Marx said, men made their history blindly, without
> knowing very well what they were doing. The effects differed
> from both the causes and the predictions, as illustrated by the

contemporary history of revolution, which is the last form of classical history. In the great strategies there appears a new rationality, full of dangers, but rational like a missile, like an atomic bomb, like a laser. This is a break with the optimism of classical reason. The relation changes from experience [*le vécu*] to conceptual thought [*le conçu*].[3]

At a time when the internationalization of information and communication systems is accompanied by the redeployment of national economies, this debate about experience and conceptual thought seems quite necessary, but it is far from having seriously begun. It would take its natural place in discussions about reindustralization policies, but also in those regarding the status of theory and the function of the intellectual in today's society and tomorrow's.

The Near versus the Distant

The return to lived experience has an impact as well on the way in which critical analyses perceive the role of the transnational corporations in their configuration of a model of development and growth. In many cases, the analyses of the strategies of these corporations seem more to reflect the paranoia of the observer, inspired by a conspiracy theory, than the reality of power. At the other end of the spectrum, the more the analysis progresses toward the microscale, the more it is reassuring, because it explores territories with which we have ties of proximity: we "know our way around," and an analysis of this sort produces for us a sense of security. Indeed, microanalysis allows each person to consider the determinations that affect his or her daily existence, his or her immediate social surroundings (family, neighborhood, office, and so forth) — determinations over which each of us maintains a certain control, whereas the determinations of macrostructures remain, for most people, superabstractions over which they have no control and which reduce them to impotence.

Taking up again the framework evoked by the Italian philosopher we quoted in the introduction to this section, one might ask if only dialectics is thrown overboard when this unambiguous celebration of the return to microsubjects occurs. For it may well be that the very existence of this transnational power and its effects in the large postindustrial societies are also cast into doubt.

An epistemological break was no doubt consummated in the field of theory when economic history was no longer apprehended as the sole determinant. However, to consolidate the gain thereby achieved, it is still necessary to include economics among the multiple determinants, of which it is not the least.

One thing is certain: doubt has taken its comfortable place in collective modes of perception. We are no longer in an era when multinational corporations are stigmatized as being the bearers of all evil. The time is already distant when ITT was spoken of in denunciatory tones for its role in the plot against Salvador Allende in Chile. Distant as well are the vituperations against the cartel of the "Seven Sisters" when oil prices were deregulated. The condemnation of the transnational giants has been succeeded by the recognition of their necessity. The era of accusatory testimony against the imperialism of the transnationals has given way to an era of banalization of the transnational phenomenon, which tends to become further diluted under the appellation of "globalization of the economy." In countries such as France, the change in perspective was just as rapid as it was radical.

Limiting ourselves to semantics, the changes we refer to have been traced in a study analyzing the discourse of the French press regarding the transnationals in the past ten years.[4] In 1976, "corruption," "imperialism," "abuses," "colonialism," and "profits" were the words most frequently used by journalists to describe the action of transnational corporations. By 1979, references to the illicit practices of these companies had practically disappeared; the transnationals were viewed from an economic angle, as witnessed by the frequent use of terms such as "market," "industry," "products," and "prices." In 1982, to speak of transnationals was to recognize their dynamism and their prodigious ability to adapt to circumstances imposed by crisis; but most of all, transnational corporations meant jobs. The same study shows that the evolution of the image of these companies as observed in the press (and which was particularly clear for the periodicals with ties to the left) was reflected by a similar evolution in attitudes. There are no more passionate reactions. The transnationals were taken for granted as fixtures of the modern economic world. The pragmatic outlook prevails. The transnational is seen as the enterprise that has shown it can withstand the effects of economic crisis.

Numerous factors explain this evolution in ideas, which has occurred even as the power of these corporations has continuously grown, along with their impact on the overall restructuring of our societies. These factors include the emergence of transnationals from countries other than the United States; the fact that these corporations appear to be sure sources of employment in a climate of generalized recession (although in reality things are more complex: transnationals originating in one's own country are criticized for exporting jobs when they open branches abroad, but foreign investment and the opening of foreign transnationals in one's country are appreciated because they create jobs); the fact that these corporations are now part of a system of power in which the differences of interest between states and the private sector are much less marked than ten years ago; and finally, the fact that the relation between transnationals and society as a whole has evolved greatly—they have ceased to be exogenous agents and have blended into the national environment.

But if the idea of the macrosubject is in sharp decline, it must nonetheless be observed that this is not the case for all macrosubjects. Some of them continue to stay afloat after the wreck. The interpretation of contemporary world reality according to the East-West polarization has led to an implicit accreditation of the natural, metabolized character of the transnational enterprises as the vanguard of a model of growth that continues, in spite of all, to ensure the coziness of daily existence in the West; but at the same time, it leads to an identification of the supreme macrosubject in the sphere of absolute power—a blind power that operates without even the mediation of diplomacy and aims to destroy Western life—Soviet military power.

[Authors' note: These paragraphs were written in 1986. The fall of the Berlin Wall and the collapse of "real socialism" in Eastern Europe have revealed a much more complex world than the one the Manichean vision of anti-Communist thought had accustomed us to. But the end of the East-West rivalry has by no means abolished the reflex of creating specters and diabolical forces. International confrontations make it necessary to invent new "Evil Empires."]

The French public was watching on April 18, 1985, at a prime-time hour on Channel FR3, when the program entitled "La guerre en face" (The war facing us) featured actor-singer Yves Montand. Using news footage, interviews and political-fiction scenarios, the program tried to demonstrate the threat of apocalyptic military operations against a Europe that had fallen into the trap of its own defense policy. Spectators saw a simulated invasion in which the Soviet Union executed a blitzkrieg across Germany, which was reduced to impotence, and drove its Russian tanks into the heart of Paris.

One might have thought that the finesse demonstrated in the past twenty years in the analysis of power and how it results from negotiations and transactions between countervailing forces would have irretrievably discredited, in France, a representation of power inspired by manipulation and conspiracy theories. But nonetheless it made a comeback, accompanied by the deployment of the whole arsenal of psychological warfare. This propagandistic discourse, playing on a single register, that of fear, had the added effect of conspicuously ridiculing the aspirations of young European pacifists. These real microsubjects found themselves interpreted as the puppets of the one great macrosubject of History, the military command of the Warsaw Pact.

We are under the influence of a metaphysical representation of society: the latter is seen as a theater in which the mythical drama of the confrontation between Good and Evil is played out in the guise of democracy and freedom versus totalitarianism. As anthropologist Gérard Althabe has pointed out, such is

> the framework in which a scholastic intellectual production is developing to feed an imaginary political field. . . . We are outside history, outside the world of domination and exploitation; we are elsewhere. . . . Concrete situations are reconstructed as reflections of a metaphysical struggle; the components of this struggle and the nature of its two actors, Good and Evil, are the object of endless commentaries (as witnessed by [recently published] essays on the individual and his freedom, the state and its totalitarian nature, and civil society and its stifled potentialities).[5]

It cannot be denied that any theoretical work today that seeks to reconcile the macro and micro approaches, micro-and international logics, is undertaken in a context marked by Manichean visions of the international field: visions inspired by both the rationality of the new Cold War and the reality of trade war. One could dream of the possibility of approaching the macro level with the sense of nuance provided by the new paradigms in their study of microconflicts. One could also dream that the end of the opposition between positive heroes and negative heroes, already quite clear for microsociology and micropsychology, could also become clear in approaches to macrostructures. But the new fascination for the media performances of conservative America keep us at a great distance from this ideal.

Local Microsubjects

If there is a theme in France that reflects the evolution of the perception of tensions between the state macrosubject and microsubjects, and between conceptualized and experienced reality, it is the theme of local concerns (*le local*), which appeared on the scene in the 1970s. The local dimension, defined — and especially, experienced — as a counterpower, appeared to be the space in which the "possible-impossible dream of changing your life" could be made to come true.

It is not at all surprising that "alternative communication" and the quest for popular cultures were the theater of operations for this movement. As one active participant in the local press explained when retracing the history of local newspapers,

> The pathways were multiple and the motivations various. For some "activists," it was the need to establish "roots" [or] the will to forge a "different life"; the need for some to "find themselves" or to leave their sphere of political activity. . . . [It provided] a new possibility for activists from intellectual circles to be no longer estranged from their social status, but rather to engage in common practice with activists from other milieux, without resorting to voluntarism or a spirit of sacrifice. [There was also] the discovery of local struggles that had been given little or no consideration by political organizations; the more "human," more concrete dimension of this new type of intervention, the discovery that the neighborhood, the locality, or the region is a place where there are concrete problems, struggles, experiences, and a place where there are associations, unions, and forces on the move. A place where bonds have been established and people of different horizons have come together, where common aspirations have been found. . . . One must begin with dominant ideology as it is experienced and felt by people in order to find the fault lines that make it possible to open a path to changes in attitudes. . . . One must begin with local reality in order to find the "values" of resistance to oppression in popular struggles, songs, and games.[6]

The return to the local dimension upset the exclusive schemas of strategies centered on social class and analyses that reduced the forms of oppression to the sole, class-determined field of exploitation in the sphere of production. At the same time, it challenged the infallibility of working-class parties as organizers of social struggles, designating a quite inhabitual terrain for the left: geographic space, rootedness, daily life, and memory.[7]

This return to the local seemed all the more paradoxical in that France was, at that time, being swallowed up in the internationalization of its economy. France's rediscovery of the diversity of its territories and its cultures—the explosion of local specificities—coincided in time with the growing homogeneity that accompanied the integration of the nation into the world economy—integration that began to accelerate in the 1960s after a period of protectionism and loss of empire. While both the local and the national levels were being increasingly dispossessed of their decision-making capacity in questions of management and modification of the system of production, the return to the notion of local needs and demands seemed to make it possible for ways of life and the very structures of daily life to escape from economic determination. For certain social movements that claimed to be rooted in local relations, the problem was having to swim against the economistic current of policies planned by the central state in the attempt to adapt to the pressures of the international market. These movements also had to swim against the economistic current of the major labor organizations—the current flowing from the idea that industry had to continue producing, that production was the top priority. This refusal of economic determinism could only be interpreted as a radical critique of the consensus on the left about ways of life, and as the will to bring back into the discussion the constantly repressed theme of growth, because, for this left, the problem was to improve the standard of living rather than to change the way of life. The left had indeed always warned that questioning growth could only result in more unemployment. The debate was open once again; it could not be avoided by rallying to the quantitative conception of growth, behind which lay the tired old ideas of the "development of productive forces" and their "obstruction."

There was a sense that the media were as they were not only because of the manipulation of a dominant class. As an article in the review *Alternatives* stated in 1977,

Information, which springs from a certain mode of production
and which, like all products, needs a technique for its
elaboration, is delivered by specialists who, in spite of their
diversity of opinion, are unable to challenge its ideological basis.
. . . We are not attacking people of the left; but their logic should
lead them to question the product called "information," that is,
its mode of production, the practices that engender it, and their
consequences: centralism as opposed to *the local*, the sensational
as opposed to *the normal*, ideas as opposed to *lived experience*.[8]

In the same manner, it was vaguely felt that neither the duplicity of manipulators of capital nor the insufficient quantity of goods produced explained why capitalist production did not have as its objective the well-being of the people. In contrast to the sector of the left engaged in its usual blind productivism, there was opposition to the idea of infinitely reproducing the conditions, habits, and modalities of that kind of development. A new image became compelling: history, rather than following a proudly progressive line to a radiant future, was caught in a reproduction cycle that had to be broken, escaped from. The conceptions of time that emerged from all these observations came within the framework of a break with evolutionism that was de rigueur in "progressive" thinking.

Because the movement to develop local relations failed to think about context and thus ignored the stakes of economic production, it declared the pseudoautonomy of the sociocultural instrument. It was there, in the local sociocultural space, that the first intuitions arose regarding the rise of a "new petty bourgeoisie," the control over cultural apparatuses becoming a privileged instrument in the constitution of its political legitimacy. The redefinition of power relations was preparing its terrain. The mission of this class, as we have written elsewhere, was to

> ensure the management at the local and cultural level of the consequences of a global strategic orientation that had grown out of the process of internationalization. . . . There is a strong temptation to culturalize the social and the political, that is, to treat in a cultural mode the problems that one does not wish to (or that one has an interest in not being able to) treat in political terms. Certain tendencies in the organization of cultural activities, certain conceptions of cultural action, a certain neoworkerist mythology of self-management, and a certain overevaluation of culture that goes together with an underestimation of social consciousness—these are its most salient manifestations.[9]

Many people failed to notice that the local was caught in a double and contradictory movement, both localist and universalist: advertising agents would interpret it as a tension between globalization and personalization.

There was a rude awakening for those who had seen work at the local level as a refuge on the margin of macrosubjects and balances of force. As the policies of technological modernization began to take definite shape, the sociocultural domain ceased to be the bastion of cultural work under the banner of public service. Other forces struggled to assume this role as well, without much concern for wounded sensibilities; for example, a representative of the Havas-Ecom advertising agency in 1979 declared in a debate, later published in the review *Autrement* under the title of "La vraie action culturelle, c'est nous" (The real cultural action is us):

> We, too, I think, engage in cultural action. Moreover, we respond to people's needs because we have the means to know what they are. You could even say that we're the ones who practice real sociology and make it effective. In my opinion, cultural workers are behind the times. They claim to know people better than we do, but they don't use modern techniques; they are limited to their own world; they're afraid to express themselves, afraid to use the media, although the media are means of mass expression much more than the theater, for example. They are defensive about us and stick a commercial label on us, but that doesn't bother me at all because our approach is perfectly honest. We begin by listening to people and recording their desires, which means that the messages we emit can't be accepted unless they

correspond to an expectation, unless they fulfill a desire. It can't be said, then, that we are engaged in manipulation. If people buy chewing gum, it's because they feel like buying chewing gum. Cultural workers are immersed in a Christian, anti-money ideology, but that shows a total ignorance of society today: we have an ideology of profit, and that's all. To speak of anything else is to enter into some sort of dialectic that I find much too complicated! (*laughter*).[10]

The imperative of profitability appears to be one of the pressures that will make themselves felt henceforth on sociocultural organizations. We may thus observe a gradual slide, in the local domain, from a logic of proximity as community of meaning to a logic of the market. The first logic, which structures the supply of these organizations' services according to the needs and the demands of the surrounding population, is in the process of being replaced by the logic of mercantile efficiency, which structures supply according to the areas of activity in which these organizations estimate they will best perform. This new logic challenges the reference to the surrounding areas as the structuring criterion for a supply of services. At the same time, the profile of the clientele is restructured along with the instruments for measuring and evaluating demands and local needs.

More generally, the pressures of efficiency and profitability impose themselves more clearly than in the past on all the small enterprises eager to develop alternative products or services in the framework of self-managed labor, although at the outset they were simply able to deny these pressures in the name of refusal of the logic of profit. This exclusive opposition between freedom and profit in fact caused a great deal of damage. It is possible, after all, to imagine a project for an alternative enterprise that is not obsessed by the profit imperative but is able to assume the imperatives of responsible management. This is particularly true for enterprises with a "cultural" vocation: press, publishing, radio, video, and the like.[11]

Crises of Legitimacy: The State

The way in which the debate on the state is being conducted today has another major disadvantage: by making the withering away of the state the condition for the revival of freedoms, one forgets that the state has already begun to change and that the logics that inhabit it are evidence more of its complicity in being stripped of some of its functions than of an unconditional attachment to some sort of essence for which its opponents habitually give it credit. To think that the ramparts of the state must be knocked down in order to emancipate society from its power is to give one's blessing to the idea of the state as citadel. And yet it is from inside that the doors have begun to open.

The very forms of the legitimacy of the state have evolved rapidly. But in order to understand the framework of this crisis of the legitimacy of the state, it is necessary to view it in the context of the legitimation crises of all forms of large organizations, private as well as public.

Parasitism, nonchalance, irresponsibility, ineffectiveness, inhumanity, interference with the lives of individuals: these are the accusations that have been made against the state in the persons of its diverse agents. Too much importance has been accorded to profit, the efficacy of production, and the income of higher-echelon managers, and not enough to the consumer, the environment, and the least privileged social categories: these are the reproaches formulated against private corporations, *a fortiori* when they have an international status. The notion of public service is now no more of a protective shield than that of profit.

Against the accusations of waste and inhumanity, the state will seek from private management the instruments to rationalize its action, but also to sell its services. Since the crisis of large organizations is also a crisis of image, remedies will be sought in new strategies of communication. In order to restore its image the state will call on marketing strategies, with the object of improving the quality of its relationship with the citizen. There is a double paradox. On the one hand, the state imports its techniques of personnel management and opinion management from the private sector, while the private sector, under pressure from the social environment, undergoes an evolution in its management toward forms that resemble those used in the public sector. Both are contested in their objectives and their methods, and each exchanges its objectives and methods with the other. As R. Laufer has written, "The private sector must take inspiration from the finalities of the public sector; the public sector must utilize the methods of the private sector."[12]

In order to cope with the crisis of traditional administrative languages, the state has turned to advertising language to launch its campaigns to raise public awareness on subjects as diverse as the promotion of reading, equal opportunity for women, auto safety, and so on. By doing so it confers on the advertising approach a public legitimacy that the market alone cannot provide. Moreover, in a society where the very idea of profit collides with those of culture and public service, this rapprochement between administrative language and marketing language results, so to speak, in an act of "laundering money."

With the rise of advertising rationality in state management, a new relation to civil society has been established. As Yves de la Haye has remarked, these advertising campaigns make the public think that new technical procedures [are involved] whereas they acquire meaning and dimension only through the old history of mechanisms by which the state in its constitutional form instrumentalizes the communication of its power and organizes the representation of the people, the fictional foundation of this power. [This old history] causes people to believe that these public communication activities have no other aim than the transparency of decisions and administrative regulation, as if the "transmitter-state" were all of a sudden becoming a pedagogue armed with the talents of an advertising agent, among others, in order to address itself to the "citizen-receiver," who is often inattentive, and thus to enhance its chances for the success of the message![13]

Crises of Legitimacy: The Nation-State

What is happening on the territory of the nation-state is unintelligible, as we have already stated, unless it is understood in the context of deep tendencies that transcend national borders. This brings us to the process of redefinition of the state according to the demands and pressures of supranational actors. This is an aspect—an essential one—that the debate about the state, locked in the national ideology of the late nineteenth century, tends to pass over in silence.

Important spheres of decision are already no longer the institutional responsibility of the nation-state. Moreover, the latter is, here again, often an accomplice to its own dispossession. In this process of remodeling, the technologies of communication and information, as structuring systems, occupy a decisive place.

The nation-state finds it more and more difficult to master its own system of communication. As proof we offer the process of deregulation of the national telecommunications (and broadcasting) monopolies. The explicit values, the modes of perceiving the world, and the concrete forms of articulation between the national level and the international level which characterized the nation-state have inspired institutions and regulatory systems that are hardly able to respond to the needs created by the globalizing logic of the new historical mode of realization of capital. With the internationalization of economies, both a new sense of dimensions and new notions of space and time are emerging. The universe of real time, of the round-the-clock global markets and the process of production conceived at the world level, finds it hard to accommodate to juridical-political arrangements based on the idea of national sovereignty. By the same token, it accommodates badly to another, corollary idea, that of popular will. These ideas founded an institutional mode of representation of national opinion, a "public sphere," which was in turn indissociable from the procedures of legitimation of the nation-state. This conception of politics, sanctioned by representative institutions and by the "code," is implicitly called into question by the pragmatic behavior of transnational actors, who reason in terms of use, forms of concerted action, and expeditious, directly operational decision making.

Certain thinking habits may prevent us from correctly perceiving the novelty of the present phase of globalization in the area of production and dissemination of cultural goods. For an entire tradition of thought about national independence and cultural sovereignty, the prevailing idea was that the degree of dependency of a nation could be measured above all by the rate of import of foreign cultural products (television series, films, video games, etc.). This tradition has its own semantic field, delimited by notions such as invasion, cultural imperialism, and cultural colonialism. This criterion, however, is now revealing itself to be insufficient. At the present stage, although there are still dominant poles that export more cultural products than others and are also able to disseminate references of a universal character, the most decisive process is the setting up, at the national, regional, and international levels, of new forms of organization of production and distribution better suited to a global logic. That is how we must interpret the various processes of privatization and the different forms taken by the transfers of competence and exchanges of know-how between the state and the private sector: they are the beginning of a socialization of "universal" norms and matrices, as opposed to the "particular" norms that legitimated the organization of monopolies and national public services.

The battle for the international harmonization of technical standards and norms for communication equipment is a reflection of the more complex battle for the alignment of national territories to internationally shared references. This globalizing trend and this search for synergies between systems that had up to now been compartmentalized, confirm — but at the same time contradict — the tendency toward more centralization and more concentration (illustrated by the formation of transnational multimedia conglomerates). Since the norm is the essential thing, the logic of centralization can accompany a logic of decentralization and autonomy. Since performance requires a combination of different orders of magnitude, the notion of flexibility masks the persistence of rigidities and compartmentalizations that originate in the deep and fundamental imbalances among the different local, national, and international apparatuses of information and communication. These inequalities are in danger of becoming aggravated with the setting up of new systems of communication. Just as money seeks money, technology seeks technology.

The theoretical stake in the question of these shifts in hegemony (from public to private actors, from national to transnational ones) is a great one. The problem is to understand the process of deterritorialization and reterritorialization, decomposition and recomposition of territories as meaningful units for collective identities.

Communication research is not the only field that is confronting the problem of the articulation between the national and international, regional and local levels. Other disciplines are posing similar questions. As geographer Yves Lacoste writes:

> This problem is posed just as much, for example, in history and in economics as in geography: How do we combine the "long time" and the "short time"? How do we find the articulation between macro- and microeconomics? In fact, in most of the areas of science and knowledge, we are becoming aware of the importance of the problem of the hiatuses between the different hierarchical levels that we are called upon to distinguish. The problem has been posed, but its theoretical solution has not yet been found.[14]

The geopolitical theory of this school of geography, which recognizes the need to approach reality on various different scales, no doubt constitutes an interesting step forward in the strategic analysis of the articulation between different levels of complexity of world space. Another essential contribution is of course that of Fernand Braudel.

The difficulty that continues to threaten this theoretical framework is conceiving the new functions of the nation-state only in an instrumental perspective within the world economy. Such a functionalist outlook would risk eliminating from the field of analysis numerous social actors who, at particular levels, through the play of struggles and negotiations, prevent the process of internationalization and the organization of new national and local structures from always functioning according to the impeccable rationality of theories of reproduction. These mediations prevent us from regarding a national territory as nothing more than a base of operations for the new macrosubjects.

The stake is also a practical one. It concerns the perception of the link between realities of each individual person and the more and more distant and abstract determinations. The local level, with all its connotations of proximity, thus takes its place in the chain of meaning that puts the singular into perspective with relation to the universal, the concrete with respect to the abstract, and the individual with respect to the collective.

In order to avoid the temptation of simply retreating back into the local level, with its subtle forms of refusing the Other, it is becoming indispensable to think of the local level with the world level in mind. We are constantly reminded of this by other forms of globalization that are seeking their paths in the margins of the transnational space of the new macrosubjects and state-to-state relations. The multiplication of direct exchanges between civil society and civil society, between local community and local community, between social movement and social movement—all these new modes of decentralized cooperation indicate that other social actors participate in international relations. Bearers of the new paradigm of the critique of the transnational model of development and productivist growth, and of a new approach to relations among different cultures, these actors extend to the international level the questionings that, at the national and regional levels, had challenged the centralizing Jacobin state's monopoly of representation and its nationalist ideology. These interrogations have been formulated by very diverse movements and currents of thought: national cultural ideologies, ideologies of identity, demands for a pluriethnic society, demands for multiple community identification, and so on. This type of impulse, which brings a new dimension to both the national and the international levels, expresses beyond a doubt the search for new modes of political expression.

13

The Logic of the Industrial Actor

From "Social Alliances" to "Industrial Synergies"

The historians who examine the first years of the 1980s will have good reason to meditate on the formidable infatuation that seized French society — which up to then had been rather reserved, and even reticent — for modern techniques of communication. France had always appeared a rearguard figure with respect to its great European neighbors and rivals, the United Kingdom and Germany. Advertising, radios, televisions, VCRs, microcomputers, and the use of audiovisual techniques in the schools had all been adopted in the United Kingdom before they had taken hold in France. Some, seeking only the simple clues, attempt to explain this retarded technological development as a function of relative standards of living. Others add to this the incapacity of the national bourgeoisie to provide the country with a modern technological and industrial infrastructure. These are very insufficient explanations, and rather too mechanistic to account for an anthropological context in which culture and industry formed a problem-couple.

Along with this liberation of technological space, there occurred a series of chain-reaction decompartmentalizations: between private industry and nationalized industry; among industries within a single sector; between local industries and branches of transnational corporations; between industry and the university; between industry and the schools; among design, industrialization, and marketing; but also between users and builders, producers and consumers. This is the context in which many intellectuals and researchers have made their peace with the world of industry and trade.

Anticipated to a large extent as early as 1975 under the heading of

137

"the computerization of society," France's technological explosion was taken over in May 1981 by a socialist government turned captain of industry. The discourse of the previous regime about "computerizing society" was succeeded by a discourse about "democratizing computer technology."

When this movement began, one had the impression that all the major questions of the previous fifteen years within the different sectors of civil society about the interface between democracy and communication were indeed being taken into account. A symposium entitled "Research and Technology" held in early 1982, which mobilized scientific, industrial, and trade-union circles and informal associations, was a typical expression of this movement of thought, which, having originated at the regional level, engendered discussion at the national level. At this symposium, the subject of "an alternative development" was raised—a type of development based on respect for cultural identity and the satisfaction of people's own needs. The imperative of not separating cultural traditions from scientific and technical progress was also spoken of. The regional level was spoken of as a place where "something called by an ugly name—the vulgarization of knowledge—and which should rightfully be named popularization" could develop "with the greatest chances of success."[1] The region was also spoken of as the place where social demands (to which all present promised to be attentive) could be best listened to and decoded. The relations between science, technology, and culture were also discussed, along with those between scientific and technical culture on the one hand and artistic creation on the other. In particular, the participants spoke of the necessity of not letting only specialists define the relations among science, technology, and the other major areas of social activity. The necessity of favoring the social appropriation of new technologies, with the deepening of democracy in view, was discussed. There was a debate about the double logic affecting research: the logic of freedom—that is, that of the researcher engaged in work, a freedom "apparently capricious and almost always unpredictable"—and the logic of needs, "that of social demand, which cannot be reduced either to economics or, less still, to a sort of market-guided steering mechanism."[2] Finally, reference was made to the necessity of "harmonizing the movement from above with the social movement, the momentum provided by the state being relayed, developed, and taken in hand by the entire collective group."[3] Most of all, participants spoke of "a French path out of the crisis"—via high technology, with new communication and information technologies constituting one of the bridgeheads of the strategy.

The first trace of this "telematics"[4] solution *à la française* can be found in the report drafted by Simon Nora and Alain Minc, *L'Informatisation de la société* (The computerization of society), commissioned by President Valéry Giscard d'Estaing in late 1976 and submitted in January 1978.

The Nora-Minc Report was constructed around a double certainty: "Computerization makes both possible and necessary a new type of growth. ... Computer technology is necessary but not sufficient for resolving the French crisis."[5] The principal merit of this report—a contradictory document in many ways—is no doubt to have attempted to place the arrival of computer technology not only in the context of the economic crisis, but also in what the authors called "a crisis of civilization," "a crisis of the social consensus," and "a crisis of the system of adherence of citizens to the social rules of the game." They thus envisioned new technologies of communication as having the potential to provide diversified political solutions, adaptable to all forms of command or regulation.

> With the movement it is provoking in information circuits, telematics is at the heart of power considerations. It displaces the balance in competitive markets and among collective public entities. It influences certain professions by modifying their social position. It increases the transparency of relationships among social groups and the vulnerability of large organizations. But it would be illusory to expect from computer technology alone a transformation of the structure of society, that is, of the pyramid of powers that governs it. ... Telematics can facilitate the rise of a new society, but it will not build such a society spontaneously or by itself.[6]

The government of the left introduced a correction: the strategy of locating particularly promising sectors of development, proposed by Nora and Minc, was replaced by an overall strategy for the electronics industry. This unitary strategy was made imperative, according to the Farnoux report, by the interpenetration of the different sectors composing the industry (media electronics, satellites, computers, robots, weapons, mass-consumption electronics, and so on). It had certainly not been the intention of Simon Nora and Alain Minc to propose a socialist model for resolving the crisis. The objective of the industrywide electronics strategy was precisely to offer a socialist option. For this strategy, the only way out of the crisis was via technology.

The economist Alain Lipietz argued in reply,

> The way out of the crisis cannot be technological because the crisis is not of a technological nature. ... Between technology and the model of development, there are a number of connecting links that contain the essential part of the cultural and political content of production: social relations. Between technology and

the technical execution [there are] the immediate relations of production (Who decides? How is the group of workers organized?); between production and the economy [there are] the overall socioeconomic relations (Will there be enough consumers? Enough investors? To produce what? To ensure what kind of full employment?). And even if a new model of development has been conceived, how can the passage be ensured from the old which is dying to the new which is having such trouble being born? How can the restructuring process be controlled, financially and above all humanly? And who are the subjects of such a transformation?[7]

A New Mode of Production?

New technologies + democracy = new model of development. Here is an equation that obviously evokes the old formula: electricity + soviets = socialism. In more up-to-date language reflecting the systemic utopias of the 1970s, this becomes: Ecosociety = conviviality + telecommunications.[8] As usually happens with this type of equation, the failure to give any content to the expression "new model of development" makes democracy the dependent variable. When, in the second half of 1984, the slogan of "modernization" was launched, "more democracy" retreated to "more technology."

Social participation, social demand, and social appropriation were reduced more and more to an incantation while electronics took off with blinding speed. The discourse of modernity escorted a policy of reindustrialization that drew an equal sign between technological innovation and new social relations, masking the contradictions of technological and industrial choices.

"Will there be enough consumers?" This is by no means certain, because not everyone is ready to submit to the pace dictated by the industrial imperative to produce the infrastructure of a communications apparatus. The history of the formation of social uses in the domain of communication shows that the time factor is decisive.[9] It is decisive not only for the broad public but also for affluent groups as well. According to estimates, the amount of money available for spending by these consumers is double what can be counted on as a result of advertising. And we now know with certainty that new systems of communication cannot be financed solely by advertising investments and state funding.

"What sort of consumption will it be?" The panacea of technological interactivity assuming the role of prototype for a new type of social interactivity is too present in discourse and experimentation not to cause doubts about the way one replies to this question. This narrow conception of interactivity falls far short of certain practices of social interactivity that very diverse social actors in the field of so-called alternative communication have attempted to develop in the past fifteen years using other techniques, and outside the technical domain. This leads to the question, "Who produces what, and how?" It took only a short time for the suspicions of actors of a real decentralization of audiovisual production to be confirmed: the incentive to produce in order to feed the new and increasingly numerous broadcast channels, means profits for the program industries, which are able to manage and exploit already existing program formulas and formats. The need to broaden the social base of audiovisual production is not taken into account, nor is the need for preserving the all-too-rare projects in which social and cultural differences are expressed.

Will the local and national levels become places from which one can really consider maintaining specificities with respect to the logics of internationalization, or will they be merely broadcasting areas, or places where prototypes already patented in foreign markets are subcontracted?

These contradictions exploded when the debate about national production arose. Faced with the threat of globalization in the form of foreign competition, the culture industry has allowed a discourse of patriotism to flourish. The national level and national independence, alias "reconquering the internal market," has become a rallying cry in the field of cultural production.[10]

Such debates, when they occur, reflect a real malaise. There is a great distance between the discourse of high government officials about national cultural sovereignty and the actual industrial policies for producing programs supported jointly by the state and the private sector. There is still a reliance, in discourse, on the old juridical-political ideology of the nineteenth century, while one floor below, at the level of pragmatic industrial decision makers, the national level is seen from the point of view of market logic as no more than a share of the market.

It seems that the cultural production industry, faced with the necessity of integrating itself into an international market, finds it difficult to perceive future paths unrelated to the needs of this market, which imposes an already accredited model of production thanks to its long experience. There is a great temptation to limit activity at the national level to adapting to predominant models that have become universal. The best example of this is the case of the French serial "Chateauvallon," explicitly patterned after the American "Dallas," the international success of which was already confirmed.

In the current phase of industrialization of cultural production, the definition of the national level tends to be the one given by the corporation in quest of a good performance.

Such hasty approaches to thinking about the national level, conditioned by the market, can only lead to a reductive reading of the history of public service, seen as a history of handicaps on independent initiative. The new requirements for good performance, combining the viability of a national industry with internationalization, give rise to a perception of the heritage of public service as nothing more than a series of obstacles preventing enterprises from positioning themselves successfully in international competition, unlike commercial television networks better equipped to produce exportable products.[11]

While the nation-state and the program industries seem to grope in search of a national norm—if they seek one at all—the advertising industry and its research branch have already developed their own idea of relations between the local and national levels and the increasing internationalization. The national level is a variable that figures both in its strategies of globalization and in its strategies of personalization. The scenarios of communication addressed to all territories on the basis of a mass marketing model are well known; what is less known are the segmented or even individualized and personalized models offered by advertising via new technologies. The "International of life-styles" accomplishes the fusion of these two tendencies. As one advertising specialist explains, "We seek to address people who have a certain life-style in France and those who have the same one in Germany and Italy."[12] To resolve the problem in this manner is to deny that there can be a national problem or that the national level poses a problem. Socio-styles throw a single-arched bridge between groups in affinity with each other, sharing the same subculture in another national society. In this perspective, there is a passage from a mass society to a segmented, multipolar society—from mass culture to diversified culture, from messages addressed to the smallest common denominator to individualized messages, from the absence of response to high feedback. As we have seen, the new targeted media define themselves, through the mouths of advertising agents, as media with "high imaginary and qualitative value added."[13]

The exponents (avowed or unavowed) of neoliberal theories, who occupy in this debate the position of refusing a high degree of state intervention, hasten to avoid another debate that seems necessary, being content to draw the following summary equation: state = totalitarianism = oppression; nation = aggression = the fascist past. In this context, to raise the question of the relation between the national and the international, and the corollary question of the international balance of forces, is to expose oneself to criticism for supporting the thesis of the positivity of the nation-state and being a prisoner of the old Leninist conception of "the national question." One thing is certain, however: in considerations whose stake is the definition of the national, one reference is absent: the accomplishments of the past twenty years in bringing out distinctions among different cultural areas within the national perimeter.

The New Legitimacy of Advertising Rationality

It is undoubtedly within the matrix established by the model of reindustrialization that grand logics are born that delegitimate certain theoretical questions about the evolution of systems of communications and legitimate others.

"With capital accumulation, economic growth is institutionalized in an unplanned, naturelike way," Jürgen Habermas has written.[14]

With the model of growth brought up to date, the forms of communication that were problematic only yesterday are naturalized, and institutionalize themselves in a spontaneous manner. The first of these is the advertising regime, which is the natural linguistic space of this growth model. The theoreticians of the American advertising industry even go so far as to say that advertising is the voice of technology. Laurent Fabius, during his term as minister of industry and research in 1984, gave prizes to the five best advertising agencies in France and made the following statement:

> You give people a positive image of France as a country that loves the freedom to create and believes in the will to succeed. Aside from its financial, industrial, commercial, and cultural stakes, I personally believe that advertising involves an essential dimension of what freedom is. I do not mean to say that everything is perfect in the world of advertising, but I believe that throughout the world, the political regimes that refuse advertising outright are usually those that do not tolerate plurality of discourse and refuse innovation and the unexpected. . . . Your profession will be remodeled by innovation in the information industries, which will cause both national boundaries and local monopolies to explode and will allow you to reach more specific publics. Advertising will be different in a world at once more international and more decentralized.[15]

A significant step forward had been taken in building a consensus around this new cultural mode of mercantile rationality. Its importance is measured better when one takes into account the resistance of French society to allowing as legitimate the rapprochement between money, trade, and culture. The advertising industry at its outset had to deal with this resistance.

In this regard, American advertisers have often noted the profound difference between American-style and French-style advertising. The latter is seen as taking a more aesthetic approach, as more flexible and more innovative, as opposed to American pragmatism, which, according to one author, J. Stratte, envisions only one solution to a problem whereas the French envision dozens of solutions.[16] Mostly, however, they noted the resistance to the rise of the logic of advertising caused by a social context deeply marked by political divisions and the tradition of social criticism. This argument was exposed in simple and familiar terms by the same author as follows: "Eighty percent of the teachers in the French school system are socialists. You can't get the type of spirit necessary for competitive advertising from that type of education."[17] How ironical this statement seems when juxtaposed to the above remarks of Socialist party dignitary Laurent Fabius!

The historical specificity of the French advertising apparatus[18] is already present in the etymology of the word *publicité* (French for advertising). In the United States, of course, "publicity" means something different. According to the International Chamber of Commerce, following the American Marketing Association, advertising is defined as "a nonpersonal, multiple presentation to the market of goods, services, or commercial ideas by an identified sponsor who pays for the delivery of his message to the carrier (advertising medium)." According to the same sources, advertising should be "distinguished from publicity, which does not pay the medium and does not necessarily identify the sponsor."[19]

The term *publicité* preferred by the French clearly indicates the historical originality of French advertising, difficult to dissociate from the statist tradition. The generalized adoption of this term is all the more significant in that the old French word *advertissement* was long used as well.

There has been little research shedding light on the history of the French model of advertising. One study, however, unpublished to date, provides precious material for understanding the formation of this type of communication in France. Whereas the American advertising apparatus was born directly in the spirit of competition, and rapidly included commercial and political marketing, the French apparatus took shape as an extension of public charitable institutions. As G. Lagneau writes:

> Since the nineteenth century, conflictive advertising (that which is engaged in the logic of the market) progressively extended its empire, eclipsing in the process an older model, but one that had left many traces since we had invented it at the end of the Renaissance. The inventor of the advertising agency [*agence de publicité*], in a form that seems primitive to us, was none other than Théophraste Renaudot, better known as the founder of the *Gazette*. Both inventions take on their full meaning within a network of public services set up with the encouragement and the protection of the government. This attempt to bring secular rationalization to charities that up to then had been managed by

the church apparently had only a distant relation to our modern advertisements; it belongs rather to the modern history of the Welfare State, because its avowed objective was "regulating the poor." This "old regime" of advertising [*publicité*] had a social finality; the means of advertising, in helping the development of exchanges, had a deeper aim than material prosperity: the improvement of commerce among men. In this sense, all advertisement is commercial; but in entering the field of political economy, it elevates the means into an end and the incitement of the consumer becomes the instrument of sales promotion. Public assistance yields to private enrichment, and advertisement becomes a source of fortune.[20]

These lines suggest that it is above all in the irresistible rise of conflictive advertisement that one can best grasp the slow transformation of the idea of public service and understand how it forged its path through various sorts of resistance, opposed by a certain historical tradition and cultural heritage.

From Popular Memory to Mass Culture

When it came to power, the French left took a liking to the media and made its politics into a spectacle. A brilliant example of this was President François Mitterrand's television appearance on Sunday, April 28, 1985, when he was interviewed by host Yves Mourousi in the first segment of "Ça nous intéresse, monsieur le Président" (We're interested, Mr. President). It was the first time that a head of state being interviewed on television agreed not to be the manifest center of attention and not to engage in political discourse. With the pace of the questions, the use of music videos and excerpts of recent films as illustrations, the use of synthetic images and commercials, and heavy recourse to design and computers, the public witnessed the death of a certain way of conceiving politics and took the plunge into its new version, defined by advertising rationality. The president's role that evening was not to develop ideas but to reply with the speed of advertising slogans and to offer as good a performance as his host, a television veteran who knew the ropes of the profession and for whom the president was simply another guest to interview, albeit a particularly interesting one. It is clear that when we are faced with such media fireworks, certain questions seem quite obsolete.

In the studio audience were some actors of the latest version of "modern society": dynamic industrialists, advertising agents, best-selling authors, sports champions, stars of show business, and a government minister who, viewers were reminded, was enjoying great success in the polls.

On the media scene, the immediate interlocutors of the presidential spectacle are no longer his fellow actors in political and social history.

We seemed to have come a long way from a certain idea of popular culture. Were we not already experiencing another? It took the frankness of a journalist from *Le Monde* during a debate in the spring of 1984 to show that the Rubicon had been crossed. What he said, quite simply, is that popular culture today is an advertising creation—those little compact stories in commercials that, like the popular narratives of yesteryear, captivate our children.

Much effort was put into resisting this evolution in France. But on the other side of the Atlantic, it had already occurred at the dawn of the massification of culture, when the expressions "popular culture" and "mass culture" became interchangeable. As Geneviève Pujol observed during a colloquium on popular cultures organized in 1977 by the Institut d'éducation populaire (Institute for popular education): "It seems impossible for a French researcher to confuse—like many Anglo-Saxon researchers still do—mass culture and popular culture."[21]

Consider, for example, the following argument: "When we turn to our popular culture, what do we find? We find that in our nation of consumption communities and emphasis on gross national product (GNP) and growth rates, advertising has become the heart of the folk culture and even its prototype. American advertising shows many characteristics of the folk culture of other societies: repetition, a plain style, hyperbole and tall talk, folk verse, and folk music. . . . How do the expressions of our peculiar folk culture come to us? They no longer sprout from the earth, from the village, from the farm, or even from the neighborhood or the city. They come to us primarily from enormous centralized self-consciously creative (an overused word, for the overuse of which advertising agencies are in no small part responsible) organizations. They come from advertising agencies, from networks of newspapers, radio, and television, from outdoor-advertising agencies, from the copywriters for ads in the largest circulation magazines."[22]

The author of these lines is the American historian Daniel Boorstin. All those who interpret advertising as "the rhetoric of democracy," in Boorstin's terms, do not display the same discernment he does, or take the same care to distinguish the experience of American society from that of European societies. For example, Boorstin remarks astutely that in places other than the United States, and in the Old World in particular, it was high culture that contributed to organizing consensus among the different social groups, whereas the United States represents no doubt "the first people in history to have a centrally organized mass-produced folk culture."[23]

Boorstin is honest enough to point out the different weights of the universities, the educational system, intellectuals, and the church in the shaping of a national consciousness and modes of social regulation in the United States and in Europe respectively. In another issue of the same journal, *Advertising Age* (the bible of American advertising agents), an issue devoted to the past fifty years of advertising in the United States, another academic, depicting mass culture as the experience of the majority, did not hesitate to defy the critics of advertising, such as the Civil Rights Commission, with the argument that criticizing the media is a disguised manner of criticizing American society.[24] One *Advertising Age* editorialist developed the following point of view: "I've always felt that advertising is one of the greatest democratizers our society has ever known, for it brings to the masses information on new products and services formerly reserved for the elite." He concludes: "What some critics object to, I've discovered, is not advertising itself but the fact that it enables everyone to have access to the same information, thereby breaking down one more barrier between the great unwashed and the self-proclaimed chosen few."[25] Advertising is thus the language of the *democratic marketplace*. Another advertising specialist, whose concern was clearly not to place the emergence of the advertising system in the context of its historical function, concluded that "all these criticisms are based on the fallacy that 'advertising' has a substance and meaning by itself. Advertising is merely a tool and a technique, and attacks on advertising *per se* are therefore meaningless. It can equally well be used to promote materialism or asceticism, the purchase of cosmetics or U.S. bonds, the sale of smut or scriptures."[26]

This legitimation of the advertising model corresponds with all the unspoken and unthought notions of the left regarding the technological mode of communication. Inclined to conceive of it in its functional use, the left has usually been content to approach it as a vessel in which only the content counts. By so doing, it has avoided asking about the nature of technical-commercial logic, instead trying to distinguish "good" from "bad" uses of advertising. But whether it is good or not, advertising is a manner of marrying the order of commodities with the order of the spectacle—producing commodities as spectacle and the spectacle as a commodity.

Advertising rationalities give rise to new conformisms, disarming the critical spirit and undermining peoples' will to understand what is happening around them. Working-class culture and the popular memory are not welcomed into the new public sphere constituted by the advertising scene. In a 1974 interview Michel Foucault invited intellectuals to help the popular classes repossess their memory.

People—and by that I mean those who do not have the right to express themselves in writing, write their own books, compose their own history—nonetheless have a way of recording their history, remembering it, experiencing it and using it. . . . But a whole series of apparatuses have been established ("popular literature," cheap literature, but also school curricula) to block the movement of popular memory. And it can be said that this enterprise has met with relative success. The historical knowledge that the working class has of itself has not ceased to shrink.

And referring more particularly to the audiovisual expression of this memory, he continued: "Every film functions as a potential archives, and in a perspective of struggle one can seize this idea and move to a higher stage where people organize their film like a court exhibit and seek to constitute their own archives."[27]

The archeologists of knowledge will no doubt try one day to clarify the reason Foucault's words today sound so strange and anachronistic. In the heat of modernization, many have preferred to write off this long, and of course contradictory, accumulation of memory as a loss (while still drawing dividends). Turning to look back is forbidden, under penalty of suffering the punishment of Lot's wife. And in a world where modernity constantly bypasses itself, a frozen position is never pardoned!

14

The Cosmobiology of *Homo Deregulatus*

A New Darwinian Theater

Political and industrial scenarios for the creation of new systems of information and communication throughout the world are dominated by a key word: deregulation. Earlier we pointed out the danger of confining the definition of the process of deregulation to the technical sphere.[1] We stressed the fact that new theoretical references are becoming established, carried forward by the logic of deregulation. Among the references on the rise, there is that of biology. The language of the social no longer suffices to describe the reconquering of industrial markets and the new strategies for overcoming economic crises through high technologies of information. Biological vocabulary is called up to describe the metabolic regulations of the immense cosmic organism known as capitalism. The chosen land for this discourse is Reaganite America.

One might have thought that American capitalism had long since perfected its philosophy of the market. Norbert Wiener, the father of cybernetics and the new science of information, had after all written in 1948, in the prologue to the French edition of his book *The Human Use of Human Beings: Cybernetics and Society,*

> My book is intended mainly for Americans, living in the
> American environment; questions about information are
> appreciated there according to the standard American criterion:
> something has value as merchandise through how much it brings
> on the free market. That is the official doctrine of an orthodoxy
> against which, for an inhabitant of the United States, it is
> becoming increasingly dangerous to resist. It may be useful to
> note that this doctrine does not represent a universal basis for

149

human values; it corresponds neither to the doctrine of the church which seeks the salvation of the soul, nor to that of Marxism for which a society has no value except through the realization of specific ideals of human well-being. The fate of information in the typically American world is to become something that can be bought or sold. It is not my role to quibble about the morality or immorality, the vulgarity or the subtlety of this mercantile attitude. But it is my duty to show that it leads to incomprehension and mistreatment of information and related notions.[2]

One might have thought that the law of the market was an integral part of the social nature of this new nation. But now we learn that this law has up to now been restricted by excessive intervention of the state. If we are to believe American economic and financial magazines, the liberation of market forces is only beginning. "Deregulation," wrote *Business Week* in 1985, "from banking to telecommunications, opened once-restricted markets to the 'animal spirits' of capitalism."[3]

The biological reference has lodged itself in the heart of deregulation. It is deployed against the background of the new Darwinian theater. The new freedoms granted by the market consecrate the "freedom to triumph": may the best man win. The tension between freedom and equality that had marked American democracy since its origins has been resolved to the advantage of the former: the discourse of freedom has taken off like a rocket and become hyperbolic while equality has failed to leave the ground.

There is a topic that haunts the discourse of industrial conversion through new technologies: that of adaptation. When workers from the steel plant in Longwy, France, came to Pittsburgh to observe firsthand the reality of American-style industrial redeployment—a key concept for the French Socialist government in its modernization program for the disaster areas of the steel industry—here is what an American professor told them: "One, perhaps two generations have been sacrificed. It's like with animals, to survive you have to adapt."[4]

The America of the "New Frontier," having become once again the symbol of the vitality of capitalism, proclaims aloud that the crisis is only an accidental phenomenon—a normal adjustment to the cycle of organic autoregulation of capitalism. Europe, by contrast, experiences the crisis as a manifestation of its own anemia. During a trip to the United States in 1985, the president of the Schlumberger corporation made an uncomplacent evaluation of European defeatism.

As opposed to these worlds in expansion, European defeatism is despairing to behold. Despairing because it engulfs all of Europe,

from the north to the south, conservative or socialist. It is not by
chance that the prophets of doom are almost all European. In
order to justify their pessimism, indeed, all they have to do is
wait for the others to collapse.[5]

The Youth Effect

A new factor has appeared in the economy: the generation effect. In the
United States, the yuppies are the emblematic group: young urban professionals between 25 and 40 years of age, new captains of industry
whose magical sense of improvisation has produced marvels, particularly
with the boom of the high-tech industries. Youth has become an explanatory category for recapturing lost economic ground. The biological vitality of youth, which propels its spirit of enterprise, has accommodated
itself to a forceful return of conservatism, the "natural" ideology of the
younger generations.

With deregulation and the new fields of competition it has opened—
for those who have the privilege of staying within the system of
production—what is occurring is the discovery of "power-as-value," or
better yet, the pleasure of power. Fordist society not only stripped the
worker of his or her know-how and allowed bosses to appropriate the
intellectual component of industrial labor; it also imprisoned the actors
of industrial production in a hierarchical framework, although of course
the bearers of technology, the engineer and the technician, are not in the
same position with respect to the boss as the "specialized laborer," who
simply executes the work. For the new enterprise, "smashing the management pyramid is a war cry heard from Silicon Valley to Monongahela
Valley."[6]

What the crisis taught—and made a reality—is that the small unit is
"complementary" to the large one, and vice versa. A double evolution is
taking place: on the one hand, the rise of conglomerates and transnationals; on the other hand, that of small, autonomous units, sometimes included within the large structures.

The earlier mode of organization of labor was characterized by the
search for greater productivity through the progressive decomposition of
tasks into elementary gestures and through the simplification of norms of
labor; the division of the functions of planning and execution; and the
exercise of direct control and surveillance of the worker. The more recent
trend is to seek the same productivity, only this time with a simplified or-
ganizational chart, with relatively indistinct gradations, where the different levels of authority and privilege lose their rigidity. The objective is to
succeed in making the company spirit penetrate the mind of new managers to such an extent that they perform their work as if they were man-

aging their own companies, each person identifying with his or her own position as if it were a small business. This results in a new morale and a new mode of channeling energies. The trend is toward deconcentration of powers and decentralization of decision making.

It is within this new architecture that a certain value that had been falling precipitously is now rising again: the attractiveness of labor, because now it is no longer merely the activity through which one earns a living and attains prosperity, but also that by which one becomes a "winner," that is, an actor in the sphere of power. The older generation agreed to put off until tomorrow the compensation for daily toil; the new generation is finding its compensation in the satisfaction of labor, now a synonym of challenge, creativity, continual personal development.

A new corporate culture is emerging. Its birth process is often painful because, contrary to certain dithyrambic declarations about the "new age" found in American financial and economic magazines, the resistance of the old industrial hierarchy is real.

This new culture includes a portrayal of the "new corporate elite," whose distinctive features could be described as follows. Contrary to the old elite, which had no horizon beyond the United States, the new elite is "totally international." The market in which it moves is the "world economy." Contrary to the reserve and the legendary ascetic tendency of most captains of industry of earlier times, the new corporate manager considers advertising and celebrity—in other words, high visibility—to be essential ingredients of success. The new elite declares itself to be "egalitarian," and this egalitarianism, defined as the reign of merit or meritocracy, is allergic to large organizations such as the state and labor unions (which are, incidentally, relatively absent from the leading sectors in technology). Presenting itself as populist, this new elite proposes to workers the status of associates or partners. Participation, in the form of profit-sharing incentives and "participative management," has become a key notion. The new elite is the enemy of any macrosubject that submerges the individual in collective bureaucracy, and of the old class of bosses who were willing to nullify their personalities in exchange for the security and recognition offered by a corporation modeled by business bureaucracy. Most of all, however, this new elite has a new relation to the social and the political. It takes positions on issues of immigration, protectionism, defense, and technology transfer, as well as in debates within the major international organizations.[7]

For the partners of the largely internationalized corporation, acquiring the values specific to the corporate culture becomes more important than learning technical skills. Although the culture respects national specificities, they constitute little more than national subcultures within the matrix of a common culture. This common culture is expressed in the internationalization of life-styles of this new class, which recognizes its peers in any part of the globe.

This new way of conceiving the relation with the corporation did not wait for the "small is beautiful" vogue in order to develop its basic founding features: already in the seventies large organizations such as IBM had been thinking about "the optimal sociomental system" for mobilizing all the resources of the individual. From this perspective, it is interesting to recall the analyses of four French researchers who for more than five years observed the modes in which power was exercised within IBM, already at that time a hypermodern organization.

The most salient feature was the spectacular extension of the power of the economic sphere to the political, ideological, and psychological spheres. At the political level, for example, a dialectic of centralization and decentralization was put into execution: the growing decentralization took place within a growing centralization at the level of rules and strategies. The researchers discovered the ways in which the organization made a deep impact, at the psychological level, on the individual unconscious, and how it restructured the individual's systems of defense. The organization acts both as an anxiety machine (through its objective power, through the state of dependency in which individuals find themselves with respect to it, through its omnipresent system of control) and as a pleasure machine, for it offers certain types of pleasure—mainly sadomasochistic (through the conquest of markets, the possibility of bypassing others in career pursuits, victory over oneself in the pursuit of an inaccessible ideal)—that are in keeping with its logic and protect its members from the anxiety it otherwise maintains. One can speak of a veritable sociomental system, since the policies of the organization and the unconscious structures of the individual are closely intertwined.[8]

This sketch of an often little-known aspect of *Homo deregulatus* pertinently reminds us that in the contemporary world the pleasure principle not only operates in the guise of the desire to consume leisure, but is also the very foundation of the reality principle in the game of destruction and construction of the structures of power on the national and international scenes.

Behind the backs of the prophets of doom, the yuppies are making converts in the Old World. Alain Minc earned from *Business Week* the title of "intellectual leader of the French yuppies." After becoming a top manager of Saint-Gobain, one of the most important French companies nationalized by the Socialist government, Minc asserted that he had turned away from some of the "public service" scruples that were still present in the report he coauthored with Simon Nora in 1978; his diagnosis was clear: "If the French left doesn't adapt itself to the free market, it faces extinction. . . . The future lies with the rebels of the 1960s, or *soixante-huitards*, who in the 1980s are turning their restiveness on the French business establishment. If given the chance, they will be the foundation of an economic revival as they have been in the U.S."[9]

The new hero of the recovery from crisis is the decision maker, whose primary quality is the spirit of enterprise. And according to the editor of the magazine *L'Entreprise*, launched in 1985, such a decision maker has the following "mixture of desires": "that of wager and risk, that of autonomy and responsibility, that of profit and capital, that of innovation and distinction. All these converge toward the taste for change—change as opportunity, as a lever, as a challenge, and as a method."[10]

The corporation, and consequently the particular form of the corporate spirit it inspires, becomes the motor of history. The memory of social struggles fades away as if historical movement had served only to sublimate all the contradictions in this irresistible rise of those "whose most ordinary daily act is to decide."[11]

Youth, a category neglected by theoreticians of the left for decades, with all its connotations—vitality, the spirit of initiative, innovation, the enterprising spirit, audacity, risk, and the taste for gambling—becomes a mythical category. As Barthes would have been the first to say, it makes it possible to see smoothness where in fact there is unevenness and social segregation. It also makes it possible to purify and render innocent the history of successive slides of the generation that began in 1968 with the project of reinventing the world and found itself in the 1980s reinventing the corporation: a generation that reconciled itself with the idols it had smashed. It fell to an American historian, Arno Mayer, to describe this new fascination.

> For French youth, America is today a very attractive country, because of a certain mode of social life and cultural and artistic activity. This is the angle from which Americans have succeeded—perhaps unintentionally—in defusing the anti-Americanism in French youth. And as these young people attain more important positions in your country, they bring in an open-mindedness about American life. This, I think, is one of the phenomena of the post-'68 period. It can be said, of course, and with reason, that 1968, like 1848, was a turning point in history that didn't turn; but there was nonetheless a change, in particular between America and France—their youth, their intellectuals.[12]

Neoliberal History

"History is bunk," declared Henry Ford in 1920. The Fordism to which he gave his name and with which he experimented on auto assembly lines may now be in decline, but his pronouncement about history seems to be faring better.

During a symposium on American documentary drama, Gore Vidal reminded everyone of what they already knew, that is, that history is "what we choose to remember."[13] With the new era opened up by institutionalized deregulation, the new class decided not to remember certain events that made the present what it is. The past is reconstructed from the central planet around which all institutions realign: the market. Explaining why women's wages have risen considerably faster than men's in the United States in the past several years, a University of Chicago economics professor wrote in *Business Week*

> that largely silent market forces, not the political activity that captures so much publicity, have mainly determined the economic position of women in our society. . . . The growth in the employment and earning of women over time is explained mostly by market forces rather than by civil rights legislation, affirmative-action programs or the women's movement. . . . Nor can equal-pay-for-equal-work legislation alone explain the narrowing in the earnings gap between men and women in the past fifteen years. For one thing, this gap also narrowed in countries such as Italy and Japan [*sic*—this is untrue], that did not introduce such legislation.[14]

This "bio-economic" brief for the recognition of the progressive potential of the market was directly intended to justify the Reagan administration's opposition to the Equal Rights Amendment from the beginning of Reagan's first term—opposition that set off active protest from the women's movement. Deregulation means the retreat of law, for law is what is considered oppressive. Less state, less legislation, more market means investing one's confidence in spontaneity. By one of those curious tricks history often plays, here we have an economic determinist position claimed not by orthodox Marxists but by their adversaries, the heirs of Adam Smith!

And that is only the tip of the iceberg. History is the history of facts and "a fact is a fact." The old principles of positivism are making a strong comeback. The idea of a society epistemologically assimilated to nature is taking root, mixing together archaism and postmodernity, reappropriating the old metaphysics of Auguste Comte, the biological organicism of Durkheim, the social-Darwinist model of "the survival of the fittest" in "the struggle for life," and the cybernetic model. The law of the state (which is—we often forget—that of its agoras) and of human action are delegitimized to the benefit of natural laws, that is, invariable ones, independent of human will and action.

Society, thus conceived in this natural order, selects the institutions best adapted to its welfare. There is no need to intervene, since natural selection operates in this area too, and here too, "the best man wins."

Just as a fact is a fact, a factual assessment is not a value judgment. This debate not only mobilizes the different schools of sociological and economic thought; it concerns just as much the different philosophical conceptions of information. It revitalizes the idea of the transparence of media systems. A fact is a fact: information is facts in the material form in which we recognize them. This neat logic, which has the charm of simplicity, is based on a total refusal to admit that information is first of all a production of meaning rather than the exhibition of a discovered object. One has to subscribe to the idea that individual freedoms blossom on the great tree of a society located under the sign of peaceful, ahistorical relations in order to acknowledge as legitimate the idea of freedom of communication defined by nature as transparent and given *a priori*, obliterating the weight of symbolic violence, or material violence, in human relations.

Free Flow and Self-Regulation

Since 1970, the American state administration and American business circles have not ceased to proclaim that if there is one rule that must govern relations among nations, it is that of the "free flow of information." This doctrine, born at the end of World War II, accompanied the international expansion of American power which, having emerged from the war with increased economic and military might, gave up protectionism and set itself up as the leader of the "free world." This doctrine of the free flow of information complemented the related doctrine of the free flow of capital, commodities, and resources.[15]

The 1970s were particularly fertile in questionings of this doctrine, which claimed universal application. New nations, emerging from processes of decolonization or liberation, retorted to the United States that the freedom of one nation ends where the freedom of the others begins. Borrowing the expression used by Rosa Luxemburg in the 1920s, a delegate from India, during one of the many debates on the free flow of information that took place throughout the decade, demonstrated the limits of the liberal sophism by declaring: "Free flow is like a free fox among free chickens!" For if everyone is equal before this doctrine, the existence of major imbalances and the realities of the balance of forces among nations, signify that some nations are freer than others. But this argument was advanced to no avail. The U.S. government, after a short eclipse, decided—or threatened—to pull out of all the international organizations that challenged the doctrine of free flow. It broke with UNESCO, the institution that had served as main host to the Third World countries expressing such a challenge.

Whether we like it or not, we can no longer pose the question of international communication systems in the same way we did before the demands of the South appeared on the international scene. In this respect we are in full agreement with the British professor James Halloran, who has written,

> In some quarters it is now suggested that UNESCO research should be shifted away from such questions as "the right to communicate" to "more concrete problems." But what are these "concrete problems"? The same as, or similar to, the safe, "value-free," micro-questions of the old-time positivists who served the system so well whether they realized it or not? All this represents a definite and not very well disguised attempt to turn the clock back to the days when the function of research was to serve the system as it was, and not to question, challenge or attempt to improve it. This then is the political arena in which mass communications research operates. It is not that research has suddenly become politicized; it is more a question of the emergence of a balance, as *latently politicized* research is challenged by the more *overtly politicized* development.[16]

In this context it is impossible to divide the participants in this dispute along an East-West axis. For if, in these debates, the Soviet Union was able to back the demands of the Third World in contesting the free flow in the name of the necessity of closing its borders, it was quite reticent when certain representatives of nongovernmental organizations from both the Third World and the large industrialized countries maintained the necessity of accompanying the rebalancing of the flow of information in the world with its internal counterpart, that is, the right to different social groups constituting each nation to communicate freely as well. The diatribes of the U.S. representatives against the new concepts of "popular communication," "alternative communication," "communication at the grassroots," and "horizontal communication," accused of comforting international communism, were matched by the suspicions of the Soviets, who returned to the slogans of "the infantile malady of spontaneism," that old ruse of capital.

Behind the American criticism lay a proposal for a neoliberal alternative in international cooperation. As William Harley wrote, defining the views of the U.S. Department of State, "The divorce from UNESCO may well foster a greater willingness on the part of the U.S. business and industry interests to support communications development projects." He further noted that "the U.S. government has recently established in the

State Department a new Office of Private Sector Initiatives."[17] And that was quite logical. For what the debates on the new international order of information teach us is that, far from concerning only the U.S. state administration, they have mobilized the entire industrial, media, and advertising establishment of the United States. This is one more confirmation of the fact that the industrial actor today must make his voice heard in matters in which he is not traditionally competent.[18]

One cannot interpret the U.S. decision without taking into account the counterstrategy of privatization that consecrates the rise of a new full-fledged actor on the international scene: large private corporations. This way of destabilizing the idea of democratic representativeness on the international scale — on the pretext that debates must not become excessively politicized — is coherent with the process of deregulation. The market and its law are put forward as a replacement for politics. The principle of self-regulation of the market is counterposed to the principle of establishing the rule of international law over international relations of information and communication.

At the center of thought about free flow is an implicit postulate: the nonexistence of power relations in the planning and development of the world. Until the end of the 1960s, this doctrine had been tempered by welfare-state policies of assistance and international cooperation. With the philosophy of the market ("trade, not aid"), it reveals itself in a stark light. Economic macrosubjects become the natural elements of the postindustrial universe. If, in the sixties, they committed abuses of power, and if they plotted against certain popular regimes, these were only youthful sins. Now that they have reached adulthood, they have acquired the discipline of habit, indistinguishable from the discipline of the market. Having acquired this naturelike character, they lose the character of historical agents of a certain mode of accumulation of capital and thus of a particular model of development.

Who can deny that there has been a change in the relations between transnational corporations and the nation-states and civil societies of the countries where they establish themselves? American capital is no longer the only one active on the international scene. The other large industrialized countries have their own transnational corporations. The Third World, which many thought of as a compact economic reality, has become fragmented, revealing within it a number of relatively privileged countries and a great mass of the hungry. And the "new industrialized countries" also have a few transnationals, which serve to discredit the idea of a bipolar world.

The countries that continue to be mired in misery have been given a star to follow. Commenting on the remarks of President Reagan about the rise of a "new model of development." *Fortune* magazine wrote in 1981,

President Reagan surely had Hong Kong and Singapore in mind when he pointed out in a recent speech that "the developing countries now growing the fastest in Asia, Africa and Latin America are the very ones providing more economic freedom for their people—freedom to choose, to own property, to work at a job of their own choice, and to invest in a dream of the future." The private enterprise approach to development is not just ideological fetishism. It is the only approach that has worked.[19]

All means are fair for praising the market and its regulation of inequalities at the national as well as the international level. But the new industrial countries usually cited as examples are not exactly models in which the state has dropped off ballast, whether one considers Taiwan, South Korea, Brazil, or Singapore. An omnipresent state has been the great helmsman of the technological and scientific takeoffs of these countries, often at the price of a muzzled opposition or even bloody repression.

The celebration of market discipline and the idea that the large transnational firms practice self-regulation purposely mask the struggles between these firms and their host countries, which since 1970 have marked the forced (and never natural) regulation of these major actors of international capitalism's model of development.[20] It is indeed because in India and Brazil, the state, scientists, and professionals as well as civil society groups have imposed the norms of a strategy of recovery of industrial capacity on the large transnationals dealing in the technology of information that these nations have been able to become producers and exporters of microcomputers and even, already, certain data-bank systems. And it is certainly not the principle of self-regulation that forced the transnational firm Nestlé to regulate its advertising campaigns for infant formula. The idea of spontaneous regulation is in fact denied by the transnational firms themselves, because they confess to having learned lessons from their struggles with the movements of protest against their abuses.[21]

The discourse of crisis favors a view of the Third World as a group of nations whose external debt has brought them to their knees and forced them to capitulate. The idea that the Third World no longer makes demands or starts conflicts draws strength from this image. But this view is negated every day in reality. The average inhabitant of the Third World experiences the weight of these firms in a concrete, tangible way.

The debates that have taken place since 1970 about the strategies of transnational firms in the field of information and communication have left us with an important theoretical lesson. Today, the transnational model of development is more than the sum of the individual transnationals. As these firms—all national origins included—become integrated into national environments and into specific social fabrics, the terrains of mediation and negotiation shift about in an incessant war of position provoked by the internationalization of economies and modes of life. Today, the transnational model of development is increasingly a structure borne by multiple actors with crossing alliances, in which the private sector and the public sector, national capital and international capital, combine their roles to redefine the nation-state. The state maintains its power of management and at the same time becomes a transit zone for strategies of power and counterpower which either transcend it or simply no longer recognize it as a perimeter of reference. We concede that Daniel Bell perceives this point clearly when he writes, "What is happening today is that for many countries, the national state is becoming too big for the small problems of life and too small for the big problems of life."[22]

Security versus Market Freedom

Beneath the lines traced by the carefree and adventurous paths of the liberated market one can distinguish the familiar topography of the military macrosubject.

The idea of national security weighs much more heavily on the future of communications systems than one might gather from the discourse about the electronization of daily life. In that pioneering French document, the Nora-Minc report, the question of national security is largely eluded, the two authors having been content to treat the civil by-products of the development of information technologies. At most, they allude to the imperative of national security as representing a limit in defining and circumscribing the individual's right to information. National security here becomes the argument of authority from which it is no longer possible to demand the protection of an individual right.

On the other hand, in the report that American experts see as the equivalent for their country to the Nora-Minc report in France, a full chapter is dedicated to national security. Of the six major objectives proposed for an American strategy in the area of international telecommunications, two mention national security: "To assure the free flow of information worldwide, subject only to the most compelling national security and personal privacy limitations" and "To assure that the necessary growth of the national security, public service, and commercial interests of the U.S.A. occurs in a manner commensurate with the U.S. leadership role in the world."[23]

Commenting on this report, British political scientist M. Naraine remarked quite correctly that "national security is the crux of the problem." It concerns not only the free flow of news, but especially the circulation of commodities and technologies of information. "For a very long time," Naraine continues,

> national security has only been conceived of in terms of territorial integrity, in spatial terms. However, when the "information revolution" is perceived as a threat to the structure of societies such that the ideological and social foundations are in jeopardy, then this becomes an issue of national security and states are justified in taking preventive action.[24]

"The East-West conflict is replacing the politics of markets," noted a German expert in 1985,[25] commenting on the competition between the project of a technological Europe (the Eureka project) and the SDI (Strategic Defense Initiative, dubbed "Star Wars"), promoted by President Reagan.[26] Military strategies thus tend to explode the theoretical purity of neoliberalism. One would have to have a bad memory to see in the American communication and information industry merely a leisure-oriented activity. With the setting up of a new system of strategic defense using detective satellites and "killer" satellites, powerful lasers and electromagnetic cannons, space radars and spatial command systems, communication and time control, the entire genesis of the information industry calls itself back to our memory.[27] American industry built its power on the rediscovery of the industry-defense-university troika and on the certainty that the state as federator always had a major role to play. A further certainty is that in strategies for recovery from economic crisis via high technology, the most promising sector for electronics remains—in spite of the media boom—the industry of electronic warfare.

The idea of national security serves to remind us that, in state practices in the area of communication and information, two logics combine effectively. The first has reference to the image of a strong state, in which new technologies of information allow the state to strengthen and modernize its apparatuses of internal and external security. The second puts forward the image of a weak state, in the process of effacement, delegating more and more of its public functions to private actors.

In the East as well as in the West, the security imperative tends to constitute a natural component of the apparatus of international production and dissemination of information. Not only do we note a generalized and obsessive fear of total war, but the proliferation throughout the world of regional or local wars multiplies the number of territories where it is difficult to distinguish rumor from fact.

In the East: the occupation of Afghanistan by Soviet troops upset, in its own fashion, the fragile equilibrium of international press agencies since December 1979. More and more, journalists and reporters depend on what are identified in news bulletins by the euphemism "Western diplomatic sources." Since information is under the control of military authorities, the only sources on which the correspondents of the large international agencies can base their stories are those that filter through the personnel of Western embassies in Kabul, Islamabad, or New Delhi. As a journalist of the *International Herald Tribune* noted in May 1985, "Many reporters in Southern Asia have become suspicious of the figures supplied in the regular briefing by Western diplomats, particularly those originating in remote areas of Afghanistan."[28] Some examples:

> In November, 1982, Western diplomatic sources in New Delhi reported a major disaster in the Salang Pass tunnel through the Hindu Kush mountains in northern Afghanistan. Witnesses were quoted as saying that more than 700 Soviet soldiers and 400 Afghan civilians had died in an explosion, and that as many as 2,700 people might have been killed. The story, emphasizing the death toll, received wide attention in the international press. A month later, the Western diplomatic sources scaled down the casualty total to 350.

And in the West: in October 1983, during the invasion of the island of Grenada, the American military authorities, openly renouncing the application of the principle of the free flow of information, made the unilateral decision to prevent the press from having access to the island. For nearly a week, the Pentagon released a great deal of information that it hastened to deny a few days later.[29] The conflicts in Central America offer a more durable example. How many items of international news, repeated throughout the world in newspapers, on television, and on the radio, have emanated from broadcasting units set up in Honduras, Costa Rica, or Belize and whose deliberate intention has been to disseminate propaganda against the Sandinista regime in Nicaragua or the guerilla movement in El Salvador? This panorama is even more elaborate since the U.S. government's launching of an anti-Castro radio station based in Florida, Radio Marti,[30] under the auspices of the U.S. governmental radio, the Voice of America. This propaganda station was born in 1985 in spite of pressure from the powerful lobby of commercial radio stations in the U.S. who feared that in reprisal, Havana would interfere with the wavelengths of private stations in the southeastern part of the country. Once again, the market had a brutal encounter with propaganda battles and the logic of war, this time in the form of a war of the airwaves.[31]

One might think these are exceptions that prove the rule. But in liberal capitalist societies, such crisis strategies, such exceptional situations of disinformation in which the norms of psychological warfare prevail over the application of the liberal doctrine of information, are growing in number. In the name of national security, pockets of exception, in which the state influences the functioning of the laws of the free market, are appearing more and more, poking liberal-capitalist normality full of holes.

[Authors' note: These analyses, as we have already noted above, were written in 1986. Clearly the collapse of "real socialism" that has shaken the Soviet superpower has changed the terms of the problem. Thus Zbigniew Brzezinski could write, in December 1990, "Washington is the only superpower," challenging those who think that the concept of superpower is dead and that the new world order will be multipolar, with no hegemonic power.

The geopolitical schema that presided over the launching of "Star Wars" is dead indeed, but the new danger—the multiplication of "midintensity conflicts" or regional wars—is more present than ever as the 1990s begin, as witnessed by the first international conflict of the post-Cold War era: the war of the Persian Gulf. This type of conflict will very likely generate favorable conditions for the development of new forms of war propaganda and psychological warfare. This will be particularly true if the North-South cleavage resulting from the immense gap between the "haves" and the "have-nots," replaces the East-West bipolar relation.]

PART 5

The Refuge of the Dialectic?

Introduction to Part 5

The contemporary rise of certain postindustrial currents of thought goes hand in hand with the idea that if macrosubjects are disappearing from the horizon of the great high-technology countries, they nonetheless continue to mold realities and attitudes in the so-called underdeveloped zones. Hence the idea, usually implicit but sometimes made explicit, that the dialectical theory that accompanied the formation of macrosubjects (the state and social classes) is no longer valid except in societies where state and class have not yet been "metabolized," because these societies have not yet transcended the prehistorical phase of the formation of individual and collective identity. "Our" Western countries have complex new topologies of individuality. Those "other" places have infinitely simpler topologies, proper to the era of development and to a history oriented toward a goal to be reached and in which the "masses" are still present on the scene.

This kind of thinking represents an important variation from the first conceptions of postindustrial society. Daniel Bell and Zbigniew Brzezinski have both built their vision of the international field on the notion of interdependence. This notion, invented by American political science, is intimately linked to strategies of legitimation of state policies; it is eminently geopolitical, for it served to sweep the idea of inequality from the universe of references in international relations. It also served to nullify the notions of imperialism and colonization, which are relegated to an earlier, "pretechnetronic" or industrial era, and thus to place all the different nations on an equal footing of mutual and reciprocal dependence.

Ever since the emergence of the concepts of postindustrial society, "technetronic society," the "information society," and the like, American political science had in fact insisted on pointing out that the scientific and technical revolution marked the end of the idea of imperialism, or at least that imperialism the United States was blamed for practicing. Zbigniew Brzezinski, creator of the concept of "technetronic society," wrote at the end of the sixties that

> the concept of "imperial" shields rather than reveals a relationship between America and the world that is both more complex and more intimate. The "imperial" aspect of the relationship was, in the first instance, a transitory and rather spontaneous response to the vacuum created by World War II and to the subsequent felt threat from communism. . . . It is the novelty of America's relationship with the world—complex, intimate, and porous—that the more orthodox, especially Marxist, analyses of imperialism fail to encompass. To see that relationship merely as the expression of an imperial drive is to ignore the part played in it by the crucial dimension of the technological-scientific revolution.[1]

The era of the strategy of domination by the gunboat was thus placed in a museum display case. The strategy of commercial and financial domination would soon be nothing more, Brzezinski claimed, than a memory. With information technologies, the era of the so-called third generation of world networks had begun.

15

The Crisis of the Paradigms

"Here" and "There"

The idea of a split between the developed world and the Third World could only have been reborn in Europe, and particularly in Latin Europe, in the context of the crisis of the intellectuals, which affects all relations between the latter and the other social groups and classes.

More than a decade now separates us from the moment when Michel Foucault wrote the following in *Les Cahiers du cinéma*:

> A battle is now occurring for history and around history, and it is very interesting. . . . Popular struggles, until 1968, were folklore. For certain people, they were not even a part of their immediate system of current reality. After 1968, all popular struggles, whether they occurred in South America or in Africa, have found an echo, a resonance. No longer can the separation, the geographical cordon sanitaire, be established.[1]

In ten years, this "geographical cordon sanitaire" Foucault sought to revoke seems to have insidiously reestablished itself. The link he sought to point out between "here" and "there" has dissolved into the idea of a gap between what is happening "here" and what is happening "there" — between what one thinks and does "here" and what one thinks and does "there."

A wind of ethnocentrism is blowing over the West. Some might seek to justify this by saying: an eye for an eye, a tooth for a tooth; in other words, the new mood is simply the legitimate response to the rise of ethnocentric violence committed by all manners of fundamentalists. Who has forgotten the crowd on the runway of the Beirut airport, fists raised, in front of the TWA airliner taken hostage in July, 1985, chanting "Death to the Americans"? Who has forgotten the interview with the spokesman for the Lebanese Shi'ite fundamentalists who defied, all at once, imperialism, Marxism, and the "white superman"?[2]

We have here the image of a Third World that deliberately flees all terrains of negotiation and closes itself into forms of radicalism that exclude any mutual understanding. It is such an excessive image that it justifies the end of Western guilt feelings (an end that in any case did not wait for these events in order to manifest itself). In the meantime, caught between political apocalypses and the great paternalistic gestures provoked by natural disasters, the image of the Third World in the West bears very little relation to the thought the Third World produces about its own experience. And this misunderstanding is felt more and more painfully by the Other. For example, at the end of a press conference at the Cannes film festival in 1985, María Luisa Bamberg, scriptwriter of the Argentinian film *The Official Story* (directed by Luis Puenzo), anticipated the reproach that no one would ever have formulated against her but which seemed implicit in this sort of debate about Third World film productions.

> Film is divided by zones. The disaster zones speak of their disaster; the zones of peace allow themselves the luxury of art and metaphysics. We leave metaphysics and anguish of the soul to Bergman. We who are threatened, persecuted, diminished, we Latin Americans, must speak of what is threatening, diminishing, or persecuting us. But from this standpoint, people continue to treat us as "natives" and have doubts about whether we have a soul. We, too, have a soul and we want to talk about it. We are not just the spectators of the soul of the rich countries.[3]

Many elements conspire against the comprehension of that face of the Third World: the ideologies of retreat nourished by economic crisis; the old fear of the disorderly demographics of the proletarians of the world; the refusal of the South as embodied in their representatives in our countries, the immigrants; the logics of reindustrialization policies that tighten the bonds between the major countries controlling the most advanced technologies; the realities of competition in international markets, in which the presence of young industries of certain Third World countries, in particular the "new industrial countries," perturbs the old equilibria of a West that had long benefited from a highly favorable situation; and the theoreticians of the "information society" who explain the evolution of the world by the determinism of science and technology and point out that it is henceforth improbable for the Third World to assume the function of a critical subject.[4]

But what contributes above all to misunderstanding the Third World is an interpretation of international relations according to a reductive schema in which the coherence of the overall situation is derived from the planetary confrontation between totalitarianism and democracy. Gone is the subtlety that had earlier inspired thinkers such as the Socialisme ou Barbarie group.

With the rise of ethnocentrism, not only the history of struggles is rendered mute; silence is also maintained about the genesis of the notions that had allowed the actors of this history to identify the breaks that have marked the past thirty years. Where there was diversity, a certain West saw a homogeneous whole. This led to the creation of the notion of underdevelopment, which can only be imagined by those who consider themselves developed.

Modernization

The notion of underdevelopment was not born in university research groups but in the White House, where it was unveiled in the midst of much publicity by President Truman in 1949, in a speech that has gone down in history as "Point Four." At that time, the U.S. government was asserting that poverty played into the hands of Communism. (An entire sector of the American establishment still affirms this. The hawks never believed it.) It was therefore necessary to support governments threatened by liberation movements of a new type. The notion of underdevelopment was first conceived as a means for mobilizing public opinion, financial resources, and brain power. But it did not become operational until 1957, eight years later. Europe had had its Marshall Plan; the Third World was to have its Agency for International Development (USAID), which designated Latin America as its primary field of action. In 1959, when Fidel Castro marched into Havana, things began to accelerate. In 1962, the Alliance for Progress inaugurated by President Kennedy undertook explicitly to stop the threat of the violent, Cuban-style alternative. By financing modernization plans in the areas of health, education, urban planning, and agriculture, the American state assumed the role of a welfare state in the international arena. The birth certificate of the notion of underdevelopment was thus a political one, in the narrowest sense of the term. It was only later that it acquired a scientific content.

It was in this precise context that the theory of modernization appeared and deeply influenced perceptions of the evolution of communication systems.

The concept of "modernity" was born in direct opposition to that of "tradition." It was also constructed on another bipolarity: folk versus urban, which in turn may suggest the opposition popular culture versus mass culture. Development, a synonym of social change, is precisely the passage from the traditional pole to the modern one.

The seminal work was that of Daniel Lerner, *The Passing of Traditional Society*, published in 1958. It was to be followed by other classics: David McClelland's *The Achieving Society* (1961); *Communication and Political Development*, edited by Lucian Pye (1963); and Wilbur Schramm's *Mass Media and National Development* (1964). Little known in Europe (none has been fully translated into French), they were broadly disseminated throughout the Third World.

The economic and cultural references attached to the poles of tradition and modernity are well known. Less simple to grasp are the political connotations attached to these poles. It is interesting in this regard to return to Lerner's book. Like many American sociologists and anthropologists, Lerner joined the psychological warfare division of the U.S. Army during World War II, becoming chief editor in the intelligence section. Unlike other social scientists, Herbert Marcuse above all, who took their distance from this framework once the hostilities were over, Lerner attempted to draw theoretical lessons from the experience of psychological warfare. In 1949 he published *Sykewar*, and undertook for the Voice of America a broad research project that led him to most of the Middle Eastern countries as well as Greece and Germany. *The Passing of Traditional Society* is the result of his analysis of 1600 interviews performed in Turkey, Lebanon, Egypt, Syria, Jordan, and Iran.[5] It was a study of audiences, intended to test the comparative popularity of the Voice of America, the BBC, and the Soviet radio stations. It classified the populations according to three strata: the moderns, the transitionals, and traditionals. In the Middle East, affected by the Mossadegh revolution and the Nasser regime, the transitionals appeared to Lerner to offer the alternative of a different path to social change. The continuity with his earlier work, *Sykewar*, was clear, since the three categories he used to classify the targets of psychological war during World War II are also adapted to the necessity of identifying the targets of social modernization. As Rohan Samarajiwa of Sri Lanka has noted:

> The threefold classification of Middle Eastern populations into "moderns," "transitionals," and "traditionals" was analogous to the German classification. The moderns were similar to the anti-Nazi categories; they were already converted. The traditionals were the Middle East's equivalent of the 35 per cent of the German population identified as Nazis. The transitionals, like the unpoliticals, were pinpointed as the most likely to yield the greatest return on propaganda effort.[6]

In the international context of the Cold War that prevailed at the time when modernization theory appeared in the field of communication, one's attitude toward the United States or the Soviet Union indicated, respectively, one's disposition to modernity or to the traditional. Harold Lasswell, one of the founders of the science of communication in the United States, wrote in 1952:

> Research on communication has its most direct function to fulfill by modifying the attention structure of the non-Soviet world at strategic points. . . . A common frame of world attention . . . will clarify the identity of genuine allies and enemies in the actual and potential alignments that arise in the building of a united body politic for the free world.[7]

This brief reference to the first work that drew a relation between the notions of modernity (or its synonym, development) and that of communication is valid both for history on a small scale and history on a grand scale.

Initiated at a time when the U.S. was preoccupied by a Middle East in movement, the theory of modernization was to find a privileged field of application in Latin America. Another pioneering work of the time was by Everett Rogers, trained in economics at the University of Chicago. After Lerner's borrowings from political science, Rogers used elements of industrial marketing that had begun to prove their effectiveness in the great metropolitan countries. It was in 1962, and in Spanish, that his work on the diffusion of innovations appeared.[8]

With the theory of diffusion, more commonly referred to as diffusionism, the concept of innovator makes its entry. The definition of an innovator was purely nominal and tautological: the innovator is the person who first adopts or utilizes an innovation, not the person who produces it. An innovation is defined by Rogers as an "idea, practice or object perceived as new by an individual." This is the concept that made it possible to classify individuals according to five categories, whether they live in Latin America, Asia, or the United States: the innovators, the early adopters, the early majority, the late majority, and the laggards. Mechanically superimposed onto extremely diverse agrarian structures, this concept suggested a society in which belonging to a class or group disappeared in favor of a set of personality profiles, more or less favorable or resistant to change. With the theory of diffusion, the ideology of modernity penetrated into projects of agrarian development, community organization, literacy campaigns, family planning, public health policy, and the like.

The experts in diffusionism elaborated strategies for causing people to adopt "positive values and attitudes," these terms being synonymous with change and progress, associated in turn with technology, science, rationality, cosmopolitanism, and empathy. At the same time that they tried to sell a modern personality, they also prepared markets for the mechanization of the countryside and the reduction of family size, while also surveying the reproduction of labor power.

A reply to this diffusionist idea of communication-development, defined according to the power of the sender and the one-way direction of the sender-receiver relation, was offered by a Brazilian organizer of literacy campaigns, Paulo Freire. At the beginning of the sixties, Freire made his reply by setting up educational activities whose aim was to bring the learner to express him- or herself. Freire's pedagogy, which had and continues to have a great impact, first in Brazil and later in the rest of Latin America, the United States, Europe, and Portuguese-speaking Africa, is based on a refusal to view education as a "lever to progress." It embodies a refusal of the idea of modernization in vogue in American-inspired sociology—that is, the opposition between a "closed" society and an "open" one, between a "traditional" society and a "modern" one—an opposition in which the constituents of the definition of one of the terms are obtained by a simple formal negation of the other.[9]

One cannot understand this current of thought and action unless one links it to the history of the Brazilian Catholic left. As early as 1962, during the populist government of João Goulart, the Popular Culture Movement undertook a vast literacy campaign among adults in the Nordeste, the poorest region of Brazil, which at that time had 16 million illiterates out of 25 million inhabitants. The program directed by Freire mobilized an important sector of committed teachers and students in the National Student Union as well as the Movement of Education at the Base supported by the Brazilian episcopate. This movement was only one expression of a host of questions and initiatives that were beginning to interest numerous Christian groups at this time. It was also in this cultural and political context that the basic principles of liberation theology were elaborated in Brazil and other Latin American countries. It would take twenty years for the authorities of the Vatican to become worried about the subversive effects of this "new doctrine" of a poor people's church, suspected of having gone Marxist. The post-aggiornamento church, caught in the ready-made schemas of thought about East versus West, considers that it is not poverty but indoctrination that plays into the hands of communism.

In 1976, Everett Rogers, the pioneer of diffusionist theory mentioned above, published an article entitled "Communication and Development: The Passing of the Dominant Paradigm,"[10] in which he confessed the bankruptcy of the theoretical and practical approach inspired by diffusionism and noted the rise of new models of development inspired by the idea of self-reliance or endogenous, self-centered development. A number of new references dotted this text—Paulo Freire, Mao Tse-tung and others—and so the page was turned. The abandonment of the diffusionist conception, characterized as centralizing and command-oriented, and of the linear model of "persuasive" communication, occurred to the benefit of a new model, called the convergence model. According to a former student of Rogers, "The unilateral communication of persuasion corresponds to the old model of development, while the model of convergence is better suited to the theoretical conception of new development, conceived as participation, self-fulfillment and justice."[11] Dialogical communication and participatory communication became the new key notions. To feedback was added "feed-forward," which means that messages must be elaborated starting from the needs expressed by the people themselves.

For the first time, representatives of American functionalism recognized signs of a crisis of dominant categories, and this recognition grew out of direct experiences in the Third World.

However, these converts from the dominant paradigm did not now pose questions about power any more than they had before. Noting the potential of new microtechnologies of communication, they extrapolated their decentralizing virtues to the totality of social relations, confusing decentralization with the redistribution of power and interpersonal exchange of information with democracy. Having begun with the theory of diffusionism, born out of strategies of persuasion in industrial mass marketing, they followed an evolution toward increasingly personalized and participatory forms, according great importance to "response"—that is, the return of the receiver's reactions to the sender. This no doubt explains why the new paradigm continues to speak of these receivers as "clients"; the problem is to help them determine their own needs and formulate their demands for technology. It need hardly be added that this revision of the paradigm has gone well beyond the framework of the academic community and spread toward the large development agencies of the American state, in particular USAID. Here is one more opportunity to note how the principle of "small is beautiful" was incorporated very early into reformulated strategies of imperial power.

Dependency

One notion definitely failed to survive the recent epistemological ruptures: the notion of cultural imperialism. Not a rigorously defined concept, this notion, which appeared at the end of the sixties as the result of an alliance of engaged intellectuals on three continents,[12] was above all a mobilizing notion intended to orient a certain kind of analysis of the new types of relationships between cultures in an economy in the process of globalization; it thereby brought a new dimension to classic studies of the relations between metropolises and their former colonies.[13]

At the time, to speak of cultural imperialism was to break with the economistic tradition of an international workers' movement that was quick to condemn any attempt to place culture before economics, consciousness before infrastructure. The notion drew support from Che Guevara's condemnations of socialist realism in the early sixties as well as from the idea of cultural revolution, which intrigued the nonorthodox lefts throughout the world. It also echoed Frantz Fanon's analyses, as prefaced by Jean-Paul Sartre, and was not unrelated to the black movement in the United States.

Some people believed erroneously—and still do—that the notion of cultural imperialism descends directly from the Leninist theory of the imperialism of finance capital. We may surprise a number of people by revealing that it owes perhaps just as much, in both its virtues and its faults, to Keynesianism as to Leninism. Factors of a psychological nature that have historically propelled expansionisms in their cultural domination drew the attention of Keynes more than that of Lenin.[14] In any event, the notion of cultural imperialism at its origin had more to do with the anthropologists' notions of ethnocentrism and ethnocide than with economic theory.

The notion of cultural imperialism had the merit of helping to open new fronts of resistance by artists and intellectuals in the Third World countries, particularly in Latin America. It interested the young Latin American film industry, which was struggling against an unbalanced and segregative system of international distribution. It interested sociologists, economists, anthropologists, and educators who were in the process of breaking with the functionalist ideology of science. In the sciences of communication, this notion was just as important in the analysis of international balances of forces as the concept of internationalization of communications systems and cultural industries would become ten years later in critical research circles in Europe, particularly in France.

If Latin America and other regions of the Third World—India, for example—were sensitive to the notion of the international balance of forces starting in the late sixties, this was not only because of political radicalization. It was also because, earlier than other regions, they experienced the challenge posed by the arrival of new technologies. Indeed, it was at the end of the sixties that the question of satellites was raised openly in Latin America and India. As the promoters of these projects noted, experiments in developing countries would help to accumulate knowledge that could be used in developed countries as well as elsewhere in the Third World:

Even if these experiments being proposed to India and Brazil have different objectives, dimensions and costs, they will hopefully be able to furnish the necessary approach to the operationalizing of satellite systems for the developed and developing countries. The future of these systems depends on the result of these studies and other, similar studies. All the errors, deficiencies and successful accomplishments must be recorded if the results are to be really beneficial to the planning, conception, development and establishment of future systems.[15]

The notion of cultural imperialism was not without its faults, of course. It has been criticized for laying too much stress on the sender and not enough on the receivers. It has especially been criticized for having emphasized a single actor on the international scene—the macrosubject known as the United States—thereby sheltering from criticism power practices *within* Third World countries. But to condemn the notion for having allowed this is to fail to understand the close relation it had to the vast movement of critical theoretical production that developed starting in the sixties and took shape around dependency theory.[16]

Dependency theory, an original contribution of Latin America, was the first attempt by Latin American social sciences to refute the postulates of functionalist sociology and the neoclassical school of economics, which eluded the historical dimension of development and underdevelopment. It was thus the first attempt to interpret the total reality of a subcontinent from an autochthonous point of view. Born in Brazil and Chile, it was criticized precisely for having generalized its hypotheses to the heterogeneous whole of Latin America and for having transposed its models of interpretation to other continents.[17]

Dependency theory was also held responsible for its tendency to privilege the international element as the single actor of the transnationalization of economies, minimizing the role of the host society. It should be noted, however, that this tendency to focus on international macrostructures is not attributable only to dependency theory. It has been pointed out, with good reason, that the theory of the development of the capitalist world-economy, elaborated by Immanuel Wallerstein, falls into a similar trap. Reducing the state to a mere instrument and defining it as a synthetic fabrication reflecting the needs of social forces at work in the capitalist world-economy (as Wallerstein might put it)[18] implies unmediated domination by the economy in which politics is instrumentalized. Once the twentieth-century state is portrayed as an economic superinstitution, there is no more room for a conception of the state as a place of mediation and negotiation among social actors, national and local, with divergent interests and projects. (We refer the reader to our earlier exposition, in part IV, of the difficulty of articulating the different levels of reality.)

The major criticism that can be addressed to many analyses inspired by the theory of dependency is thus their imprisonment within political economies that pay little attention, in fact, to politics and neglect the analysis of social classes, systems of power, and state systems. As a Brazilian anthropologist has noted,

> It may not be too farfetched to state that the basic dualism of dependency theory and the poverty of its political approach largely derive from an "economistic" view of the social process which considers economic development as an essentially quantitative type of phenomenon and, in a sense, as a "natural" one. In this sense, the concept of dependency appears to work in a way quite similar to the concept of modernization, as used in North American political science. Between the center and the periphery, between dominant and dominated countries, there flows the stream of economic development: some will catch it, others will block its course; it will be available to some, but not to all. To go beyond dependency is seen as a synonym for "having another chance" at development, just as the overcoming of traditionalism is the indispensable condition for becoming "modern." Among the few "dependentist" authors who manage to escape the poverty of its political theory are F. H. Cardoso in his work on social classes and the state and economist Celso Furtado in his most recent formulations.[19]

For Chilean economist Gonzalo Arroyo this economic reductionism explains why cultural and popular resistance have been of very little interest to the economic and political research marked by this particular idea of dependency. Arroyo writes, "The analysis of the historical process, especially popular social movements—the way they constitute, structure, and express themselves, and their ideological, cultural, and religious dimension—has in general been left aside by the economists, sociologists and other intellectuals identified with the dependency current."[20]

And this repressed dimension is precisely what returned with the crisis of the dilemma between revolution and reformism in left-wing political thought and led to a new critical observation of the plurality of new historical subjects closer to the base, more "popular," closer to concrete collective groups, and closer to the daily experience of oppression and injustice than the traditional parties and trade-union organizations had been.

Between the moment when the notions of dependency and cultural imperialism appeared and the new phase, there was a long period of incubation during which the Third World was not content to denounce the mechanisms of its international subjection, but actually began to create a more favorable balance of forces in economic negotiations with the economic macrosubjects. This shows, once again, that concepts correspond to states of consciousness. The merit of dependency theory is to have paved the way to the emergence of this new phase.

16

Rediscovering Popular Cultures

The Chilean Popular Unity: Both a Classical and a Modern Experience

The fact that the notion of cultural dependency moved on a separate path from that of popular resistance and popular culture was altogether normal in the sixties, when the Latin American left was torn by contradictory strategies in which the people did not occupy a preponderant place. On the one hand, the far left, inspired by the Cuban revolution, stressed the purely military aspects of the struggle. This was also the time of the theory of revolutionary *focos*, in which an enlightened group thought it could move masses who were normally difficult to mobilize. On the other hand, the workers' parties were convinced of their vanguard role in preparing for the taking of state power. Finally, the dominant conception of politics deliberately rejected the idea of progressively creating a popular hegemony, postponing this until after the revolution. This conception favors what Gramsci called the "war of position" at the expense of the "war of movement," which takes into account the contradictory trends within civil society and the state.

The arrival of the Popular Unity government in Chile in 1970 began to create fissures in this overly solid bloc of convictions. It was a classical process in many ways. It was classical, first, in terms of its actors. The Chilean left reflected the image of the international left. The organization and the history of its workers' parties could be understood in terms of the genesis of the Western workers' movement. In this respect it had nothing in common with its neighbors, Argentina and Bolivia in particular, the former because of its forms of populism, which had reduced the Communist Party to a tiny minority, and the latter because of the strength of the miners' trade-union movement, which affected the whole of civil society. Nor did it have anything in common with Brazil, where populism under Getulio Vargas and João Goulart had deeply marked the political organizations of the right as well as the left.

From another standpoint, however, Chile was no longer classic. The question "What is to be done with the media?", inherited by the left, provided an opportunity to measure just how useless the classical approaches were when the problem became how to find an alternative to the hegemonic media. The Popular Unity faced a bourgeoisie that was, of course, dependent, but also armed with a political intelligence acquired during its long history of managing public affairs in a true representative democracy. For the left, the problem consisted in confronting a bourgeoisie that had remained in place while also accepting the rules of political pluralism. What separated the writings of classic Marxists from the reality experienced by the Chilean people was the fact that mass culture, in its most varied forms, continually made its presence felt in Chile. There could be no question of repeating the experience of Cuba, which had begun to build socialism on an island by sweeping away the existing media, both out of conviction and because its hand was forced by the American embargo. It was even less conceivable to ignore the weight of mass culture and to adopt the conception that prevailed in the countries of "real socialism," where democratization of culture meant access to high culture. What separated the realities of Eastern Europe from those experienced by popular Chile was precisely that the Chilean experience took place in a cultural context in which industrialized culture and a model of democratization of cultural goods via the marketplace had affected collective mentalities, shaping a certain relationship between leisure and work.

The ideological and cultural question thus acquired the highest importance, and it defied the mechanistic approaches according to which ideology and culture were a by-product of the economy. It was necessary to take into account mass culture, which had become an element of everyday culture. For the first time, the question of the contradictions between consciousness and desire, consciousness and taste, appeared, in outline at least, in the debates about the transformation of the forms and contents of the media. As was frequently observed, the people—even in their most mobilized strata—appreciated the products of this culture. There was a contradiction between the political analyses of leaders and intellectuals, who spoke of alienation, and the subjective experience of the consumer.

The strategy put into effect by the right-wing opposition was not dictated to it from outside the country, even if it did owe something to the logistical support of the United States and certain multinational corporations; rather, it grew out of an analysis of the balance of forces among the diverse actors of Chilean society itself. This strategy, combining a broad alliance between the organized groups of businessmen and the professional associations of the petty bourgeoisie, was an eminently modern form of resistance to a socialist project. It was modern because it was based on the defense of the interests of groups in their professional function rather than in terms of a vague sense of belonging to the middle class. It was modern as well precisely because it broke with the idea of an amorphous, passive, depoliticized middle class, pictured as the soft underbelly of mass society.[1] It was indeed the massive presence of this middle class and the diverse interests of the groups composing it that conferred a preponderant significance on the question of culture and ideology.

Three years—1970 to 1973—was a short period historically, but still long enough to raise certain questions that have continued to haunt theories and practices of transformation of the media. Confronted in the sixties with the sources of French structuralism (Althusser, Barthes, Greimas, and others), certain sectors of the left involved in the Chilean process were able to measure the distance between the labor of ideological interpretation and the building of practical alternatives. For the first time in a revolutionary movement, the question of singular, active, and even resistance-oriented interpretations adopted by consumers to counter the unilateral logic of the stimulus-response schema emerged as a crucial issue.

For the first time as well, the difficulty of dissociating form from content became apparent, opening a rift between those who envisioned the alternative merely as a change in content and those who could not conceive of it short of a profound modification of the social relations of production. Soon afterward, the same question would be raised by the European left, during the first experiences of free radio stations (*radios libres*).

After the Chilean Popular Unity experience, it was no longer possible to speak of the history of alternative communication exclusively in terms of the use of the media by liberation movements. Popular Chile provoked thought about their alternative use within the power configuration of a parliamentary democracy.

The Chilean experience was a modern process, but also a classical one. It remained locked within a conceptual framework defined by class and failed to adopt a framework of movement.

New Historical Subjects

The unitary conceptions according to which ideology is a powerful element of aggregation tend to give way today to a multiplicity of ways of seeing the problem, originating from many very different perspectives. What has been defeated in the past few years is the image of state power without fissures or contradictions; much attention is now paid to these fissures and contradictions which, while they ensure the survival of a regime, also expose it, making it visible and vulnerable. This way of stating the problem has become a meeting ground between the "disaster zones" and the "zones of peace," as referred to by the Argentinian filmwriter we quoted above.

Martin Barbero of Colombia has clearly expressed the tensions that had arisen and the theoretical shifts they implied by identifying three points of rupture: the first refutes the left-functionalist view according to which the system reproduces itself inexorably, within and by the social; this traditional left view produces monolithic, instrumentalist conceptions of the state as well as conceptions that attribute a mythical omnipotence, ubiquity, and omniscience to transnational corporations. The second point of rupture sees in the emergence of social movements the expression of a multiplication of contradictions; the third consists in a growing awareness of the activity of the "dominated," not only as accomplices to their domination but also as subjects of a riposte to the discourse of their master.[2]

This questioning echoes another which, in the field of political action, challenges the centrality of the working class, interpreted as the exclusive bearer of historical consciousness. Just as the primacy of the working class and workers' struggles was called into question, so was the generally uncritical acceptance of the modes of industrial development and growth promoted by the most developed nations of the Western world (as well as by the countries of "real socialism"). At the same time there was a questioning of the meaning of "social identity" and "cultural identity"; at the heart of the matter was a questioning of the correspondence between state, nation, and people, but also the identification of the people with a single social actor.

In the seventies, the influence of the structuralist school may well have prevailed (the Althusserian school and the school of semiotics in particular), but in the eighties a more anthropological approach, related to Gramscian thought, distinguishes the various vanguard currents in critical research in Latin America.

The existence of these critical currents should not, however, cause us to forget the increasingly marked influence of systems theory in its different variants. At a time when the intellectual class is undertaking basic redefinitions, the cleavages appearing in Latin America are the same as those found in the debates in Spain, Italy, and France.

No one can deny that these new critical interrogations coexist with collective modes of perception inherited from the classical paradigms that reintroduce into the definition of "the popular" the particularisms of localist and nationalist ideologies. And that is no doubt one of the paradoxes of the present moment.

Nor can it be denied that these new interrogations are affecting groups of very different natures, in every continent on the planet, from the church-affiliated grassroots communities in Latin America to the consumer associations of Southeast Asia. And it is precisely this proliferation of viewpoints and centers of interest that has made possible the emergence of new conceptions of international "interdependence" which, in attempting to move away from the balance of forces among nation-states, bring together the converging interests of civil societies located at very different geopolitical and cultural latitudes.

This new paradigm affects each reality in a specific way. To be convinced of this one can peruse the abundant theoretical production that refers to it, but also the new forms of communication and artistic expression to which this new sensibility gives rise. Regarding reflection on media culture, the personal testimony of Martin Barbero, whom we quoted in part III, provides a good idea of the new fields being opened up to research in this area.

This new sensibility has affected realities in very different types of political regimes, since it is shared (in Latin America, for example) among the movements of opposition to military dictatorships waving the banner of neoliberal capitalism, movements for popular education and communication, ethnic communities in the Andean countries, Christian grassroots communities in Brazil, and intellectual movements in most of the countries in the region.[3] This new sensibility has inspired the activity of numerous actors in the Nicaraguan revolution, torn between the logic of war and the plural logics of democracy, between the reproduction of vertical schemas of agitation and propaganda and the inventiveness of new social movements—ethnic movements, women's movements, Christian movements—that are replacing a narrow notion of the vanguard with the demand for the plurality of democratic subjects.[4]

In the face of the negation of the political embodied in the rise of neoliberal theses in countries such as Chile, where the public exists only in the form of "publics" and advertising targets, the challenge to social movements lies in reconquering the spaces of publicly exercised communitarian sociability and in re-creating a public sphere. This is explained well by the Chilean author José Joaquin Brunner in his essay "Daily Life in Authoritarian Regimes," where the only community allowed is that of the market and its specific interests—a market "which depersonalizes while valuing personal differences." In 1982 he wrote:

All the activities and institutions that create, maintain, and transform public communitarian sociability have come to fulfill a function of generating politics: churches, solidarity activities, trade unions, cultural activities, academic centers, artistic movements and movements of ideas, alternative means of communication, youth and women's groups, human rights activities and institutions, etc. This is what explains the emphasis placed on social movements: it is recognized that under current circumstances party politics does not suffice for completely renovating politics in society. Indeed, the party organizes publicly exercised communitarian sociability but it is without strength when this sociability does not exist, for it is incapable of creating it by itself.[5]

A common concern inspires the multiple expressions of this return to thought about the public sphere: the attention to lived experience and everyday language in the concrete space of the family, in the urban district, in relations within the neighborhood and surrounding area, in religious and secular holidays, in marketplaces and in the multiple manifestations of popular religious sentiment. As Peruvian sociologist Rosa María Alfaro noted, after having completed a critical analysis of the forms of leadership within popular organizations in the urban districts surrounding Lima, inhabited mostly by people of Andean culture and who come from rural zones where Quechua is spoken,

Sports, love relationships, the frustrations of love, encounters and conversations on the doorstep, at the marketplace, at the school gate, at the provincial club, Andean music, festivals, and wakes for the dead—these are things which do not seem to be of much interest to the leaders of popular organizations. This daily universe is expressed according to a different logic, with another language, in other semantics and other means and forms of communication radically different from those proposed by the district [party] organization, which is ever more empty in content.[6]

She concludes: "Understanding the social requires an interpretation of daily life."

Daily life, the current developments of social movements apart from or in the place of political parties, the plurality of subjects and ideologies: these are all expressions of the reconquering of subjectivity in contemporary culture. The developed world has no monopoly on the return to the subject.

Conclusion

The questions society asks about the media changed radically in the 1980s. The configuration of actors who are interested in the media changed as well. There have been new questions, but also new formulations of old ones.

Research activity reflects this evolution. Here and there, new hypotheses are advanced and new fields of thought are proposed. The project of studying the economics of cultural industries is no longer just wishful thinking. Interest in the practices of users has brought new life to the interrogations about the intersubjective processes of communication and the participation of different social actors in the choices of new networks. Renewed inquiry about consumption procedures has made it possible to consider in more depth the idea that the moment of reception is indissociable from the moment of production and that both are managed in social space-time. Reflection on the modalities of innovation in audiovisual production has taken off; it has developed an interest in the modes of production of genres, the effects of the new media on the more traditional ones, and the role of advertising creation in models of television creation. We are beginning to better understand the sociology of the professional groups involved in communication. The fragile balance between creation and programming, between directors and producers, is more clearly perceived. A better understanding has emerged of the balance of forces that condition industrial strategies. More accurate evaluations are made now of the specificities of national communication apparatuses with respect to international markets. There is a better appreciation of the problems posed by the internationalization of communication systems — within Europe at least, and sometimes outside Europe — sometimes even to the detriment of interest in other realities. With deregulation, the juridical aspect of the problems of communications is better taken into account. In short, the forms of knowledge about communications have grown.

Although this extension of forms of knowledge is indeed more and more tangible, it is inhabited by contradictory tendencies. Even as these tensions have deepened, the practical and theoretical stakes of the elaboration of the epistemological foundations of these forms of knowledge have become clearer.

Almost a half century later than in the United States, administrative research in France about the institutions and practices of communication has reached its true dimensions. The growing functionalization of science, its integration into the state-industrial command system, are now realities. More and more research on communication assumes the character of expert advice commissioned by decision makers; this has naturally upset both intellectuals' attitudes toward these questions and the conditions of production of theory.

Reflecting in 1969 on his first experience of participation in administrative research—a project on radio communications financed by the Rockefeller Foundation and undertaken in association with Lazarsfeld in 1938—Theodor Adorno described the kinds of problems he had encountered.

> Naturally there appeared to be little room for such social research in the framework of the Princeton Project. Its charter, which came from the Rockefeller Foundation, expressly stipulated that the investigations must be performed within the limits of the commercial radio system prevailing in the United States. It was thereby implied that the system itself, its cultural and sociological consequences and its social and economic presuppositions were not to be analyzed. . . . I was disturbed . . . by a basic methodological problem—understanding the word "method" more in its European sense of epistemology than in its American sense, in which methodology virtually signifies practical techniques for research.[1]

Adorno's comment helps us grasp what is at stake in the rise of administrative research. This rise of "practical knowledge" is taking place in a context where the margin for maneuver of critical thought, and its very legitimacy, are shrinking more and more. The problem of integration is on the agenda in societies that for a long time had tolerated the existence of a broad category of individuals, in the intellectual class and within civil society more broadly, who did not conform to the existing order of things. The factors that stimulated this development are numerous: the necessity, imposed by a certain model of development and growth, of tightening the links between an apparatus of production in the process of reindustrialization and human reserves of social creativity; the structural necessity of redefining the relationship between the sphere of production and all the social spaces that had remained relatively protected from the law of value and the valorization of capital. Above all, however, there has been a change in the status and function of the production of knowledge and symbolic resources in the determination of political power—a very concrete power that tends to be obscured by the rising idea of the sovereignty of individuals over their destinies and choices.

With these changes, the very conditions of the exercise of social criticism are now being upset. The once relatively autonomous territories of intellectual activity—free, that is, from industrial and market-related contingencies—from which many representatives of the intellectual class conceived the function of critical consciousness, are tending to become immersed in the new economic and political configurations of the so-called postindustrial society.

This effervescence of decision-oriented research is far from satisfying the needs for knowledge—and, it must be said, for theory—that are arising in numerous sectors of society that desire to take some distance from the uncontrolled acceleration of technological change in order to understand its meaning.

The genealogy of forms of knowledge about the media shows that they are subject to a pendulum-like movement. After having witnessed the neglect, or even the rejection, of technological data, we are now observing—throughout the world, no doubt, but particularly in France—a fascination for it. From the initial project that caught the fancy of Roland Barthes (that is, a science of the symbolic, which, it must be admitted, hardly took into account material conditions of production), we are in danger today of veering toward a neopositivist project that would tend to evade the symbolic dimension—that is, the very substance of culture.

This tension is particularly visible today. Research seems to be oscillating between a retreat into methodology aiming to dissect and decode operations, and the return to abstract speculation on the destiny of culture. On the one hand, exhaustive exploration of infinitely small problems; on the other, the tendency to dissociate the imaginary from the new modes of technical production and their social and economic dimension, with the risk of turning the imaginary into a ritual invocation.

One detects here the disarray of the intellectual class, which has suddenly discovered that the media exist and that the cultural industries have instituted a different idea of culture from the one on which their own status of intellectual was constructed in the past. Contrary to what was still true a few years ago, every intellectual now feels the need to develop a discourse on the media, *a fortiori* when his function puts him into frequent contact with the younger generations.

In French society where, unlike the Anglo-Saxon countries, the discourse of the market has very little symbolic legitimacy, the arrival of the "information era" shows every sign of being a godsend for those seeking to establish such legitimacy. The very immateriality of information suggests the image of a transfigured market, become transparent. It provides the perfect opportunity to reintroduce into the informational conception of the world the old demons of idealism. It is thus possible to speak of commodities without speaking of the the segregations they provoke, without referring to those who consume them or produce them, in short, without referring to power (now called "energy"). This is a doubly opportune era, because commodities themselves have become elusive, making possible a reunion between capital and that which it had alienated. In this universe of sociological and historical weightlessness, the fluidity of social relations seems to derive from the fluidity of "flows."

It is no longer possible to limit communications to the conceptual framework the sociologies of the media have tried to establish in the past two decades. The field was occupied, and will be more so every day, by the interests and concerns of disciplines bearing their own conception of communication and information. The subject of communication and information is undoubtedly one of the areas in which one perceives most sharply the growing interpenetration among different sectors and disciplines. The problems now emerging are rendering obsolete the traditional specializations of scientists, economists, administrators, and politicians, as well as the customary distinctions between different sectors and disciplines of science. These new problems give us a sense of the new challenges raised by the study of the interaction of complex systems.

Given this rise of transdisciplinarity, epistemological distance is more and more necessary. The very notions of communication and information refer to a multiplicity of theories that are rarely made explicit or mutually coherent. Within the human sciences, these notions serve as bridges from one discipline to another, but often assume divergent contents. These divergences or shifts in meaning are great, one suspects, when these notions travel through the life sciences and the physical sciences before reaching the engineer!

We obviously do not mean to object to the multiplication of disciplinary encounters. The question is rather to determine the positions from which this association can be sought. Indeed, the transdisciplinary approach can represent a forward flight, an avoidance of disturbing social and scientific questions, or it can represent an essential step forward in the fertilization of a discipline. Some transdisciplinary enterprises are centrifugal and end up drying out the disciplines involved in them; but there are others that, as they push back the frontiers of a discipline and multiply the areas of common observation and reflection, do allow an internal enrichment of the specific field itself. The question of the balance of forces among disciplines is more than ever on the agenda.

Certain specialists of the analysis of discourse, whose work is located at the crossroads between the behavioral sciences and linguistics, have become aware more quickly than others of the consequences of upsetting the boundaries between disciplines. Moreover, they have defined the conditions that would allow an encounter, on new theoretical and practical bases, between the life sciences, the engineering sciences, and the social sciences. The question of the subject, a focal point of the new approaches to processes of communication, stands out in relief. In the social sciences, the paradigm of the return to the subject and to individual and collective psychic processes has provoked a burst of interest in language (*le langagier*) and discourse (*le discursif*) as relation to the Other. But in order to take fully into account the complexity and the ambiguity of the epistemological break that this paradigm implies in a transdisciplinary perspective, one must also look at recent developments in cognitivist and neurobiological models, without, of course, abandoning the whole terrain to them *a priori*.

The new paradigms call for transversality. They upset the unilateral relations that linear thought had established between cause and effect, source and receiver, center and periphery. They challenge the exclusive determinism that had marked a certain conception of history and progress. All these linear visions had long accommodated themselves to the compartmentalization of conceptual categories and disciplines. But these new paradigms will not be able to express this new consciousness of the multiplicity of causes and effects, the plurality of historical subjects, unless an elementary epistemological precaution is taken: acknowledging that in the new relations and exchanges they give rise to, the different approaches do not meet on equal terms, for the simple reason that behind the debates over the definition of concepts lie new regimes of truth, new forms of the exercise of power, and new modes of integrating human societies.

NOTES

Introduction to Part 1

1. M. Nivat, *Savoir et savoir-faire informatique* (Paris: La Documentation française, 1983), pp. 44-45.

2. R. Carraz, *Recherche en éducation et socialisation de l'enfant* (Paris: La Documentation française, 1983), p. 53.

3. A. M. Thiesse, *Le Roman au quotidien: Lecteurs et lectures populaires à la Belle Epoque* (Paris: Le Chemin Vert, 1984), p. 173.

4. Quoted by P. Mallein, P. Corset, and M. Sauvage, "Sociologie d'un corps de professionels," in the review *Réseaux*, Department of Studies on Social Practices, Centre national d'études sur les télécommunications (CNET), Paris, no. 9, 1984. [Monoprix is a chain of inexpensive department stores, like the " 5 & 10." — Trans.]

5. Two reports have analyzed in depth the state of communications research: M. de Certeau and L. Giard, *L'Ordinaire de la communication*, (Paris: Dalloz, 1983); and A. Mattelart and Y. Stourdzé, *Technology, Culture and Communication: A Report to the French Minister of Research and Industry*, trans. David Buxton (Amsterdam, New York, and Oxford: North Holland, 1985; originally published in French in two volumes, 1982-83).

6. See, for example, the research published in the journals *Correspondance Municipale* (editor Jean-Paul Simon) and *Cinémaction* (editor Guy Hennebelle). Yves de la Haye's work *Dissonances: Critique de la communication* (Grenoble: La Pensée Sauvage, 1984) is a good introduction to this approach.

1. On the Difficulty of Reflecting on Communication

1. For an analysis of the genealogy of research in Great Britain, see N. Garnham, "Towards a Theory of Cultural Materialism," *Journal of Communication*, vol. 33, no. 3, Summer 1983.

2. M. Pêcheux, "Discourse: Structure or Event?", in *Marxism and the Interpretation of Culture*, ed. C. Nelson and L. Grossberg (Urbana and Chicago: University of Illinois Press, 1988).

3. H. Assmann, "Evaluación de algunos estudios latinoamericanos sobre communica-

ción masiva," paper read at the 11th Latin American Congress of Sociology, July 8-12, 1974, San José de Costa Rica.

4. This is not true, however, of the French functionalist school, which has imported its American homologue to France. This French school was led by sociologists or social psychologists such as Jean Cazeneuve and Jean Stoetzel. On the American texts disseminated in France, see the (dated) anthology by F. Balle and J. Padioleau, *Sociologie de la communication* (Paris: Larousse, 1973). For a critical view, see J. M. Piemme, *La Télévision comme on la parle* (Brussels-Paris: Labor/Nathan, 1978); and more recently, P. Béaud, *La Société de connivence* (Paris: Aubier-Montaigne, 1984).

5. See, for example, Stuart Hall (editor), *Culture, Media, Language* (Centre for Contemporary Studies, Birmingham, U.K., Hutchinson University Library, 1980).

6. Nicos Poulantzas, "Le déplacement des procédures de légitimation," *Le Nouvel ordre intérieur*, a colloquium held at the University of Paris-Vincennes (Paris: Alain Moreau, 1980), p. 141.

7. Louis Althusser, "Ideology and Ideological State Apparatuses," in *Essays on Ideology*, trans. Ben Brewster (London: New Left Books, 1971; London and New York: Verso Books, 1984), p. 18.

8. [ORTF, Office de la Radio-Télévision Française, was a French state monopoly corporation until it was split into autonomous units in 1974.—Trans.]

9. J. Rigaud, *Les Relations culturelles extérieures* (Paris: La Documentation française, 1979), pp. 12, 24.

10. See, in particular, P. Flichy, *Les Industries de l'imaginaire* (Presses Universitaires de Grenoble, 1980) and A. Mattelart, *Multinational Corporations and the Control of Culture*, trans. Michael Chanan (Atlantic Highlands, N.J.: Humanities Press, 1979). The research for this latter work was begun in Latin America in 1972.

11. Louis Quéré, "Les sociologues et l'analyse des problèmes locaux et régionaux," *La Recherche en sciences humaines 1979-1980* (Paris: CNRS, 1980), p. 69.

12. A. Frémont, in *Le CNRS et la communication* (Paris: CNRS, 1984), p. 69.

13. Ibid.

14. R. Brunet, "La géographie," in *Rapport Godelier, Les sciences de l'homme et de la société en France: Rapport au ministre de la Recherche et de l'Industrie*, ed. G. Delacote (Paris: La Documentation française, 1982), p. 408.

15. Important representative works of the "histoire des mentalités" current include Emmanuel Leroy-Ladurie's *Montaillou, un village occitan (1294-1324)* (Paris: Gallimard, 1975); E. Leroy-Ladurie, *Le Carnaval de Romans. De la Chandeleur au Mercredi des cendres (1579-1580)* (Paris: Gallimard, 1978); Michel de Certeau, Dominique Julia, and Jacques Revel, *Une politique de la langue. La Révolution française et les patois* (Paris: Gallimard, 1975); Arlette Farge, *Vivre dans la rue à Paris au XVIIIe siècle* (Paris: Gallimard, 1979); Dominique Julia (ed.), *Atlas de la Révolution française. L'enseignement 1760-1815* (Paris: Ecole des Hautes Etudes en Sciences Sociales, 1987). The journal *Annales*, also published by the Ecole des Hautes Etudes en Sciences Sociales (Paris), has published numerous articles drawing inspiration from this current.

16. D. Julia, "L'histoire de la culture à l'époque moderne et contemporaine," *La Recherche en sciences humaines (1979-1980)* (Paris: CNRS, 1980), p. 84.

17. G. W. F. Hegel, *Philosophy of Right*, trans. T. D. Knox (London: Oxford University Press, 1962).

18. Roland Barthes, *Mythologies*, trans. (London: Paladin Grafton Books, 1973), p. 153.

19. Pierre Bourdieu, *Distinction: A Social Critique of the Judgment of Taste* (Cambridge, Mass.: Harvard University Press, 1984), p. 338.

20. Henri Mercillon, "Industrie culturelle et littérature économique," *Communications*, no. 2, p. 24.

21. M. Vessillier, "Musique et arts du spectacle," *La Recherche en sciences humaines, sciences sociales (1976-77)* (Paris: CNRS, 1977).

22. The difficulties encountered in legitimizing the field of research on mass communication have also been illustrated by the pioneering experiment of Pierre Schaeffer, within the very sphere of radio-television public service—the former ORTF.

23. Vessillier, *Musique*, p. 104. Among the research institutes that have formulated the same wish, at the same time, are the seminar on the economy of labor, whose director was Professor Bartoli; the Center for the Sociology of Innovation (Ecole des Mines) and the European Center for Historical Sociology (with Raymonde Moulin).

24. Annie Cot and Bruno Lautier, "Métaphore économique et magie sociale," in *L'Empire du sociologue* (Paris: Editions La Découverte, 1984), pp. 73-74.

25. A. Lefebvre, A. Huet, B. Miège, and R. Péron, *Capitalisme et industries culturelles* (Presses universitaires de Grenoble, 1978).

26. *Les Réseaux pensants*, ed. A. Giraud, J. L. Missika, and D. Wolton (Paris: Masson, 1978), pp. 255-83.

27. [The Sixth Plan, drawn up in 1969, was one of a series of indicative economic plans adopted by the French government in an effort to ensure industrial growth.—Trans.]

28. L. Brams, in *Les Réseaux pensants*, ed. Giraud et al., p. 224.

29. Y. Stourdzé, in *Les Réseaux pensants*.

30. Flichy, *Les Industries de l'imaginaire*.

2. The Quest for Transdisciplinarity

1. Ecole Pratique des Hautes Etudes, 6th section, *Le Centre d'études des communications de masse 1960-1966*, Paris, p. 2 (mimeographed). To retrace the genealogy of this French project, we relied on the report authored by A. Mattelart and P. Roussin on the state of research in the sciences of information and communication, commissioned by the CNRS, 1983.

2. Ibid., p. 2. The choice of the Ecole Pratique des Hautes Etudes as the institutional anchor of this center is already an indication of the difficulty it had in having this field of investigation recognized as legitimate by traditional research institutions (such as the university or the CNRS).

3. Ecole Pratique des Hautes Etudes, *Le Centre*.

4. "A Georges Friedmann," *Communications*, no. 28, 1978, p. 2. Let us recall that for the American school of functionalism, of which Berelson is a representative, content analysis is characterized as the objective, systematic, and quantitative description of the manifest content of communications. This is precisely what would be refuted by studies of the ideological level of discourses. See B. Berelson, *Content Analysis in Communication Research* (Glencoe, Ill.: Free Press, 1952).

5. Editorial in *Communications*, no. 1, p. 1.

6. Ecole Pratique des Hautes Etudes, *Le Centre*, p. 6.

7. With the noteworthy exception of E. Verón, *Construire l'événement, les médias et l'accident de Three Mile Island* (Paris: Editions de Minuit, 1982).

8. The evolution of the themes around which issues of the review *Communications* were constructed over the years attest to this gradual reduction of the initial object, contained in the very title of the review, and reflecting the image of the founding principles of the Center.

9. Reconciling the instrumental and technical approach with the "literary penchant," this new field of application opened by semiology made it possible to overcome both the

mercantile aspect of advertising production and the gratuitous aspect of literature. If this new path of legitimacy for the advertising environment is so decisive in our view, it is because of the link it maintains with the notion of creation and creativity. This is a most sensitive notion in the French context, where the cleavage between "creative" and "commercial" is present in the minds of all advertising agents. Ten or fifteen years after the fact, this argument may seem rather feeble next to the powerful movement of legitimation constituted by the rise of market ideology. Nonetheless, it does represent a landmark in the prehistory of the attitudes of corporations and consumers.

10. See *Les Apports de la sémiotique au marketing et à la publicité* (Seminar of the IREP: Paris, 1976).

11. M. Pêcheux in ADELA (Analyse de discours et lectures d'archive), *Rapport d'activité et perspectives de recherche*, 1983, p. 16 (mimeographed).

12. Lucien Goldmann, "L'importance du concept de 'conscience possible' pour la communication," in *Colloque de Royaumont: Le concept d'information dans la science contemporaine*, Paris, Editions de Minuit, 1965.

13. Edgar Morin, "L'Evénement," *Communications*, no. 18, p. 4.

14. Ibid., pp. 4-5

15. Serge Moscovici, "Nos sociétés biuniques," *Communications*, no. 22, p. 149.

16. Ibid.

3. The Temptation of Metaphor

1. The contributions of François Jacob as well as those of Roman Jakobson, and that of Claude Lévi-Strauss (which follows), were originally published, in part, in *Critique*, March, 1974, and in *Linguistics*, November, 1974. They were published together with contributions by Michel Foucault and Georges Canguilhem by Joan Senent-Josa of Spain under the title of *Lógica de lo viviente e historia de la biología* (Barcelona: Anagrama, 1975).

2. Ibid., pp. 25-40.

3. F. Jacob, "El modelo lingüístico en biología," in *Lógica*, p. 15.

4. Ibid., p. 21.

5. C. Lévi-Strauss, "Conversación entre F. Jacob y C. Lévi-Strauss," in *Lógica*, p. 42.

6. *Construire l'avenir: Livre blanc sur la recherche présenté au président de la République* (an official report on the state of research in France, presented to the president of the Republic) (Paris: La Documentation française, 1980), p. 142.

7. A. Danchin, *L'Oeuf et la poule* (Paris: Fayard, 1983), p. 228.

8. A. Danchin in *Le Débat*, no. 2, p. 75.

9. Interview with the professor Jean-Paul Lévy, "La guerre des sciences est déclarée," *Le Monde Aujourd'hui*, May 14-15, 1984, p. 6.

10. A. and M. Mattelart, *De l'usage des médias en temps de crise* (Paris: Alain Moreau, 1979), p. 18.

11. For this section we are particularly indebted to Philippe Roussin for his valuable contribution in investigating the links between communication and progress in biological theories.

12. F. Jacob, *The Logic of Life: A History of Heredity*, trans. Betty E. Spillmann (New York: Vintage Books, 1973), p. 307.

13. Ibid., p. 306.

14. On the fate of this formula, see A. Danchin and P. Slonimski, "Les gènes en morceaux," in *La Recherche*, no. 155, May 1984. See also J. P. Changeux, *L'Homme neuronal* (Paris: Fayard, 1983), p. 246.

15. Jacob, *Logic of Life*, p. 320.

16. Ibid., p. 321.

17. J. Ruffié, *De la biologie à la culture* (Paris: Fayard, 1983), p. 354.

18. Ibid., p. 356.

19. Review of M. Godelier's book *L'Idéel et le matériel: Pensées, économies, sociétés* (Paris: Fayard, 1984).

20. R. Thom in *Le Débat*, no. 15, September-October 1981, p. 116.

21. R. Thom, "Halte au hasard, silence au bruit," in *Le Débat*, no. 3, July-August 1980, p. 127.

22. Ibid.

Introduction to Part 2

1. "Ferment in the Field," special issue of the *Journal of Communication*, Summer 1983, vol. 33, no. 3.

2. R. K. Merton, *Social Theory and Social Structure* (Glencoe, Ill.: Free Press, 1949), pp. 442, 446.

3. See, in "Ferment in the Field," an astute critique by two young American professors of the uses made of the critical schools, especially the Frankfurt School, by the university establishment in the United States: J. D. Slack and M. Allor, "The Political and Epistemological Constituents of Critical Communication Research," pp. 208-18.

4. See the comments of M. Pêcheux, in part I above, on the crisis of structuralism in France and its success in the United States.

5. While this structuralist approach was at its apogee, certain critics from within the field of anthropology itself pointed out that the complexity of social facts was not served by a reduction to systems of communication. There was a real danger of eliminating the political and the social from the analysis. See D. Sperber, *Le Structuralisme en anthropologie* (Paris: Le Seuil, 1968), and in particular chapter 3, "Systèmes et modèles de communication."

4. The Theory of Information

1. C. Shannon and W. Weaver, *The Mathematical Theory of Communication* (Urbana: University of Illinois Press, 1949).

2. It was in fact as early as 1943 that the vocabulary of information made its appearance in biology. In his book *What Is Life?*, physicist E. Schrödinger wrote: "The chromosomes . . . contain in some kind of code-script the entire pattern of the individual's future development and of its functioning in the mature state. Every complete set of chromosomes contains the full code" (New York: Doubleday Anchor Books, 1956), p. 18.

3. Roman Jakobson, *Selected Writings II: Word and Language* (The Hague: Mouton, 1971), p. 556. It is in this same perspective that Jakobson, who was a colleague of Claude Lévi-Strauss in the United States, took advantage of the discoveries of molecular biology—one of the strong areas of French scientific research—and proposed his analogies between the genetic code and the linguistic code (see the previous section).

4. Noam Chomsky, *Entretiens avec Mitsou Ronat* (Paris: Flammarion, 1977), pp. 132 and 134-35.

5. A. Lichnerowicz, F. Perroux, and G. Gaddofre (editors), *Information et Communication*, interdisciplinary seminars at the Collège de France (Paris: Maloine, 1983).

6. J. F. Barbier-Bouvet, "Beaubourg—BPI modes d'emploi," *Revue Cadres CFDT*, March-May 1983, p. 12.

7. Jacques Derrida, interview with François George, *Le Monde*, October 21-22, 1984 (reprinted in *Entretiens-Philosophie* [Paris: La Découverte-Le Monde, 1985]).

5. Postlinearity

1. Daniël Bell, *The End of Ideology* (New York: Collier, 1960); *The Coming of Post-Industrial Society* (New York: Basic Books, 1973).

2. Seymour Martin Lipset, *Political Man* (London: Heinemann, 1960).

3. For a history of the birth of the concept, see P. A. Julien, P. Lamonde, and D. Latouche, "La société post-industrielle: un concept vague et dangereux," *Futuribles*, no. 7, Summer 1976; M. Marien, "Les deux visions de la société post-industrielle," *Futuribles*, no. 12, Fall 1977.

4. M. Crozier, S. P. Huntington, and J. Watanuki, *The Crisis of Democracy: Report on the Governability of Democracies to the Trilateral Commission* (New York: New York University Press, 1975).

5. Within this current of thought particular attention is given to the universe of consumption and its modalities. Indeed, consumption (that is, cultural consumption, but also, more broadly, models of consumption) has hardly been taken into account by the left's major parties and trade unions. Two important reasons may perhaps explain this historical failure of the workers' movement—that is, its lack of interest in the "consumption" dimension and more generally in the "quality of life" and the problems of people's daily existence: on the one hand, the principal mission of the party was considered to be the taking of state power; on the other hand, the mission of the unions was considered to be representing workers in the sphere of production. It was to remedy this neglect of other issues by the workers' movement that the new social movements were born and that certain groups have demanded that the socialist project include a "quality of life unionism."

6. M. Pleynet, "A propos d'une analyse des *Mystères de Paris* par Marx dans la *Sainte Famille*," *La Nouvelle Critique*, special issue, 1968. [See chapter 10, note 9, in this volume for a discussion of serial literature.—Trans.]

7. According to the expression of J. de Rosnay in *Le Macroscope* (Paris: Le Seuil, 1975). This term is used to designate the dynamic vision introduced by the "systemic revolution."

8. One need only compare several works that have become classics on postindustrial society, postmodern society, and modernity, by authors as different as Alain Touraine, Jean Chesneaux, Alvin Toffler, Jean-Jacques Servan-Schreiber, Jacques Attali, and Jean-François Lyotard, to see the contradictions at work, and their extension into differing conceptions of social change.

9. One may refer in particular to Ernest Laclau and Chantal Mouffe, *Hegemony and Socialist Strategies* (London: New Left Books, 1985). See also *Les autres marxismes réels* by a collective group, edited by André Corten et al. (Paris: Christian Bourgois, 1985).

6. Negotiated Power

1. R. Luperini, "Critica marxista e critica structuralista," *Nuovo Impegno*, November 1966-April 1967.

2. Michel Foucault, *Discipline and Punish: The Birth of the Prison* (London: Penguin, 1977), p. 27.

3. Henri Lefebvre, *De l'Etat* (Paris: 10/18, 1976), vol. 2, p. 78.

4. K. Naïr, "Marxisme ou structuralisme," *Critiques de l'économie politique*, October-December 1972, p. 82.

5. Our allusion to Sartre is far from fortuitous. He remained one of the rare French intellectuals in the postwar era who developed thought about the media and encouraged intellectuals to go beyond their role of "strollers through history" by moving from writing to the relay arts, cinema and radio. He was also one of the rare people on the left who criticized the dogmatism of the Marxist approaches that dominated the progressive press in

the 1950s. See in particular *What Is Literature?* trans. B. Frechtman (New York, 1949); *The Search for a Method*, trans. H. Barnes (New York: Knopf, 1963).

6. Herbert Marcuse, *One-Dimensional Man: Studies in the Ideology of Advanced Industrial Society* (Boston: Beacon Books, 1964), p. 178.

7. See, for example, Goldmann's articles "Pouvoir et humanisme" and "Réflexions sur la pensée de Herbert Marcuse," in *Marxisme et sciences humaines* (Paris: Gallimard, 1970).

8. See, for example, the research by A. Cirese, *Cultura egemonica e cultura subalterne* (Palermo: Palumbo, 1976).

9. Exceptions here are the works by S. Blum, *La Télévision ordinaire du pouvoir* (Paris: PUF, 1982) and by R. Laufer and C. Paradeise, *Le Prince et le bureaucrate* (Paris: Flammarion, 1982).

10. See, in particular, C. Buci-Glucksmann, *Gramsci and the State*, trans. David Fernbach (London: Lawrence and Wishart, 1975). Another work of reference is that by E. Laclau and C. Mouffe, *Hegemony and Socialist Strategies* (London: New Left Books, 1985).

11. A. Gramsci, *Quaderni del carcere* (Turin: Einaudi, 1975), 1st notebook.

12. H. Lagrange, "A propos de l'école," *Critiques de l'économie politique*, October-December 1972, p. 142.

13. Lefebvre, *De l'Etat*, vol. 2, pp. 43-44.

14. See, e.g., J. von Neumann and O. Morgenstern, *Theory of Games and Economic Behavior*, 3rd ed. (New York: Wiley, 1964). For a critical presentation of these theories, see M. Plon, *La théorie des jeux: une politique imaginaire* (Paris: Maspéro, 1976), and E. Allemand, *Pouvoir et télévision* (Paris: Anthropos, 1980).

15. An important book for the exposition of this conception is M. Crozier and E. Friedberg, *L'Acteur et le système* (Paris: Le Seuil, 1977). It was at about the same time that Crozier took part in the drafting of the famous report of the Trilateral Commission on the "ungovernability" of Western democracies.

16. [The French union of heads of corporations. — Trans.]

17. Quoted by the journal *Cadres CFDT*, no. 275, September-October 1976 (issue dedicated to the problem of information in the enterprise).

18. [The union of newspapers and journalists from in-house corporate publications in France. — Trans.]

7. The Return of the Subject

1. Georges Balandier, "Essai d'identification du quotidien," *Cahiers internationaux de sociologie*, vol. 74, 1983, p. 8.

2. D. Julia, "L'histoire de la culture à l'époque moderne et contemporaine," *La Recherche en sciences humaines, 1979-1980* (Paris: CNRS), p. 85.

3. *La Nouvelle communication*, ed. Yves Winkin (Paris: Le Seuil, 1981), pp. 24-25.

4. M. Pêcheux, "Discourse: Structure or Event," in *Marxism and the Interpretation of Culture*, ed. C. Nelson and L. Grossberg (Urbana and Chicago: University of Illinois Press, 1988).

5. Authors who have developed this approach include R. L. Birdwhistell, E. Hall, E. Goffman, and G. Bateson. See, for example, E. Hall, *The Hidden Dimension* (Garden City, N.Y.: Doubleday Anchor Books, 1966); E. Hall, *The Silent Language* (New York: Fawcett, 1959); and R. L. Birdwhistell, *Kinesics and Context* (New York, Ballantine, 1972).

6. Handwritten note by G. Althabe, November 1984, during the launching of a joint research project by the CNRS (French National Research Council) and the CNET (National Council of Telecommunications Studies).

7. These remarks were suggested to us by the observations of Bernard Miège regarding certain projects for ethnographic research on radio.

8. See in particular the penetrating analyses of Philippe Roqueplo, *Le Partage du sa-voir* (Paris: Le Seuil, 1972), and *Penser la technique: Pour une démocratie concrète* (Paris: Le Seuil, 1983).

8. The Procedures of Consumption

1. P. Bourdieu and J. C. Passeron, "Sociologues des mythologies ou mythologie des sociologues," in *Les Temps modernes*, no. 211, December 1963, pp. 998-1021.

2. R. Hoggart, *The Uses of Literacy: Changing Patterns in English Mass Culture* (Fair-lawn, N.J.: Essential Books, 1957).

3. See the study by M. Mattelart, "Chile: Political Formation and the Reading of Tele-vision," trans. D. Burxton, in *Communication and Class Struggle: An Anthology*, ed. A. Mattelart and S. Siegelaub, vol. 2, "Liberation, Socialism" (New York: International Gen-eral, 1983).

4. Roland Barthes, *The Fashion System*, trans. Matthew Ward and Richard Howard (New York: Hill & Wang, 1983).

5. Yves Winkin (editor), *La Nouvelle communication* (Paris: Le Seuil, 1981), p. 108.

6. M. Pêcheux, "Délimitations, retournements et déplacements," *L'Homme et la so-ciété*, July 1982 (article completed in May 1980, that is, prior to the left electoral victory).

7. Michel de Certeau, *The Practice of Everyday Life*, trans. Steven F. Randall (Berke-ley: University of California Press, 1987).

8. Letter from Goethe to Frederic-Henri Jacobi, reported by G. Gusdorf in *Du néant à Dieu dans le savoir romantique* (Paris: Payot, 1984).

9. See, for example, H. J. Graff (editor), *Literacy and Social Development in the West: A Reader* (Cambridge: Cambridge University Press, 1981). This unique work includes ex-cerpts from books or articles published between 1968 and 1979 on the history of the book and alphabetization, in Europe principally. It includes, in particular, the classic studies by F. Furet and J. Ozouf in *Lire et écrire* (Paris: Editions de Minuit, 1977).

10. S. Giner, *Sociedad Masa* (Barcelona: Ediciónes Peninsula, 1979). An English trans-lation exists under the title of *Mass Society* (New York: Academic Press, 1976).

11. Claude Lévi-Strauss, preface to *Le Regard éloigné* (Paris: Plon, 1983).

12. Henri Giordan, "Culture de masse et culture populaire: Théories et expériences italiennes," unpublished.

13. ["Free radio stations" were created throughout France by independent groups in the late seventies in an effort to break the state monopoly over the airwaves; they were given a legal, if restricted, status beginning in 1981 when the left came to power.—Trans.]

14. This conception of alternative communication was criticized in A. Mattelart and J. M. Piemme, *Télévision, enjeux sans frontières* (Presses Universitaires de Grenoble, 1980), in part 3, entitled "Nouveaux moyens de communication, nouvelles questions." See also, by the same authors, "New Means of Communication: New Questions for the Left," *Media, Culture and Society*, special issue on alternative media, vol. 2, no. 4, October 1980.

15. Collectif A-Traverso, *Radio Alice, radio libre* (Paris: Jean-Pierre Delarge, 1977), p. 87. See also G. Cesareo, "The Form of Apparatus in the Mass-Media," in *Media, Culture and Society*, July 1979.

16. See, for example, the two colloquia organized by the Association des rencontres sur audiovisuel et mouvement ouvrier at the Maison du peuple de Saint-Nazaire in January, 1984, and January, 1986. In this perspective, see the studies and reports of the CERIAM, in particular *Une autre optique à Gennevilliers*, by G. Azémard and J. C. Quiniou (Paris: Edi-tions du CERIAM, 1984).

17. See in particular C. Hamelink, "Emancipation or Domestication: Towards an Uto-pian Science of Communication," *Journal of Communication*, vol. 33, no. 3, Summer 1983.

18. P. Hemanus, "Journalism, Knowledge and Changing the World," *The Nordicom Review*, Göteborg, Sweden, no. 2, 1984, p. 11.

19. See G. Cornu, "Analyse de la réception: Théorie des 'effets' ou théorie des pratiques de consommation?," mimeographed article, 1983.

20. Interview with A. Moles, *Le Monde aujourd'hui*, December 30-31, 1984, p. 3.

Introduction to Part 3

1. Umberto Eco, *Apocalitti e integrati* (Milan: Bompiani, 1964).

2. Pier Paolo Pasolini, *Scritti corsari* (Milan: Aldo Garzanti, 1975).

3. The reader may refer in particular to the analyses of Betty Friedan in *The Feminine Mystique* (New York: Dell, 1963).

9. Popular Pleasure as a Revelation

1. Michael Poole, "Made in America," in *The Listener* (London), November 29, 1984, p. 29. Many voices have expressed uncertainty regarding the mediating role critical intellectuals have assumed between the public and media culture. The experience of teachers has often been revealing. In 1983, in the pages of *Rolling Stone*, Susan Sontag explained why she had quit academics. Her colleagues had faulted her for having confused university research with themes dealing with popular entertainment. A teacher at the University of Illinois, Larry Grossberg, observed in 1983 that it was very difficult for him to legitimate the subject of his research, the modern forms of popular music, in a milieu accustomed to "serious" critical considerations about "high culture." He also noted the difficulty a researcher could experience when entering, with the established categories of most of the existing critical theories, into an area where, as had become clear to him in his daily contact with students, it is a question of pleasure before it is one of understanding. (L. Grossberg, "Teaching and the Popular," in press.)

2. Letters exchanged between Martin Barbero and Michèle Mattelart in response to questions formulated by Michèle Mattelart about the question of pleasure experienced in mass culture, originally included in *Femmes et industries culturelles*, UNESCO, documentary dossier no. 23 (letter by J. M. Barbero dated February 16, 1984).

3. Michel Maffesoli, Centre d'études sur l'actuel et le quotidien (Center for studies on current affairs and daily life), in a document prepared by the Centre Georges Pompidou for two weeks of activities devoted to Brazilian television, January 21-February 3, 1985, Paris.

4. Walter Benjamin, "The Work of Art in the Age of Mechanical Reproduction," in *Illuminations*, ed. Hannah Arendt (New York: Schocken Books, 1969), p. 234.

5. T. Davies, "Transports of Pleasure," in *Formations of Pleasure*, ed. Fredric Jameson (London and Boston: Routledge & Kegan Paul, 1983). It is interesting to note that there has been a fierce opposition between two cultural currents, along the classic division between the "integrated" and the "apocalyptics," regarding this literature, known in Great Britain as "railway literature."

6. Quoted by Martin Jay in *The Dialectical Imagination* (London: Heinemann, 1973), p. 211.

7. Hans Magnus Enzensberger, "Constituents of a Theory of the Media," in *The Consciousness Industry: On Literature, Politics and the Media* (New York: Seabury Press, 1974). Curiously, it has never been translated into French. The text is known in France only through the critique by Jean Baudrillard in *Pour une économie politique du signe* (Paris: Gallimard, 1972). However, other works by Enzensberger have been published in France, in particular *Culture ou mise en condition?* (Paris: 10/18, 1973).

10. Negative Culture, Affirmative Culture

1. Thorstein Veblen, *The Theory of the Leisure Class* (1899; New York: Modern Library, 1943).

2. See Adorno's article "Veblen's Attack on Culture," which first appeared in *Studies in Philosophy and Social Science* in 1941 and is included in *Prisms* (Cambridge, Mass.: MIT Press, 1981), p. 81.

3. Fredric Jameson, "Pleasure: A Political Issue," in *Formations of Pleasure*, ed. Fredric Jameson (London and Boston: Routledge and Kegan Paul, 1983).

4. D. Prokopp, *Massenkultur und Spontaneität zur Veränderten Warenform des Massenkommunikation im Spätkapitalismus* (Frankfurt: Suhrkamp, 1974), pp. 44-102.

5. Colin Mercer, "A Poverty of Desire," *Formations* (London and Boston: Routledge and Kegan Paul, 1983).

6. P. Germa, "La publicité du futur," in *Nouveaux médias et nouvelles technologies* (Paris: IREP, 1981), p. 37.

7. W. Haug, "Some Theoretical Problems in the Discussion of Working-Class Culture," in *Communication and Class Struggle: An Anthology*, ed. A. Mattelart and S. Siegelaub (New York: International General, 1983).

8. L. Silva as quoted in the Caracas review *Comunicación*, no. 2, May, 1975, p. 63.

9. This dilemma expressed itself as soon as the first form of mass literature, serial literature, appeared. In France, the newspapers that identified with the socialist movement oscillated at the end of the nineteenth century and up to World War I between two tendencies, one consisting of disseminating international culture (Tolstoy, Gorky, Sinclair, London, Conan Doyle, and Poe) and promoting the realist and naturalist literature of the end of the century (Balzac, Flaubert, Zola); the other consisted of producing serial novels similar to those published in popular commercial newspapers. But as Anne-Marie Thiesse has noted, "this policy of publishing serial novels was lacking in firmness or else did not meet with great success in the working-class public. . . . Was this an expression of disarray by intellectual editors who did not know what to do with their working-class column? One perhaps may glean here the absence of reflection on the social problem of reading by workers and peasants. Between the attempt to let the masses accede to classical culture and the temptation to seek recourse in the proven formulas of the commerical novel for 'the people,' the French socialists did not know how to choose their path, nor were they able to generate an appropriate cultural production for this unread public whom they had to win to revolutionary ideas." *Le Roman au quotidien: Lecteurs et lectures populaires à la Belle Epoque* (Paris: Le Chemin Vert, 1984), p. 119.

10. A. Gramsci, "Some Problems in the Study of the Philosophy of Praxis," *Selections from the Prison Notebooks*, ed. Q. Hoare and G. Nowell-Smith (London: Lawrence & Wishart, 1971).

11. Evidence of this may be found in the numerous studies published in reviews such as *M/F* (Great Britain), *Signs, JumpCut*, and *Radical America* (United States).

12. See Geneviève Fraisse's critique of the theses of social reproduction: "Un dangereux anachronisme: questions sur l'analyse de la reproduction du sexisme," in *L'Empire du sociologue* (Paris: La Découverte, 1984).

13. Michèle Mattelart, "The Myth of Modernity," in *Women, Media, Crisis: Femininity and Disorder* (London: Comedia, 1986).

11. The Heavy and the Light

1. I. Ang, "The Battle between Television and Its Audience: The Politics of Watching Television," in *Television in Transition*, ed. R. Patterson and P. Drummond (London: British Film Institute, 1985).

2. D. Vicas, in *Nouveaux médias, nouvelles technologies* (Paris: IREP, 1980), p. 46.

3. Ibid., p. 47.

4. Gilles Deleuze and Félix Guattari, *Anti-Oedipus: Capitalism and Schizophrenia*, trans. R. Hurley, M. Seem, and H. R. Lane (New York: Viking, 1977; Minneapolis: University of Minnesota Press, 1983).

5. These expressions are taken from D. Wolton and J. L. Missika in *La Folle du logis* (Paris: Gallimard, 1983).

6. Pierre-André Taguieff, "Néo-libéralisme," *Enjeu*, February 1985, p. 39.

7. A. and M. Mattelart, *De l'usage des médias en temps de crise* (Paris: Alain Moreau, 1979), p. 9.

8. Jürgen Habermas, *The Structural Transformation of the Public Sphere: An Inquiry into a Category of Bourgeois Society*, trans. Thomas Burger and Frederick Lawrence (Cambridge, Mass.: MIT Press), 1989.

9. On pleasurable pedagogy via television as a remedy to the crisis of education, see M. Mattelart, "Education, télévision et culture de masse," in *Technologie, culture et communication*, vol. 2 of the Report by Mattelart and Stourdzé (Paris: La Documentation Française, 1983), pp. 151-88. For an analysis of computer-assisted teaching see J. Perriault, "L'école dans le creux de la technologie: À la recherche d'un nouvel équilibre entre école et technologies de la communication," *Revue française de pédagogie*, September 1981.

10. Roland Barthes, *Mythologies* (New York: Hill & Wang, 1972), p. 155.

11. On the concept of modernity and its relation to the women's movement, see M. Mattelart, "Notes on Modernity," in her book *Women, Media and Crisis: Femininity and Disorder*, trans. Mary Axtman, David Buxton, and Keith Reader (London: Cornelia/ Routledge, 1986).

12. In an interview with two journalists from *Le Monde*, the American historian Arno Mayer drew attention to this gap: "When Mr. Fabius [then French Prime Minister] preaches the gospel of modernization, that is sweet music to the ears of Americans. It rings rather false because the concept of modernization and modernity had its moment of glory in the United States in the 50s and 60s and was completely taken apart by the social scientists. We know very well that there is always a mixture of ancient and modern and that it is the amalgams that count." "Un entretien avec l'historien Arno Mayer" (Interview with the historian Arno Mayer) by J. Amalric and M. Lucbert, *Le Monde*, October 30, 1984.

13. Félix Guattari, "L'impasse post-moderne," *La Quinzaine littéraire*, February 1-15, 1986, p. 21.

14. Martin Jay, *The Dialectical Imagination* (London: Heinemann, 1973), p. 216.

15. Annie Ernaux, "L'écrivain en terrain miné," *Le Monde*, March 23, 1985, p. 21.

16. Bertolt Brecht, *Ecrits sur la critique et la société* (Paris: L'Arche), p. 133.

17. Michel Foucault, "Du pouvoir," an interview with P. Boncenne conducted in 1978 and published in *L'Express*, July 6-12, 1984.

Introduction to Part 4

1. R. Bodel, "Stratégies d'individuation," *Critique*, January-February 1985, pp. 125, 128.

12. The State as Macrosubject

1. Henri Lefebvre, *De l'Etat*, vol. 2 (Paris: 10/18, 1976), p. 100.

2. François Châtelet, "Remarques sur les philosophies de l'histoire," paper delivered at the colloquium entitled "1970-1980: Les années gauches" (1970-1980: The left years), organized by the DIRE group, May 8, 1980.

3. Lefebvre, *De l'Etat*, vol. 2, p. 70.

4. J. M. Cotteret et al., *L'Image des multinationales dans une France socialiste* (Paris: PUF-IRM), 1985.

5. G. Althabe, in *Enjeu*, no. 13, May 1984, p. 52.

6. "Utopies!" in *Alternatives*, issue on the local press, 1977, p. 10, 12.

7. On the question of local relations, see the collective work coordinated by Lucien Sfez, *L'Objet local* (Paris: 10/18, 1980).

8. In *Alternatives*, p. 8.

9. A. Mattelart and J. M. Piemme, *Télévision, enjeux sans frontières* (Presses Universitaires de Grenoble, 1980), pp. 225-26.

10. C. Quénard, "La vraie action culturelle, c'est nous," *Autrement*, no. 18, April 1979, p. 149.

11. On this subject, see the critique by a small English press and publishing house, Comedia, of ideas which have led to the failure of many practices by the left in the area of cultural intervention: D. Landry and D. Morley, et al., *What a Way to Run a Railroad: An Analysis of Radical Failure* (London: Comedia, 1986).

12. R. Laufer, "Crise de légitimité dans les grandes organisations," *Revue française de gestion*, March-April 1977.

13. Y. de la Haye, *Dissonances* (La Pensée sauvage: Grenoble, 1984), p. 81.

14. Yves Lacoste, *La géographie, ça sert d'abord à faire la guerre* (Paris: La Découverte, 1985), p. 188.

13. The Logic of the Industrial Actor

1. "Un débat démocratique pour un grand enjeu," in *Actes du colloque national Recherche et Technologie* (documents of the colloquium "Research and Technology") (Paris: Le Seuil, 1982), p. 25.

2. Closing speech by J.-P. Chevènement, ibid., p. 194.

3. Ibid., p. 196.

4. [*Telematics*: neologism coined from the contraction of *telecommunications* and *informatics*.—Trans.]

5. S. Nora and A. Minc, *L'Informatisation de la société* (Paris: La Documentation française, 1978), p. 42.

6. Ibid, pp. 12-13.

7. Alain Lipietz, *L'Audace ou l'enlisement* (Paris: La Découverte, 1984), pp. 274-75.

8. J. de Rosnay, *Le Macroscope* (Paris: Le Seuil, 1975), p. 279.

9. See P. Flichy, *Les Industries de l'imaginaire* (Presses Universitaires de Grenoble, 1980).

10. See, in particular, the speech by François Mitterrand at the summit meeting of the large industrialized countries, Versailles, June 1982; the speech by Jack Lang (French Minister of Culture), at the conference on cultural policies organized by UNESCO in Mexico, July 1982; and finally the opening and closing speeches at the "Sorbonne Colloquium," which brought together intellectuals, creators, and high civil servants in March 1983, and whose contributions were published in *Le Complexe de Léonard* (Paris: Editions Nouvel Observateur, 1984).

11. On this problem, see M. Mattelart, "What Programs for What Internationalization?" in A. Mattelart, X. Delcourt, and M. Mattelart, *International Image Markets*, trans. David Buxton (London: Comedia-Methuen, 1984).

12. D. Vicas, "Prospective sur l'impact des nouveaux médias et les applications marketing ou publicitaires," *Nouveaux médias et nouvelles technologies* (Paris: IREP, 1981), p. 55.

13. P. Germa, "La publicité du futur," ibid., p. 37.

14. Jürgen Habermas, *Legitimation Crisis* (Boston: Beacon Press, 1973), p. 41.

15. Quoted by Philippe Gavi in *Libération*, June 18, 1984, p. 11.

16. See J. Stratte, "French Ad Traits," *Advertising Age*, March 27, 1978.

17. Ibid.

18. The specificity of French advertising is even more striking when one examines the way in which certain European countries judge their own advertising industries and speak of their difficulties in forging their own paths. For example, this excerpt from a study of Italian advertising: "In this past decade Italian advertising at the festivals did not distinguish itself very much, partly because we lost our identity. This is incredible because all the world considers us to be the best art creators. Italian design is our utmost expression, such as our coach-builders who sign the automobiles of the Japanese, the French, the Germans. For the assembling of automobiles the most complex technology does not come from Japan but from Turin. . . . The accusation that can be made to certain Italian advertisers is that they have given more importance to the affairs of others than to [their own]." R. Gavioli, in *Grands Prix i film premiati in trent'anni di festival del cinema pubblicitario* (Torino: SIPRA, 1984), p. 35.

19. S. R. Bernstein, "What is Advertising," *Advertising Age*, April 30, 1980, p. 28.

20. G. Lagneau, *Les Institutions publicitaires, fonction et genèse*, state doctoral thesis in the human sciences, Université René-Descartes, 1982, p. viii.

21. G. Poujol and R. Labourie (editors), *Les cultures populaires* (Toulouse: Privat, 1979), p. 36.

22. D. J. Boorstin, "The Rhetoric of Democracy," *Advertising Age*, April 19, 1976, p. 64.

23. Ibid.

24. R. Berman, "Advertising and Society," *Advertising Age*, April 30, 1980, p. 7.

25. R. Crain, "Advertising: The Brick and Mortar of our Economy," *Advertising Age*, April 30, 1980, p. 1.

26. S. R. Bernstein, "What is Advertising," ibid., p. 40.

27. Interview with Michel Foucault in *Cahiers du cinéma*, July-August 1974, p. 7.

14. The Cosmobiology of *Homo Deregulatus*

1. For a critical view of the deregulation of communications systems in the United States, see D. Schiller, *Telematics and Government* (Norwood, N.J.: Ablex, 1982); for a distinctly liberal-capitalist view, see I. de Sola Pool, *Technologies of Freedom* (Cambridge, Mass.: Harvard University Press, 1983).

2. Norbert Wiener, *The Human Use of Human Beings: Cybernetics and Society* (Boston: Houghton Mifflin, 1950).

3. *Business Week*, January 21, 1985, p. 61.

4. Quoted in P. Rolle, "Sidérurgistes à la découverte de l'Amérique," *Enjeu*, February 1985, p. 31.

5. J. Riboud, "La gauche et le déclin de l'Europe," *Le Monde*, February 26, 1985, p. 10.

6. "The New Corporate Elite," *Business Week*, January 21, 1985, p. 63.

7. Since the commercial success of *In Search of Excellence* by T. Peters and R. Waterman, Harper & Row, 1982, numerous works have shed light on the characteristics of these new entrepreneurs. See, for example, D. Quinn Mills, *The New Competitors* (New York: John Wiley & Sons, 1984).

8. See the work containing the results of this pioneering study: M. Pagès, M. Bonetti, V. de Gaulejac, D. Descendre, *L'Emprise de l'organisation* (Paris: PUF, 1979).

9. "The Yuppie Who's Rewriting the Socialist Agenda," *Business Week*, May 13, 1985, p. 32. On the rise of the *soixante-huitards* to power, see H. Landier, "Les babyboomers au pouvoir," in *Futuribles*, no. 87, Spring 1985; and the collective work entitled *Cycles de vie et génération* (Paris: Economica, 1985).

10. Advertisement written by Jean-Louis Servan-Schreiber on the occasion of the first issue of his magazine *L'Entreprise*, "the magazine for those who have the spirit of enterprise." The publication was launched jointly by the Expansion group and Ouest-France. See *Libération*, May 6, 1985.

11. Ibid.

12. Arno Mayer, interview conducted by J. Amalric and M. Lucbert, *Le Monde*, October 30, 1984, p. 21.

13. From Serge Daney's introduction to a group of articles on the American documentary drama in *Les Cahiers du cinéma*, January 1981.

14. G. S. Becker, "How the Market Acted Affirmatively for Women," *Business Week*, May 13, 1985, p. 10.

15. On the genesis of this doctrine, see H. Schiller, *Communication and Cultural Domination* (White Plains, N.Y.: M. E. Sharpe, 1976), chapter 2.

16. J. Halloran, *The Context of Mass Communication Research* (Paris: UNESCO, 1980).

17. William G. Harley, U.S. State Department memorandum, in *Journal of Communication*, Fall 1984, vol. 34, no. 4. This issue focuses on international relations in the light of the U.S. withdrawal from UNESCO.

18. On this point, see Colleen Roach, "The U.S. Position in the New Information and Communication Order," *Journal of Communication*, vol. 37, no. 4, Fall 1987.

19. R. Lubar, "Reaganizing the Third World," *Fortune*, November 1981.

20. On these demands and their results, see A. Mattelart, *Transnationals and the Third World: The Struggle for Culture*, trans. David Buxton (South Hadley, Mass.: Bergin & Garvey, 1983).

21. One representative of a large transnational pharmaceutical corporation, accusing certain Christian groups in the United States of being Marxists in disguise because of their campaigns against the advertising strategies of large pharmaceutical and food-processing companies, confided to *Fortune* magazine that "the activists may be doing corporations a good turn by prodding them to prove they can meet social challenges. Thus the Marxists marching under the banner of Christ may help the private-enterprise system to adapt and survive—even though that may be the last thing they want to see happen." Quoted in H. Nickel, "The Corporation Haters," *Fortune*, June 16, 1980, p. 128.

22. Daniel Bell, "Communications Technology, For Better or for Worse," *Harvard Business Review*, May-June 1979.

23. *Long Range Goals in International Telecommunications and Information: An Outline for United States Policy* (Washington, D.C.: Government Printing Office, 1983).

24. M. Naraine, "U.S. International Telecommunications Goals," in *Telecommunications Policy*, March 1985, p. 80.

25. Quoted by Pierre Drouin, "Multinationales, firmes de pointe?", *Le Monde*, May 10, 1985, p. 42.

26. On the stakes of the militarization of space and its relation to the development of communications systems, see the dossier entitled "L'espace, nouvelle frontière de l'empire américain," including articles by V. Mosco and H. Schiller, in *Le Monde Diplomatique*, March 1984.

27. We do not develop these themes here. On this genesis, see: A. Mattelart, *Multinational Corporations and the Control of Culture*, trans. Michael Chanan (Atlantic Highlands, N.J.: Humanities Press, 1980); A. and M. Mattelart, *De l'usage des médias en temps*

de crise (Paris: Alain Moreau, 1979); G. Menahem, *La Science et le militaire* (Paris: Le Seuil, 1976); A. Jaubert and J.-M. Lévy-Leblond, *(Auto)critique de la science* (Paris: Le Seuil, 1976). A more recent work on this subject is H. Schiller's *Information and the Crisis Economy* (Norwood, N.J.: Ablex, 1984).

28. W. Claiborne, "From Foreign Embassies, Afghan News," *International Herald Tribune*, May 18-19, 1985.

29. See P. M. Thivolet, "Les vertus de la désinformation," *Le Monde Diplomatique*, December 1983. In May 1985 an independent American foundation composed of former military officers and high civil servants published a report on the relations between the press and the army. This document, written after the invasion of Grenada, observed how the unilateral decision of the Pentagon interrupted a tradition going back to World War II. Until October 1983, the decisions regarding information and press censorship had always been made by civilians. Regulation of the role of the press in armed conflicts falls to the president, as commander-in-chief of the armed forces, and his civilian advisors. See A. S. Jones, "La presencia de periodistas en el frente de batalla es necesaria, según un informe independiente," *New York Times* article appearing in Spanish in *El Pais* (Madrid), May 31, 1985, p. 31.

30. The name is, of course, that of the Cuban independence fighter José Marti, who founded the Cuban Revolutionary Party and died while in command of the liberation army in 1895 during the battle of Dos Ríos. With a strength of 20 kilowatts, Radio Marti operates on middle waves with 14 hours of broadcasts per day in Spanish, covering the entire island of Cuba.

31. The necessity for the logic of war and the logic of the market to coexist on traditional networks as well as new ones is confirmed by the new projects announced by the U.S. Information Agency (USIA), which controls The Voice of America. In November 1984, this agency proposed its candidacy for the acquisition of a station on a European commercial satellite in order to launch "Worldnet," a two-hour daily television program. Its promoter, a special adviser to President Reagan, did not hesitate to present this initiative as "just as important for the Atlantic Alliance as the installation of Pershing II missiles in Europe." (Quoted by J. F. Lacan, "Les Etats-Unis à l'assaut de la télévision européenne," *Le Monde*, February 12, 1985, p. 18.)

Introduction to Part 5

1. Z. Brzezinski, *Between Two Ages: America's Role in the Technetronic Age* (New York: Viking Press, 1970), pp. 32-33.

15. The Crisis of the Paradigms

1. Interview with Michel Foucault in *Les Cahiers du cinéma*, July-August 1974, p. 13.

2. *Libération*, July 6-7, 1985.

3. Quoted by Serge Daney, *Libération*, May 11-12, 1985, p. 28.

4. See J.-F. Lyotard, *The Post-Modern Condition: A Report on Knowledge*, trans. Geoff Bennington and Brian Massumi (Manchester University Press, 1984), chap. 4.

5. All this information is taken from an unpublished article by R. Samarajiwa of Simon Fraser University, Canada, entitled "The Tainted Origins of the Communication and Development Field: The Voice of America and the Passing of Traditional Society."

6. Ibid.

7. H. Lasswell, *Public Opinion Quarterly*, 1952, p. 498, quoted by R. Samarajiwa, "Tainted Origins."

8. The most representative work by E. Rogers is, however, *Communication of Innovations: A Cross-Cultural Approach* (New York: Free Press, 1971), also written with the collaboration of F. Floyd Shoemaker; it restates the earlier theses. Many critiques of this work have been published in Spanish and Portuguese: see, in particular, J. Martins de Sousa, *Capitalismo e tradicionalismo* (Sao Paulo: Pioneira, 1975); L. Ramiro Beltrán, "Alien Premises, Objects, Methods in Latin American Communication Research," *Communication Research*, vol. 3, no. 2, 1976. See also J. Maho, "Diffusion de l'innovation: Valeur et limites de quelques concepts," *Epistémologie sociologique*, no. 8, 1969; O. Capriles, "La nouvelle recherche latino-américaine en communication," *Communication Information*, fall 1982, vol. 5, no. 1. (This journal is published at the Université de Laval, Québec.) Another important critic of the concept of diffusionism was the Paraguayan J. Díaz Bordenave, one of the great specialists in rural communication in Latin America; see, for example, "Communication and Adoption of Agricultural Innovations in Latin America," in *Communication Strategies for Rural Development*, ed. R.H. Crawford and W. B. Ward (Ithaca, N.Y.: Cornell University Press, 1974).

9. F. Weffort, "Education et politique," preface to Paulo Freire, *L'Education, pratique de la liberté*, 2d ed. (Paris: Editions du Cerf, 1973).

10. E. Rogers, "Communication and Development: The Passing of the Dominant Paradigm," *Communication Research*, vol. 3, no. 3, April 1976.

11. These are the words of a former student of E. Rogers at Stanford University, J. O'Sullivan Ryan, a counselor to the Ministry of Agriculture of Venezuela, in *Bases teóricas para la formulación de una política de comunicación agrícola*, Caracas, September 1980.

12. It was in January 1968 at the Cultural Congress held in Havana that the notion of cultural imperialism acquired its legitimacy. Present at this congress was the cream of European intellectual life, which sympathized with the Cuban revolution prior to its spectacular break with it in 1971. Among the participants were David Cooper, Eric Hobsbawm, Ralph Miliband (all from Great Britain), Rossana Rossanda (Italy), Jorge Semprun and Michel Leiris (France), and Hans Magnus Enzensberger (Germany); Bertrand Russell, Jean-Paul Sartre, and Ernst Fischer all sent messages of support. Among the many delegations from Latin America and the Caribbean were Aimé Césaire, René Depestre, Mario Benedetti, Julio Cortázar, and others. In this congress, whose theme was "the intellectual and the liberation struggles of Third World peoples," Julio Cortázar launched a phrase that was soon adopted by all the participants: "Every intellectual belongs to the Third World!" The documents of this congress were published in English and edited by Irwin Silber under the title *Voices of National Liberation: The Revolutionary Ideology of the "Third World" as Expressed by Intellectuals and Artists at the Cultural Congress of Havana, January, 1968* (Brooklyn: Central Books, 1970).

13. For an analysis of the evolution of the concept of cultural imperialism, see V. Lanternari, "L'imperialismo culturale di ieri et di oggi," in *Terzo Mundo*, no. 37-38, anno 12, gruppo 4, January-June 1979. (This journal is published in Rome.)

14. On this point see Serge Latouche, "L'impérialisme précède le développement du capitalisme," *Les Temps modernes*, September 1982. Also see Michael Barratt Brown, *The Economics of Imperialism* (Harmondsworth, U.K.: Penguin Books, 1974).

15. K. Polcyn et al., *The Use of Satellites for Educational Television in Developing Countries: Report on the Munich Conference, 1972* (Munich: Internationales Zentralinstitut für das Jugend-und Bildungsfernsehen, 1973).

16. Among the major theoreticians of dependency, we may cite Vania Bambirra, André Gunder Frank, Theotonio dos Santos, Ruy Mauro Marini, Fernando Henrique Cardoso, and, in the area of education, Tomas Vasconi. See, in particular, André Gunder Frank, *Capitalism and Underdevelopment in Latin America: Historical Studies of Chile and Brazil*

(New York: Monthly Review Press, 1969), and F. H. Cardoso and E. Faletto, *Dependency and Development in Latin America* (Berkeley: University of California Press, 1979).

17. Gonzalo Arroyo, "A propos de la dépendance," *Amérique latine*, October-December 1980, p. 32. As this author noted, "The economic and social structures and the form assumed by the state differ as much as the trade-union and political movements. The contrast is evident if one considers, on the one hand, the southern cone, Mexico, and certain Andean countries such as Peru and Colombia, and, on the other hand, Paraguay, Bolivia, and Central America as a whole. A general interpretation of dependent capitalism in Latin America is doubtless invalid, even if capitalist domination stretches over the whole region, excepting Cuba. In fact, the forms it takes in each social formation vary considerably."

18. Immanuel Wallerstein, *The Modern World-System: Capitalist Agriculture and the Origins of the European World System in the Sixteenth Century* (New York: Academic Press, 1974).

19. H. Souza, *An Overview of Theories of Multinational Corporations and the Quest for the State* (Toronto: Latin American Research Unit [LARU], February 1977).

20. Arroyo, "A propos de la dépendance," p. 34.

16. Rediscovering Popular Cultures

1. For a deeper analysis of the Chilean question, see A. and M. Mattelart, *De l'usage des médias en temps de crise* (Paris: Alain Moreau, 1979); A. Mattelart, *Mass Media, Ideologies and the Revolutionary Movement*, trans. Malcolm Coad (Highland Park, N.J.: Humanities Press, 1980); M. Mattelart, *Women, Media and Crisis* (London: Methuen, 1986).

2. J. M. Barbero, "De quelques défis pour la recherche sur la communication en Amérique latine," *Amérique latine*, January-March 1982.

3. For the record, we refer here to special issues of a Mexican review, *Comunicación y Cultura*, no. 10, and the review of the Institute of Research in Communication of the Central University of Venezuela, *ININCO*, no. 3, 1981. The reader may also consult M. and A. Mattelart, *The Carnival of Images: Brazilian Television Fiction* (New York: Greenwood Press, 1990), and the journal *Media, Culture, and Society*, no. 4, 1988, a special issue on new currents in research on Latin America.

4. See the texts gathered in A. Mattelart, ed. *Communicating in Popular Nicaragua* (New York: International General, 1986).

5. J. J. Brunner, "La vie quotidienne en régime autoritaire," *Amérique latine*, October-December 1982, p. 43.

6. R. M. Alfaro, "Democracia y comunicación en la organización popular," bulletin of the documentary service of ECO (*Educación y comunicaciónes*), Santiago, Chile, December 1984.

Conclusion

1. T. W. Adorno, "Scientific Experience of a European Scholar in America," in *The Intellectual Migration: Europe and America, 1938-1960*, ed. D. Fleming and B. Bailyn (Cambridge, Mass.: Harvard University Press/Belknap, 1969), p. 343.

INDEX

Compiled by Robin Jackson

About the Authors

Armand Mattelart is professor of information and communication sciences at the University of Haute-Bretagne (Rennes, France). From 1962 to 1973 he taught at the University of Santiago, Chile, where he worked closely with the Allende government in the attempt to create new initiatives in popular communication. He has carried out frequent missions for the governments of Belgium, France, Nicaragua, and Mozambique in the area of communication policy. He has authored or coauthored several books on culture, ideology, and communication, including *Mass Media, Ideologies, and the Revolutionary Movement* (1980), *Transnationals and the Third World* (1983), *Technology, Culture, and Communication* (1985), and *Advertising International: The Privatisation of Public Space* (1991).

Michèle Mattelart holds a degree from the Sorbonne. She is currently doing research at the Centre National de la Recherche Scientifique in Paris. From 1963 to 1973 she taught at the University of Santiago and helped to found a center for national study. Frequent trips and missions since then have maintained her close ties with Latin America. She has written extensively on women, politics, and culture, and on media and society. Among her books are *La cultura de la opresión femenina* (1977) and *Women, Media, and Crisis: Femininity and Disorder* (1986). She coauthored *De l'usage des médias en temps de crise* (1979), *International Image Markets* (1985), and *The Carnival of Images* (with Armand Mattelart) (1990). Her essays have appeared in *Sex and Class in Latin America* (1974), edited by June Nash and Helen Safa, and *Marxism and the Interpretation of Culture* (1988), edited by Cary Nelson and Lawrence Grossberg.

About the Translators

James A. Cohen received his doctorate in political science from the University of Paris-I in 1991. He currently teaches sociology and political science at the University of Paris-VIII at Saint-Denis. He has worked extensively on the relationship between Puerto Rico and the United States since 1898. He has published articles in *Les Temps Modernes*, *L'Evénement Européen*, and *Annales de l'Amérique centrale et de la Caraïbe*, in addition to having translated four books and numerous articles.

Marina Urquidi has been an independent translator and journalist for the past ten years, working primarily for international organizations, as well as in the area of market research and semiotics. She has been living in Paris for twenty years and works on media-related projects for the Club of Rome. She is the translator of "Africa Facing Its Priorities," a report to the Club of Rome by Bertrand Schneider (1988).